CW00750108

WHY I A
ATHEIST AND NOT
A THEIST

HOW TO DO
KNOWLEDGE, MEANING, AND MORALITY
IN A GODLESS WORLD

JONATHAN MS PEARCE

Why I Am Atheist and Not a Theist: How to Do Knowledge, Meaning, and Morality in a Godless World

Published by *Onus Books*

All rights reserved. No part of this publication may be reproduced, stored in a retrieval system, or transmitted in any form by any means, electronic, mechanical, photocopy, recording, or otherwise, without the prior permission of the publisher, except as provided for by UK copyright law.

Cover design: Onus Books

ISBN: 978-1-8382391-1-4

OB 18/33

About the author:

Jonathan M.S. Pearce is a teacher and author from Hampshire, UK, who has dedicated many years to studying all manner of things philosophical and theological. A philosopher with a marked interest in religion, he became a founder member of the *Skeptic Ink Network* (SIN) before moving to write for *Patheos Nonreligious* (Pearce's blog is *A Tippling Philosopher*). As a founder member of the Tippling Philosophers, from which his blog title comes, a friendly group of disparate believers and non-believers, and sort-of believers, based in Hampshire, he is a big advocate of casual philosophy groups meeting over pints of good ale. He lives with his partner and twin boys and wonders how she puts up with him. Being diagnosed with primary progressive multiple sclerosis, he would like to personally thank God for that gift, though rely more reasonably on science to find a treatment (which he did do, with successful stem cell therapy that has kept him stable for a couple of years – a resurrection of sorts but certainly not a miracle).

Acknowledgements:

Over the years, I have found that writing is a collaborative affair. I rely on the goodwill, time and effort (and not to mention expertise) of many good people. Some of these include Dana Horton, who worked tirelessly on an early manuscript, as well as (again) Jörg Fehlmann, whose eye for typos and grammar as a non-native speaker is a marvel. Geoff Benson is such a reliable ear and eye, providing always-welcome feedback. Thanks also to John Grove for looking over the manuscript. All of these people and more have been fantastic. May the cosmos shine on them before it eventually flickers out into an eternal heat death. Or something (atheism can be a tough sell). For more on that, you might need to get my book *Did God Create the Universe from Nothing?*...

Other books by Jonathan MS Pearce:

Free Will? An Investigation into Whether We Have Free Will Or Whether I Was Always Going to Write This Book

The Little Book of Unholy Questions

The Nativity: A Critical Examination

Beyond An Absence of Faith: Stories About the Loss of Faith and the Discovery of Self

13 Reasons to Doubt (ed.)

The Problem with "God": Classical Theism under the Spotlight

Did God Create the Universe from Nothing? Countering William Lane Craig's Kalam Cosmological Argument

Filling the Void: A Selection of Humanist and Atheist Poetry

Not Seeing God: Atheism in the 21st Century (ed.)

The Resurrection: A Critical Examination of the Easter Story

As Johnny Pearce:

Twins: A Survival Guide for Dads

Survival of the Fittest: Metamorphosis

Survival of the Fittest: Adaptation

The Curse of the Maya

Contents

To Julian,

without whom so much of what

I do and have done

simply would not have been possible.

He is something of a hero. To me, at any rate.[1]

---

[1] Firstly, who footnotes dedications? Well, it turns out that I do. Secondly, this reference to "hero" will become clearer throughout the text.

INTRODUCTION

This collection is a glimpse into my philosophical worldview of humanism, or scientific naturalism, or atheism with a whole bunch of add-ons. This is in no sense an exhaustive collection; far from it. I have written enough elsewhere on my blog or in almost a dozen other books and commissioned chapters that should give you a far more comprehensive account. What this volume does is give you an insight, enough to pique your interest, into my thinking that might hopefully lead you to continue thinking about these ideas and to continue your research elsewhere. Obviously, if you decide that this research should include purchasing my other books, then I would be more than delighted.

This project started as a way to compile a number of older essays into a collection. When I did this, I realised that I could order them coherently and create an overarching narrative flow – a thread through all the various pieces that connected them. From here, other pieces needed to be written and drawn in from my blog or elsewhere to flesh out what was no longer just a collection of essays but an exposition of my worldview and how I got there. Each discipline affected another until, like dominoes in reverse, they all aligned to create an interlocking pattern.

Some of the essays in here are heavier, denser affairs, but these are interspersed with lighter pieces to give you that range. This is not a case of the tortoise or the hare but the tortoise *and* the hare.

However, these topics, as with all areas of philosophy, if you really want to go to town on them, will require years of laborious research and reading. Feel free to accept that challenge. In the academic ivory towers of philosophy faculties, philosophers spend entire lives often on single niche areas, delving ever deeper into the rabbit holes they themselves have often dug. This collection is a light skip through the flowery meadows of each given topic, meadows that blow in the winds of thought, surrounding those ivory towers. If the skip leads to a towering climb, then job done. On the other hand, if you just enjoy the prance through the fields and nothing more, job also done. Just as long as you listen to those winds and feel the long grass brush against you as you walk.

Okay enough of the extended metaphor. Let's go with it.

Much of this writing here is available elsewhere, but some of it is also entirely original to this volume.

You might be forgiven for believing that these essays or chapters are disparate and unconnected, but they are not. In some sense, philosophy is hierarchical. You cannot make claims about morality without working out

1

epistemology (or figuring out what is the difference between justified belief and opinion), and without knowing what abstract objects (such as morality) are made of.

And so, with this in mind, I start off with an essay that looks to open up the realm of ontology, the investigation into existence. What reality is and what it is made up of. More often than not, theists (and nontheists, to be fair) will make claims on the veneer – moral claims, often – without having done the necessary groundwork: specifically, understanding that morality is an abstract concept and so it is probably worth understanding what an abstract concept is in order to understand what morality is.

I was once arguing with an interlocutor who took great efforts to disagree with most everything I said. Part of this was because we disagreed on pretty much all our conclusions by coming at things from completely different angles.

The problem, as far as I'm concerned, is that he argued *from* his conclusions and not *to* them. This is one of the main points I want to make here: we should approach reasoning to our conclusions from bottom up rather than top down. For me, the bottom-up approach is by far the more justifiable one.

Rationality is useless if it is not *sound*. This is what Martin Luther meant when he called reason a "whore". Pick the wrong premises, and rationality is going in the wrong direction. Therefore, *merely* that someone is "rational" means absolutely nothing about whether that person is well-connected to *reality*.

I think the goal is to have a bottom-up worldview, where you establish the building bricks and see what building arises. I think top-down approaches are dangerous, and I think this is what many people, particularly theists, do. They start with a conclusion and massage the evidence to fit. I will happily throw out conclusions, as I have done many times in the past, if that is where the path leads.

Is it better to have a conclusion that is correct but to which you poorly reason, or an incorrect conclusion to which you have argued very well (but perhaps an axiom is incorrect)? It is perhaps worth asking "What is the goal?"

If it is about finding the cure to a disease that is predicated upon correct truths, then having a poorly argued correct conclusion is *better*. If it is about fostering better critical thinking, for example, then perhaps the other option. Personally, I prefer the other option of well-argued valid and sound conclusions. Over time, arguing well will more likely reach a correct conclusion. I prefer working from the bottom up because this is about making sure everything from the bottom up is sound, leaving only the axiomatic foundational bricks unable to be fully (deductively) rationalised. We will later discuss how to ground our foundations. This approach gives a solid wall, hopefully, without any missing bricks.

As mentioned, conclusions are hierarchical. In other words, objective morality, for example, depends upon several other levels, including whether objective ideas in general *can* and *do* exist, and whether anything exists outside of our own heads.

Just like Descartes, I reason from what I indubitably know to be true and build from there. Anything else opens you up more probably to cognitive biases.

This can be seen in two ways of approaching a building construction project. A bottom-up approach would require a plan, blueprints, a firm foundation laid before proceeding with the rest of the building. A top-down approach might have all the workers turning up on day one with all the pieces they had pre-built, and trying to stick these disparate half-constructions together coherently.

We can exemplify this in a microchip construction flow chart. This is a genuine flow chart, though you don't need to know the technical terms involved in constructing microchips!

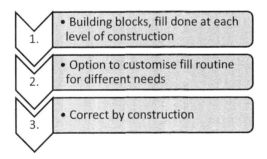

1. • Building blocks, fill done at each level of construction
2. • Option to customise fill routine for different needs
3. • Correct by construction

Above is a bottom-up approach. A top-down approach can be seen as follows:

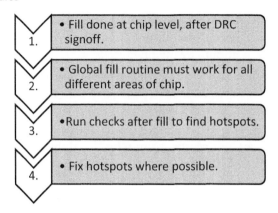

Forget the subject matter here – it's irrelevant. The point of showing these is hopefully to illustrate how the second flowchart exemplifies the problems with top-down thought; it's a case of fire-fighting and not fire prevention. "Fix hotspots where possible" can be translated as (in the context of what we will be talking about "firefight worldview problems when they pop up because you haven't thought this thing through properly".

This is what I have often said about fundamentalist evangelical Christians. Take the Westboro Baptist Church, who is the arguably the most controversial church organisation in America. They have been known to celebrate at the funerals of returning dead military service people because they are celebrating God's judgement: If God designed and created the world and is all-powerful, all-knowing and all-loving, and this is the eventuality he had brought about, then such perfect judgement is worthy of praise.

Controversially for myself, perhaps, is the claim that I make: such fundamentalist Christians are actually more consistent and coherent than liberal Christians, even though I much more closely morally align with said liberal Christians than with fundamentalist Christians like members of the Westboro Baptist Church. This is because the Westboro Baptist Church members are being logically consistent; but the problem is that they start with faulty axioms (they presuppose the truth of the Bible and the existence of their god as established by the Bible). They are taking the bottom-up approach but…garbage in, garbage out.

Liberal Christians take a different approach that looks more like a top-down affair, where they start with certain modern moral norms: Slavery is bad; we should be kind to people no matter their race, gender, sexuality; and so on. As a result, if they start with this, they then have to reverse engineer the evidence that they have (the Bible, theology, revelation to fit into this model. In microchip terms, this is "Fix hotspots wherever possible". Such an example would be squaring "homosexuality is morally fine" with "the Bible says homosexuality is a sin" or some similar incoherence. The liberal Christian ends up going through life fighting fires, mentally contorting to make the evidence fit their initially built conclusions. In short, it is mental gerrymandering.

But, you may say, in this situation, the liberal may use faulty construction to arrive at their conclusion and because their axioms are better, their conclusions are better than the fundamentalists. So what's the problem?

Sure. However, *this is my point.* It shows the importance of the axioms that exist at the bottom of hierarchies. If you start with faulty building bricks, then your worldview wall becomes shoddy. The ideal that we are heading for is good evidential bricks bonded with the mortar of sound reasoning built on robust axioms and initial foundational bricks. Both the axioms and the way that you build from there need to be well thought through.

This is the thread that runs through this book.

What I seek to do is set up the foundations by looking first at some useful ideas around definitions of key terms before examining the ontology (the existence properties) of abstract objects – ideas in our conception. This first section is hugely important as it affects the rest of the book in constructing the lens through which we will inspect the rest of reality.

After this, in the Epistemology (the study of knowledge and truth) section, we look at how I build up my system and structure of building up my knowledge. I also have a brief detour to look at how our minds deal with the external world is entirely mental or made up of matter. Proceeding are some pieces on inductive reasoning (looking at the past to inform our predictions of the future) and probability. This gives the reader the methods to analyse truth claims that they might come across, allowing them to understand how I can defend my atheistic naturalist worldview with an epistemological account.

In the section "Why I Am Not a Theist", I take the reader on a whistle-stop tour through the jungle of atheistic arguments showing that the God-concept is incoherent. This should fit neatly into the context of the rest of the book.

Next up, we have a jaunt into the world of teleology – meaning and purpose. This will be given clarity by the lens constructed in the opening section of the book, illustrating the coherence that underwrites this whole project. Meaning and purpose are abstract objects and they are constructed conceptually by the individual rather than making sense as being imposed on us by an outside agent (God).

Most philosophical arguments devolve (or evolve?) to morality – it is the inexorable direction of travel. This is largely because morality is what is important to our daily, psychological lives and how we organise ourselves. It is hard to establish morality without doing all the spadework into ontology, epistemology and teleology first. With this, in the home leg, I move into the Morality section to deconstruct theistic moral arguments before establishing my own beliefs on moral philosophy.

That is my roadmap; and off we go.

DEFINING OUR TERMS

"The beginning of wisdom is the definition of terms"

attributed to Socrates

Ordinary discourse recognizes several different kinds of things as possible objects of definition, and it recognizes several kinds of activity as defining a thing. To give a few examples, we speak of a commission as defining the boundary between two nations; of the Supreme Court as defining, through its rulings, "person" and "citizen"; of a chemist as discovering the definition of gold, and the lexicographer, that of 'cool'; of a participant in a debate as defining the point at issue; and of a mathematician as laying down the definition of "group." Different kinds of things are objects of definition here: boundary, legal status, substance, word, thesis, and abstract kind. Moreover, the different definitions do not all have the same goal: the boundary commission may aim to achieve precision; the Supreme Court, fairness; the chemist and the lexicographer, accuracy; the debater, clarity; and the mathematician, fecundity. The standards by which definitions are judged are thus liable to vary from case to case. The different definitions can perhaps be subsumed under the Aristotelian formula that a definition gives the essence of a thing. But this only highlights the fact that "to give the essence of a thing" is not a unitary kind of activity.

In philosophy, too, several different kinds of definitions are often in play, and definitions can serve a variety of different functions (e.g., to enhance precision and clarity). But, in philosophy, definitions have also been called in to serve a highly distinctive role: that of solving epistemological problems.

Anil Gupta, "Definitions", *Stanford Encyclopedia of Philosophy*

How I Define *Atheism*

I get the impression that some atheists don't like the term "belief" or "believe" because it sounds too much like religious talk. They prefer to define atheism in terms of being a lack, or not being a belief thus allowing them to avoid attack for having a *belief system*.

In a book by Franz Kiekeben called *The Truth About God,* a whistle-stop tour through atheism and counter-apologetics, Kiekeben discusses this definition of atheism, which is important because atheists often disagree on what they mean by the label itself. In the book, Kiekeben states:[1]

> Above, I said that an atheist is someone who believes that there are no gods. In recent times, however, it has become common among nonbelievers to define atheism more broadly. Rather than limiting the term to those who specifically reject the existence of any god, the new trend is to apply it to anyone who does not positively believe in a god – anyone, in other words, who is a nontheist. Consider agnosticism. Agnostics claim not to know whether there is a God. Hence, they (usually) neither believe nor disbelieve in him, but instead suspend their judgment. An agnostic does not *believe* that there are no gods, so he does not count as an atheist by the definition used in this book. But he obviously lacks a belief in any god. Thus, he is an atheist on the wider meaning of the term. So for that matter are infants (much to the horror of some parents), since infants do not yet have the conceptual ability to believe in a god.
>
> This broadening of the concept of atheism seems to be getting more popular. It is common to see debates on the existence of God in which the purported atheist maintains that he does not have to provide evidence that there isn't a deity: the onus of proof, he states, is entirely on the side of theism, for only the theist is making a positive claim. Now, if the atheist is merely someone who fails to believe for lack of evidence, then of course all he has to show is that the theist's arguments aren't convincing; he does not have to, in addition, present any arguments of his own. No wonder, then, that this view is popular among

---

[1] Kiekeben (2015), p. 16-17.

nonbelievers: it makes things considerably easier! And of course it's fine if people want to argue this way. Nevertheless, the broad definition is not the traditional meaning of the word. And besides, as mentioned, I'll be arguing that there are reasons for positively claiming that God does not exist, which means I'll be arguing for the narrower type of atheism. Therefore, it makes sense for me to use the term in its more traditional sense.

In technical parlance, these two definitions are labelled as *negative* or *weak atheism*, and *positive* or *strong atheism*. Negative/weak atheism is the lack of belief in a god; positive/strong atheism is the positive belief in the proposition that there is no god. In other words:

I do not believe there is a god.
Or
I believe that there is no god.

The first is a proposition that entails a negation of a positive statement, or a positive statement about a negation. Here, I am endorsing the second way of understanding atheism.

This is not just a lack of belief. This is saying, positively, that I believe something here; I am taking a position on an issue. I must not be the only one. People don't write books, listen to debates, and vociferously argue over merely a lack. Weak atheism entailing merely a lack of belief is not what such people hold, despite what they may say. Blogs and books and endless comments on blog threads and online forums entail more than defending a lack. These debates mean people are positively arguing for something. I also feel quite strongly about this and I appreciate that Kiekeben stated his position early on.

Children are born agnostic; they do not have the faculties to comment on the belief in God either way. Even as adults, we are agnostic about lots of things we know nothing about. For example, I am an a-unicornist. That is, I hold a firm belief that unicorns are mythical creatures that do not exist in the real world. The same with gods. All of them.

In the *Cambridge Companion to Atheism*, Michael Martin sets this out early:[1]

---

[1] Martin (2007), p. 1-2.

If you look up "atheism" in a dictionary, you will find it defined as the belief that there is no God. Certainly, many people understand "atheism" in this way. Yet this is not what the term means if one considers it from the point of view of its Greek roots. In Greek "a" means "without" or "not," and "theos" means "god." From this standpoint, an atheist is someone without a belief in God; he or she need not be someone who believes that God does not exist. Still, there is a popular dictionary meaning of "atheism" according to which an atheist is not simply one who holds no belief in the existence of a God or gods but is one who believes that there is no God or gods. This dictionary use of the term should not be overlooked. To avoid confusion, let us call it *positive atheism* and let us call the type of atheism derived from the original Greek roots *negative atheism*....

Negative atheism in the broad sense is then the absence of belief in any god or Gods, not just the absence of belief in a personal theistic God, and negative atheism in the narrow sense is the absence of belief in a theistic God. Positive atheism in the broad sense is, in turn, disbelief in all gods, with positive atheism in the narrow sense being the disbelief in a theistic God. For positive atheism in the narrow sense to be successfully defended, two tasks must be accomplished. First, the reasons for believing in a theistic God must be refuted; in other words, negative atheism in the narrow sense must be established. Second, reasons for disbelieving in the theistic God must be given.

Whilst Martin and Kiekeben may disagree on the traditional element of the term, I think they are both spot on in making an important distinction between the two. I am definitely in the camp of the strong, positive atheists. And you shouldn't, as an atheist, be afraid of using the term "believe". It is one single belief, no more, no less. It is not a belief *system* or a religion. Everything else is up for grabs. In some sense, everything is a belief outside of "I think; therefore, I am".

We have faith over certain axiomatic claims, like I am not a brain in a vat or I exist in a world like in *The Matrix*. Can I prove it? No, I can only prove, by doubting, that I exist. Can I prove that I am not in *The Matrix*? No, I take that as a self-evident truth, which is not grounded in any evidence, since by definition, it can't be. There is a little faith involved in that claim, and it is a belief.

However, my belief that gods/God does not exist is founded on a lot more rational spadework than my brain not being in a vat.

What Is "True Christianity"?

Having just discussed, albeit briefly, the label of "atheism" and "atheist", it might be prudent to spend a little time discussing a related term: "Christianity" and "Christian". Things start getting a little trickier here because there are arguably an awful lot more properties involved with a term like "Christianity" than there are with "atheism".

How does one go about arguing that their version of Christianity is the "True Christianity"™? I have discussed this elsewhere with regard to Islam and its differences to Christianity, in two essays "'True Islam' and violent extremism – redux"[1] and "Islam vs Christianity: the core differences".[2] I will now quote from the latter of the two:

Comparing the Provenance of Islam and Christianity

It starts with the holy books, the codification and revelation of Christianity and Islam. With Christianity, we have the Bible, which is the "inspired word of God". This can mean several things to different people. However, most Christians believe this to mean that the books, many and varied, were written by humans, though with some kind of divine inspiration. Perhaps not, though. The key is that it was mere humans who wrote things down, itself an interpretative process. Further, the reading of the holy book is an additional interpretative process over and above the interpretative process of writing.

The Qu'ran, on the other hand, is *the* word of God, dictated to Muhammad, and written down accordingly. You can't argue with it, because you would be arguing directly with God. In fact, to get the full effect, you really need to read it in Arabic, the original language of the book. Although there is some interpretative process going on in reading it, the scope is far less when compared to the Christian Bible. We know who took down the dictation, and supposedly lots about him. With the Bible, we can merely guess at many of the writers. And critical scholarship allows us to be thoroughly skeptical about the traditions of who supposedly wrote the books.

What this has meant is that the evolution of the religions has been quite different. And this has been the strength and weakness of both. Let me explain.

---

[1] Pearce (2015).
[2] Pearce (2014).

Christianity has been able to evolve throughout its history. Its strength, in evolutionary or memetic terms, is its adaptability. It has been able to adapt to society, such that with scientific, technological, economic and moral progress, Christianity has adapted. We can see this empirically by the fact that there are supposedly some 42,000 denominations of the religion. There is a Christianity for everyone. If you hate gays or love gays; hate slavery or love it; hate capitalism or love it; hate socialism or love it – there is a Christianity for you.

Biblical criticism, especially since reformation times, has been encouraged, by and large. Naturally, all these factions mean that theologians and Biblical scholars disagree quite considerably with each other.

The flipside of this is that the religion of Christianity is somewhat, arguably, bastardised from its purest form, whatever that may be. It has been diluted to adapt to whatever the prevalent school of thought requires. As economics and morality have undergone huge zeitgeists, so too has Christianity. And this might be argued to be its weakness, too.

Islam, however, has been very different. Due to the nature of the holy book, Islam requires that society adapts to *it*. Throughout history, Islam has remained a fairly monolithic construction (albeit with political schisms along the Sunni/Shia divide and with other interpretative schools – just fewer of them than with Christianity). For example, in the banking sector, or morally, within the context of its primarily theocratic domain, Islam has not particularly shifted from its inception in the 600s CE. Lending is outlawed in certain forms. Stoning and beheading seem to be still widely accepted in these same forms. Sharia law often prevails. And secular Islamic countries are few and far between, if at all ever properly secular (e.g., Turkey).

What this means, in evolutionary or memetic terms, is that Islam requires the environment to adapt to it. Islam has changes little in response to environmental constraints (yes, we can argue about fuzzy edges, but you get the picture). So its strength is that it appears to be a purer religion in comparison to Christianity, and purer in relation to its earlier forms. The evolution of Christianity against Islam produces two entirely different pictures: One is a large, foliage-burdened tree of evolutionary worldviews. The other is a more streamlined set of grasses, perhaps.

So when we see the moral paradigm of the modern world, we can see that Christianity is able to mould better to the environment, while Islam struggles. And where Islam and the modern world meet, there is little shaking of hands, and much bloodshed.

Islam needs a reformation, for sure, but I don't think the Qu'ran really permits such a much-needed philosophical transformation.

This is not to belittle the comparatively limited (though significant) variation within Islam, but to show that the variation within Christianity is far more widespread, and that this has its basis in textual provenance.

The Meaning of the Words "Christian" and "Christianity"

As ever, much will depend on the meaning of the word(s) so that to stop anyone claiming to be a Christian there has to be some minimum requirement. We might agree by dictionary consensus that, if I claim to be Christian, it at least means I am…

1. adj: relating to or professing Christianity or its teachings. 2. noun: a person who has received Christian baptism or is a believer in Christianity.

But this is open to a deluge of subjective interpretation. What *are* the teachings? If I *profess* them but don't *do* them, what then? If I *claim* them but don't *believe* them deep down where no one else will know this, what then? What if I think that the teachings are really left field in a way that is essentially unrecognisable from any other known Christianity as I use some "crazy" interpretative lens? Being "a believer in Christianity" becomes a circular definitional problem with no clear resolution. We get back to the definition of Christianity being:

1. the religion based on the person and teachings of Jesus Christ, or its beliefs and practices.

The most we can perhaps get from this is that a person who claims they are *not* a Christian (or who does not claim they are and bears no connection to Christianity) is not a Christian. And everyone else is somehow in…

True Christianity™

As we can see, approaching something that looks like True Christianity is problematic. It depends on whether you derive your religion and teachings from:

15

(1) the Bible as a revelatory text
(2) personal revelatory experiences
(3) extra-biblical, non-subjective sources (other books, artefacts etc.)

Or all of the above.

We can see some of the issues with #1. as stated in the introduction. Is religion subjective? Do we accept a postmodern approach whereby you make of Christianity what you want and that *your truth* is *a truth?* Or, on the other hand, is there something like an objective truth? Or, failing that, if there is no *one* particular truth, are some versions of Christianity just more wrong and more right than others even if there is no individual Christianity that represents True Christianity?

True Christianity relies on a correct interpretation of the Bible – if not all of it then at least some. For example, take Noah's Flood: it either happened or it didn't. There are five options for the Christian:

(1) Noah's Flood happened and I understood it correctly from the Bible.
(2) Noah's Flood happened and I misunderstood the theology.
(3) Noah's Flood didn't happen but it shows some other truth, that I get right.
(4) Noah's Flood didn't happen but it shows some other truth that I get wrong.
(5) Noah's Flood didn't happen and it doesn't have correct symbolic meaning and has erroneously turned up in the Bible. Oops.

Or different shades of these – we could be wrong about the literal accounts, plus wrong about the theological interpretation. We also have an issue with the variety in the Bible: we could be right on Noah's Ark but way off on slavery and the Atonement. It's a very tall order to get a full-on True Christianity right, down to every jot and tittle.

Truth

Granted, this is my interpretation of truth (my truth about truth…). The problem with defining a True Christianity (TC) is *knowing* that your TC is *the* TC. This is the case for any truth proposition. I defer to Descartes (as I did in invoking *The Matrix* in the previous short piece) in that the only thing we can know is that you, the thinking entity (whatever that is) exists – *cogito ergo sum*. Beyond that, it's all probability. We will talk about this a lot more in some of the coming essays in this collection.

Most people adhere to the correspondence theory of truth (my epistemology is a bit of a mish-mash of theories, personally, as you will see). This means what you think of truth is that some proposition you believe as true corresponds accurately and objectively to the world (outside your head). The problem here is that you cannot indubitably *know* that your truth claim is correct. I don't *know* I'm not a brain in a vat so I cannot *indubitably know* any other claim is true. For example, I would argue that the story of Noah's Ark never happened, but may contain a symbolic meaning for some people. How do I know if I have hit the target on Noah's Ark if I can't even know the world exists outside of an evil daemon injecting these ideas into my head as dreams? There will be much more talk on epistemology later.

Let's then broadly accept this state of affairs…for now…and apply it to True Christianity.

I might be right in that my views on Noah's Ark correspond precisely to an objective reality. I just can't *know* this short of God coming down and telling me so. Even then, I could be imagining that or experiencing it in *The Matrix*. And even if I am correct about Noah, I could be way out with regard to many of my other interpretations of the Bible.

And this, of course, depends wholly as to whether the Bible has divine sanction, that *it really is the inspired word of God*, that it is the best revelation with the very best interpretation. All that gets you to something approaching a True Christianity.

This is evidenced in what we see in the world around us: 42,000 different denominations of Christianity and Christians at seminaries, universities, theological institutes, homes and churches busily disagreeing with each other about what this or that means in the Bible – each and every day, for thousands of years.

Conclusion

I am an atheist, so there is no True Christianity.

But, if I was a Christian, it would depend on:

(1) The Bible being accurate.

(2) Any personal revelations (revelations of others) being accurate.

(3) Extra-biblical sources, whatever they might be, being accurate.

(4) Certain theologians and thinkers being accurate.

(5) Me being accurate in my interpretations of all of the above.

And this is a tall order. The chances of any individual Christian stumbling across a True Christianity is incredibly slim and they can never then know they have hit the jackpot. Certain sects, such as the Catholic Church, claim to have TC primacy. But establishing this beyond a reasonable doubt is tough because it essentially comes down to your exegetical approach to the Bible (i.e., how you interpret it) and the historical and theological claims therein.

To refer back to Muslims, it is somewhat easier to determine what True Islam is when you believe the holy book has the provenance of the Qu'ran. Fully-fledged biblical literalists do this too, and so are probably more akin to Islam and Muslims than they would like to admit. But if their primary axiom, that reliance on the infallible revelation of the Bible, is erroneous in some way, then they might be way off the mark.

This is a minefield. And because it is a minefield, no Christian really agrees as to what Christianity truly is (and perhaps postmodernism seems all the more appealing). Since no independent arbitration looks particularly likely, we might as well accept (certainly from an atheist position) that anyone claiming to be a Christian is, indeed, a Christian (within a reasonable definition of the word as accepted by consensus, itself problematic).

I find it easier to argue for a True Islam given the provenance of their holy book than I do for a True Christianity given the Bible is the sort of collection of books that it is.

In conclusion, there is no such thing as True Christianity. And even if there were, it would be impossible to know if you had it right. But, still, I'm sure you're right enough to go to heaven, but Martin over there has the wrong version and you won't be seeing him in the afterlife.

Naturalism and Supernaturalism

Supernaturalism and naturalism are famously difficult terms to define. Intuitively, we know what they mean, and what we mean when we use the terms. But when it gets down to the minutiae, it can become somewhat fuzzy. A trite soundbite might be something like, "The Cosmos is all that is or ever was or ever will be," as the great physicist Carl Sagan said in the ground-breaking series *Cosmos*. But it lacks philosophical clarity.

To start us off, it is worth noting that there is a difference between what is known as *methodological naturalism* and *metaphysical naturalism*. As physicist and skeptic Lawrence Lerner states:[1]

> *Methodological naturalism* is not a "doctrine" but an essential aspect of the methodology of science, the study of the natural universe. If one believes that natural laws and theories based on them will not suffice to solve the problems attacked by scientists – that supernatural and thus nonscientific principles must be invoked from time to time – then one cannot have the confidence in scientific methodology that is prerequisite to doing science. The spectacular successes over four centuries of science based on methodological naturalism cannot be gainsaid. On the other hand, a scientist who, when stumped, invokes a supernatural cause for a phenomenon he or she is investigating is guaranteed that no scientific understanding of the problem will ensue.

On the other hand, metaphysical naturalism is a philosophical commitment that the supernatural, however defined, does not exist. I will give you a long quote on naturalism from theoretical physicist and sometimes philosopher, Sean Carroll, whose book *The Big Picture* is well worth reading. He states:[2]

> *Naturalism* is a philosophy according to which there is only one world – the natural world, which exhibits unbroken patterns (the laws of nature), and which we can learn

---

[1] Lerner (2003).

[2] Sean Carroll's summary of "Poetic Naturalism", undated on his website *Preposterous Universe*, https://www.preposterousuniverse.com/poetic-naturalism/ (retrieved 02/02/2021).

about through hypothesis testing and observation. In particular, there is no supernatural world – no gods, no spirits, no transcendent meanings.

I like to talk about a particular approach to naturalism, which can be thought of as *Poetic*. By that I mean to emphasize that, while there is only one world, there are many ways of talking about the world. "Ways of talking" shouldn't be underestimated; they can otherwise be labeled "theories" or "models" or "vocabularies" or "stories," and if a particular way of talking turns out to be sufficiently accurate and useful, the elements in its corresponding vocabulary deserve to be called *real*.

The poet Muriel Rukeyser once wrote, "The universe is made of stories, not atoms." That is absolutely correct. There is more to the world than what happens; there are the ways we make sense of it by telling its story. The vocabulary we use is not handed to us from outside; it's ultimately a matter of our choice.

A poetic naturalist will deny that notions like "right and wrong," "purpose and duty," or "beauty and ugliness" are part of the fundamental architecture of the world. The world is just the world, unfolding according to the patterns of nature, free of any judgmental attributes. But these moral and ethical and aesthetic vocabularies can be perfectly useful ways of talking about the world. The criteria for choosing the best such ways of talking will necessarily be different than the criteria we use for purely descriptive, scientific vocabularies. There won't be a single rational way to delineate good from bad, sublime from repulsive. But we can still speak in such terms, and put in the hard work to make our actions live up to our own internal aspirations. We just have to admit that judgments come from within ourselves.

Indeed, Carroll's book is consistent with much of what I have will be saying throughout this collection, including with regard to my ontological outlook (see the next section, "Ontology"). Concerning the focus on the mental, it is worth bringing into play Richard Carrier, prominent atheist thinker, who offers the following:

> In short, I argue "naturalism" means, in the simplest terms, that every mental thing is entirely caused by fundamentally nonmental things, and is entirely dependent on nonmental things for its existence. Therefore, "supernaturalism" means that at least some mental things cannot be reduced to nonmental things. As I summarized in the Carrier-Wanchick debate (and please pardon the dry, technical wording):
>
> *If [naturalism] is true, then all minds, and all the contents and powers and effects of minds, are entirely caused by natural [i.e. fundamentally nonmental] phenomena. But if naturalism is false, then some minds, or some of the contents or powers or effects of minds, are causally independent of nature. In other words, such things would then be partly or wholly caused by themselves, or exist or operate directly or fundamentally on their own.*

So when we talk of any supernatural phenomena (e.g., a miracle), we are never *really* talking about some kind of observed phenomenon that may take place in the world unconnected to gods or magic, minds – say some interesting and as yet unexplained quark behaviour in a given scenario. We are talking about something happening because of a mind – whether of gods or fairies, demigods or ghosts.

Carrier concludes:

> Many naturalists have a poor conception of how to define naturalism or the supernatural. They might know it when they see it, but when they try to capture in words what exactly it is they are talking about, they often come up with a badly worded travesty. I've done what little I can to remedy this by developing and testing a precise definition of naturalism and the supernatural, providing a sensible and usable natural-supernatural distinction, which also happens to align adequately well with how people use these words in practice (as I believe our terminology ought to do as much as possible). And now I have amplified my past work on this by surveying numerous

hypothetical examples of how my proposed distinctions can be applied.

In defining the words "natural" and "supernatural" as I do, I differ from the legal and science community, as exemplified most recently in the Kitzmiller v. Dover case. There, Judge Jones was bound by legal principles to follow case precedent and the professional standards of established industries. Following the 1982 McLean decision he found the courts had defined "supernatural intervention" as intervention that "cannot be explained by natural causes, or be proven through empirical investigation, and is therefore neither testable nor falsifiable." Jones further cited the official statement of the National Academy of Sciences, which declares "claims of supernatural intervention... are not science because they are not testable by the methods of science." Thus we see the same trend in both the legal and scientific communities, to veer away from metaphysical distinctions and in favor of purely epistemological ones, but as my articles, and now examples, have shown, this does not track the real-world use of the word at all, which can tend to no good.

I think the legal and scientific communities are on a bad track with this (hence the barely coherent discussion of the supernatural in Wikipedia), especially since the same point can be made without abusing the word "supernatural." It is enough to say, for example, that creationism isn't science, not because it is supernatural, but simply because it is untestable (assuming you can prove it is). There is no need to conflate the two.

Though I understand their reasons for wanting to keep metaphysics out of it (since both enterprises are more fundamentally epistemological), I disagree with their attempted solution of coopting and changing the meaning of a popular word. That's the wrong way to go about it. Hence I believe a paradigm shift is needed in those communities regarding how the word "supernatural" is defined and applied. Both law and science must get back in line with ordinary English and real-world language, ideas, and concerns.

What is important here is that the mental world needs to be within the scope of *naturalism* (I will use "naturalism" to essentially refer to metaphysical naturalism from henceforth) and that what is claimed of naturalism is testable and falsifiable. Very briefly, if you can test it, it falls under the purview of naturalism. For example, something like prayer is unfalsifiable in many senses: I could claim prayer works, and when it does not, just assert "God works in mysterious ways". You cannot really test this hypothesis.

Conversations about naturalism often find parallels with discussions concerning consciousness and the mental realm. For consciousness, naturalists will either adopt some kind of monism, where mental *is* physical (monism refers to a sort of "oneness"), or supervenience. Supervenience is where the something (the mental) *depends* necessarily on something else (the physical). In other words, either consciousness *is* equivalent to something physical in some way, or it necessarily depends on the physical for its existence.

Dualism, where the mental and the physical are distinct in some way, can be seen in terms of *property dualism*, where a single physical substance may have mental and physical *properties*. This is opposed to *substance dualism* that suggests that there are two fundamental *substances* (i.e., matter and mind) that inhere two different sets of properties.

One might claim that naturalism is all that can be found by the methodology of science. If you can't test it, it's not natural. We might say that something that is natural is bound by the Laws of Nature.[1]

This is where methodological naturalism comes in because we might discover a new, unexplained physical phenomenon. Rather than think it might be some supernatural phenomenon, we assume it is natural and part of the natural fabric around us, and we do so based on inductive reasoning (i.e., what we have observed repeatedly).

Philosophy, as you are seeing, is thoroughly interconnected. Specifically, you can't talk about God and naturalism without dealing with epistemology (knowledge and truth), ontology (existence properties) and, very often, morality.

Steven Schafersman (in "Naturalism is Today An Essential Part of Science", a paper presented at the *Conference on Naturalism, Theism and the Scientific Enterprise*) synthesizes many definitions to create his own:[2]

---

[1] See Pearce (2020) where I discuss what Laws of Nature are and whether they describe reality or prescribe it.

[2] Sadly, his paper is no longer on the internet, though I was able to retrieve it from internet archives.

In my own definition, a synthesis of those above, naturalism is the philosophy that maintains that (1) nature is all there is and whatever exists or happens is natural; (2) nature (the universe or cosmos) consists only of natural elements, that is, of spatiotemporal material elements–matter and energy–and non-material elements–mind, ideas, values, logical relationships, etc.– that are either associated with the human brain or exist independently of the brain and are therefore somehow immanent in the structure of the universe; (3) nature works by natural processes that follow natural laws, and all can, in principle, be explained and understood by science and philosophy; and (4) the supernatural does not exist, i.e., only nature is real, therefore, supernature is non-real. Naturalism is therefore a metaphysical position opposed mainly by supernaturalism. It is not an ethical system, although a variety–pragmatic naturalism, a synthesis of pragmatism and naturalism–does develop ethical positions. Furthermore, naturalism is a subset of metaphysical realism....

Even though naturalism has two primary sources in philosophy, "materialism in metaphysics and empiricism [and skepticism] in epistemology" (Kurtz, 1990, p. 12), naturalism does not necessitate a commitment to materialism, a philosophy with which it is often confused (more on this below). Materialism recognizes the existence of non-material elements, but claims that they are unconditionally produced by or associated with material elements, that is, the non-material elements would not exist if the material elements did not exist. Certainly most philosophical naturalists today are materialists, and methodological materialism is probably universally adopted among scientists today, but idealism or dualism could be true and naturalism would still be viable.

Naturalism is pretty much a case of Ockham's Razor (where the "simplest explanation" – the one with the fewest unnecessary entities – is preferred), in one sense, being that which is required to understand our physical environment, and no more. We have no need of the supernatural hypothesis. Phil Rimmer, commenting on my article ("Concerning

Metaphysical and Methodological Naturalism" – Pearce 2020b) produced a pretty good working definition that I think is worth including here:[1]

> A good definition of natural is to say it is that which is bound by law, hence a Law of Nature.
>
> All observed natural phenomena are seen to be lawful and lawfully consistent even if the laws are not known. Even radioactivity is statistically lawful.
>
> The supernatural would be that which is not seemingly lawful and is often associated with imputations of unseen agency. Any phenomenon claimed to be innate magic possessed by objects, if seen to be lawful, would need to be re-categorised as natural. Thus sunstones and south-seeking stones.
>
> A spurious claim of supernatural for that which is natural is a technique used by hucksters, often supported by the duped, who, in their occasional slow counter-realisations, often double down for shame or for a little duping of their own.
>
> Metaphysical objects are mental might-bes. These are just thinking tools that, like all mental objects, exist in the natural space that includes brains.

Of course, one could defer back again to the example of a newfound phenomenon (any new scientific finding) – how would this fit here? Well, if the phenomenon was predictable, reproducible, observable in some way, then it would fall into the purview of naturalism. This is why, in my essay "The Argument from Format" that you will soon read, I argue that the universe and its laws qua naturalism must be deterministic. I can't make sense of any other form of reality that gives rise to such complexity as we see around us if it does not work to lawlike behaviour.

Personally, I don't rule out supernatural activity *a priori* – out of hand before any rational evidence is considered. We will soon discuss the idea that much knowledge really is an exercise in probability, and more accurately in probability inferred from observations of the world around us. The probability of the supernatural existing is, therefore, vanishingly small. Our whole world is a combinations of sensory data collections and conclusions,

---

[1] Pearce (2020b).

and so probability is the only way we can really and pragmatically makes sense of it.

You might go down the rabbit hole of wondering whether rather a-causal mental or abstract domains are part of a naturalistic worldview, such as mathematics. I would argue maths is a conceptual language that humans have developed to understand and navigate the physical world around us, and falls into the mental → physical supervenience.

My working definition, condensing the previous quotes that I agree with down to a parsimonious distillation, might be:

Supernaturalism: The belief that some mental, intentional force can and does overcome the Laws of Nature, with the caveat that science and knowledge is a changing field and that our understanding of the details of the Laws of Nature is not immutable.

In later essays, I will flesh this out to illustrate how I can evaluate truth claims that may concern the supernatural.

What we have here is a situation whereby naturalism (and by definition supernaturalism) is whatever an individual believes it is, or a group of individuals agree it is. And this, as we have seen, is exactly the same situation with Christianity. It is whatever people agree it to be. And agreement, at heart, is a pragmatic tool to get things achieved.

Where we fail to agree on a term, the term remains nebulous. Though it may be useful from a macro-perspective, it becomes a little more problematic where its usage requires a magnification of the term to lay out its individual properties.

This little discussion about labels should now have warmed you up to the first substantial piece here: a bigger discussion about labels.

ONTOLOGY

As a first approximation, ontology is the study of what there is. Some contest this formulation of what ontology is, so it's only a first approximation. Many classical philosophical problems are problems in ontology: the question whether or not there is a god, or the problem of the existence of universals, etc. These are all problems in ontology in the sense that they deal with whether or not a certain thing, or more broadly entity, exists. But ontology is usually also taken to encompass problems about the most general features and relations of the entities which do exist. There are also a number of classic philosophical problems that are problems in ontology understood this way. For example, the problem of how a universal relates to a particular that has it (assuming there are universals and particulars), or the problem of how an event like John eating a cookie relates to the particulars John and the cookie, and the relation of eating, assuming there are events, particulars and relations. These kinds of problems quickly turn into metaphysics more generally, which is the philosophical discipline that encompasses ontology as one of its parts. The borders here are a little fuzzy. But we have at least two parts to the overall philosophical project of ontology, on our preliminary understanding of it: first, say what there is, what exists, what the stuff [of] reality is made out of; secondly, say what the most general features and relations of these things are.

Thomas Hofweber, "Logic and Ontology", The Stanford Encylopedia of Philosophy

Why Abstract Objects Is the Only Argument in Town

Setting the Scene

People the world over, philosophers included, often prefer to argue about the big things: the existence of God or gods, what type of moral value system we should be using, what personhood is, what politics would serve the world the best, what knowledge is, what constitutes truth, so on and so forth.

But they are all wrong. Well, they are not wrong, but they are looking further down the line than they should be, using binoculars to look in the distance when they should be looking at the ground in front of them. It is like arguing about what colour paint you should use to cover the rust on your metal railing without arguing about what causes the rust and how to stop it from rusting in the first place.

But what could be more important than these huge ideas?

Quite simply, what these "ideas" are made of and whether they really "exist".

When talking about morality, when talking about categories of personhood or essences (what is the essence of a human being, and does it include the behaviour of being homosexual, for example?), we are talking about abstract ideas or abstract objects. It seems rather more pertinent to me, rather than arguing what constitutes the "essence" of a "human being", that we should be arguing about whether abstract ideas even exist and in what form they might do so.

Therefore, we really need to argue about ontology: the nature of existence. How do abstract ideas exist? After all, I can talk about morality, so in some sense, it exists, even if only in my mind and yours as you listen to me. But what about out there, in the aether? Does morality take on some form, outside of our minds?

If We Didn't So Much as Exist

To further set the scene for you, ask yourself this: If all sentient creatures in the universe ceased to exist right now, would the following things exist?

29

- Morality
- Love
- Loyalty
- $3 + 3 = 6$
- Quadratic equations
- Philosophy
- Human rights
- The legal age to vote
- The right to carry arms

The list is very long indeed, but you get the picture. If there was no mind capable of understanding the above ideas, would the ideas exist? Do these ideas require a mind to conceive them, or can they exist independently of such a mind? If sentient creatures died, would morality die too? And mathematics? Is mathematics just a pragmatic language we use to navigate the world around us, a map that shouldn't be confused with the terrain itself?

We might call this mind-independent existence "objective" existence. In other words, is mathematics or morality objective?

It All Started with Plato

Plato gave birth to the idea that ideas exist outside of our minds such that this idea is now called "Platonic realism". In this concept, realism is the notion that ideas *really do exist*. He claimed that everything, including numbers and geometrical shapes, had its perfect form. This was later built upon and refined into a position called "essentialism" – certain things have their essential properties or essential forms. Thus, a man and a woman each have their Platonic forms as essential properties. Men or women who fail to adhere to these forms are not being a man or woman "properly". They are not fulfilling the necessary requirements to qualify, using the property criteria of being a man or woman. We might see this in terms of discussions over gender, gender roles, biological sex (seen as a binary), sexuality, and so on.

This can apply to any label or any categorisation. For example, a hero or a chair, the number three, a human being, personhood, all have their individual essence to which such objects must qualify, or not.

These abstract forms are often seen in terms of entailing other abstracts known as universals: entities or qualities that are shared over individual things. Apples may have the universal property of redness. So redness and appleness are both universals.

Somehow, out in the aether, (or existing in God, maybe?), or however the realist wants to try to establish it, there is the prescriptive form of any given thing in existence.

Such (Platonic) thinkers believe that universals like redness exist separately from the particular objects (apples) that contain said property. This is what Platonic realism states. There are other types of realism but let's keep this digestible.

Some arguments propose that, in order to have truth value in statements, universals must exist. For example, "This apple is red" implies that the universal of redness exists for the proposition to actually be truthful. Already, we can see that the argument about universal forms underwrites arguments about truth, and perhaps, then, knowledge.

The problem: Where is the locus of these universals – where can these universals be found? And what *is* their ontology?

Conceiving These Things Subjectively

At the opposite end of the spectrum, we have the individual conceiving these ideas. As we explore this end of the spectrum, there are two positions that I will explain before conflating them. The first position is "nominalism".

Nominalism stands in stark contrast to realism in that the adherents state that only particulars exist, and not universals. Properties of particular objects can account for eventual similarity between objects (such as the green of grass and the green of a painted wall). But universals do not exist.

The second position is called "conceptual nominalism" or "conceptualism". This position states that universals and abstract ideas exist but only in the mind of the conceiver. Thus, if all conceivers were to disappear, the ideas and concepts that they were conceiving would also disappear. If a tree falls in the forest…

Whether they exist only in the minds of conceivers or not at all, the notion that these abstract ideas don't exist objectively (having "ontic existence") is important here, and what makes me conflate these two positions. Specifically, nominalism and conceptual nominalism both conclude that abstract ideas do not exist out there, in the aether, or wherever one may posit. At best, they exist in our minds. But like any clean room has its tidy boxes and cupboards, our minds need their compartments and filing systems.

We love a good label, even if the box to which it pertains contains a whole range of things that others wouldn't dream of putting there.

Categorising Things

We love to use categories. That's a blue flower, that's a red car, that's an adult, that's a child. It is how we navigate reality in a practical sense – it provides our conceptual map. However, you should not confuse the map with the terrain. Essentially, we make up labels to represent a number of different properties. A cat has these properties, a dog has a different set. Red has these properties, blue those. Often, we agree on this labelling, but sometimes we do not. What constitutes a hero? A chair? Is a tree stump a chair?

The problem occurs when we move between categories. It is at these times that we realise the simplicity of the categories shows weakness in the system.

You reach eighteen years of age. You are able to vote. You are now classed as an adult. You are allowed to buy alcoholic drinks (in the UK). But there is barely any discernible difference between you, physically and mentally, from 17 years, 364 days, 11 hours, 59 minutes, 59 seconds, and you 1 second later.

However, we decide to define that one second change at midnight as differentiating the two "yous" and seeing you move from child (and here we can assign cub-categories of newborn, baby, toddler, child, adolescent, etc.) to adult. These categories are, in some sense, arbitrary in where we exactly draw the line. Some countries choose sixteen, some younger, and others choose older. These are conceptual constructs that allow us to navigate about a continuum of time. You can look at a five-year-old and the same person at twenty-eight and clearly see a difference. But that five-year-old looks like the same person one second later, yet there is no discernible difference.

However, it is pragmatically useful for us to categorise; otherwise, things like underage sex and drinking would take place with wild abandon, perhaps. For example, sixteen for the age of consent is rather arbitrary. Why not five seconds later? Four days? Three and a half years? Indeed, our categorisations of time (a year, month, week, day, hour, second) are themselves in some sense arbitrary and constructed as a result of the context of planet Earth and how it rotates around its axis and orbits around the sun.

Speciation is exactly the same. There is no real time where a population of organisms actually transforms into a new species. Because species is a human conceptual construct that does not exist objectively. We name things "homo sapiens" but cannot define exactly where speciation occurred (when homo sapiens first came into existence, definitively, as a species). In one sense, it *does not occur*. In another, if you look at vastly different places on the continuum, it does (at least in our minds).

Conceptual nominalism denies the existence of abstracts so these categories are conceptually invented. Thus, species do not exist as objective categories. We invent them for pragmatic reasons and could use completely different criteria. Indeed, there are other proposals for taxonomy. As such, if all people who knew about the category of homo sapiens suddenly died and information about them was lost, then so too would be lost the concept and categorisation.

When we look at two very different parts of a continuum, we find it easy to say certain things are different categories. But when we look in finer detail, this falls apart. There is a fuzzy logic at play.

Species exist only in our heads. Then, we might agree about them. And, only then, so we can nicely label pictures in books, or in our heads, and in doing so communicate this idea to others. This is practical philosophy.

Labels, Labels, Labels

We may think that things like tables, chairs, humans, rocks, lemmings and so on exist. They do in one sense – an arrangement of matter/energy – but in the sense of the abstract labels of "rock" or "chair", they are only abstract labels. Their existence, in Platonic terms, as some kind of objective entity, requires the philosophical position of (Platonic) realism. As mentioned above, this means that universals such as rock or chair, redness or doghood, and abstractions ("natural kinds",[1] characteristics, relations, properties etc.) are not spatial, temporal or mental. Instead, they have a different ontology, existing separately from the objects that instantiate such properties.

---

[1] "Scientific disciplines frequently divide the particulars they study into kinds and theorize about those kinds. To say that a kind is natural is to say that it corresponds to a grouping that reflects the structure of the natural world rather than the interests and actions of human beings. We tend to assume that science is often successful in revealing these kinds; it is a corollary of scientific realism that when all goes well the classifications and taxonomies employed by science correspond to the real kinds in nature. The existence of these real and independent kinds of things is held to justify our scientific inferences and practices.", Bird & Tobin (2017).

For example, in order for the statement "John Smith is a gardener" to hold a truth value, there must be some existence property defined by "gardener" such as "gardenership". This universal is different from the instance of the universal property found in John Smith. What this means is that the molecules and atoms that make the chair, already existed in some form or other before the "chair" came to be. It is the same for John Smith. So the matter or energy did not "begin to exist". This merely leaves the label of "chair", or "John Smith".[1]

The nominalist adopts a position that denies the existence of universals, such as redness or gardenership The nominalist claims that only individuals or particulars exist. The conceptualist or conceptual nominalist, on the other hand, claims that universals only exist within the framework of the thinking (conceiving) mind.

Most philosophers agree that abstract objects are causally inert, by definition. This means that, at best, the abstract label is unable to have causal power anyway (regardless of its ontology).

To illustrate this, let's now look at the label of "chair". This is an abstract concept, the nominalist posits, that exists only in the mind of the conceiver. We, as humans, label the chair abstractly and it only means a chair to those who see it as a chair – i.e., it is subjective. The concept is not itself fixed. My idea of a chair is different to yours, is different to a cat's, to an alien's, and to a human who has never seen or heard of a chair (early humans who had never seen a chair, for example, would not know it to be a chair. It would not exist as a chair, though the matter would exist in that arrangement). I might call a tree stump a chair, but you might not. If I were the last sentient creature on Earth and died and left this chair, it would not be a chair, but an assembly of matter that meant nothing to anyone. The chair is a subjective concept existing in each human's mind who sees it as a chair. A chair only has properties that make it a chair within the intellectual confines of humanity. These consensus-agreed properties are human-derived properties, even if there may be common properties between concrete items – i.e., chairness.

What is this "chair" to a cat? I imagine a visual sensation of "sleep thing". To an alien, it looks rather like a "shmagflan" because it has a "planthoingj" on its "fdanygshan". Labels are conceptual and depend on the subjective mind.

---

[1] The idea of personal identity, particularly as to whether it holds over time, is a fascinating debate that still continues to this day without any clear resolution. For example, *how* does "John Smith" maintain as an accurate label over time, from blastocyst (or before?) to an old man on his deathbed (or after?).

To expand this idea, I may see that a "hero", for example, has properties X, Y and Z. You may think a hero has properties X, Y and B. Someone else may think a hero has properties A, B and X. Who is right? No one is right. Those properties exist, but ascribing them to "heroness" is a subjective pastime with no ontic reality, no objective reality. For the sake of interest, I have previously asked audiences at talks for their definitions and examples of what constitutes and is defined by "hero" – and I was met with a vast array of very different answers. Each to their own. Which is the point.

Dictionaries

This is how dictionaries work. I could make up a word: "bashignogta". I could even give it a meaning: "the feeling you get when going through a dark tunnel with the tunnel lights flashing past your eyes". Does this abstract idea now objectively exist, now that I have made it up? Does it float into the aether by Platonic magic? Or does it depend on my mind for its existence? I can pass it on from my mind to someone else's using words, and then it would conceptually exist in two minds, but it still depends on our minds.

What dictionaries do is codify an agreement in what abstract ideas (words) mean, as agreed merely by consensus. The same applies to spelling conventions—indeed, convention is the perfect word to illustrate the point. But without all the minds existing in that consensus, the words and meanings would not exist. They do not have Platonic or ontic reality.

Dictionaries are descriptive and not prescriptive: they describe how we use language. They are reflections of human language usage, not law books (unless you want to arm the grammar Nazis).

Thus, the label of "chair" is a result of human evolution and conceptual subjectivity.

If you argue that objective ideas exist, then it is also the case that the range of all possible ideas must also exist objectively, even if they don't exist materially. Continuing with my previous point, a "forqwibllex" is a fork with a bent handle and a button on the end (that has never been created and I have "made up"). This did not exist before now, either objectively or subjectively. Now it does – have I created it objectively? This is what happens whenever humans make up a label for anything to which they assign a function.

Also, things that other animals use that don't even have names must also exist objectively under this logic. For example, the backrubby bit of bark on which a family of sloths scratch their backs on a particular tree exists materially. They have no language, so it has no label. Yet even though it only has properties to a sloth, and not to any other animal, (Platonic) realists would claim it must exist objectively. Furthermore, there are items that have multiple abstract properties that create more headaches for the realist. A chair might well be a territory marker to the school cat. Surely the same object cannot embody both objective existences: the chair and the marker! Perhaps it can, but it just seems to get into more and more needless complexity.

Beginning to Exist

When did this objective chair "begin to exist" and who gets to decide? Was it when it had three legs being built, when 1/2, 2/3, 4/5, 9/10 of the last leg was constructed? You see, the energy and matter of the chair already existed. So the chair is merely a conceptual construct. More precisely, a human one. More precisely still, one that different humans will variously disagree with.

The Sorites Paradox

This, to me, is the most important thought experiment in philosophy and underwrites a huge number of problems and arguments that we have.

Let's take the completed chair. When will it become not-a-chair? When I take seven molecules away? Twenty? A million? This is an example of the Sorites Paradox (sometimes called the paradox of the beard/dune/heap or similar), attributed to Eubulides of Miletus. It goes as follows. Imagine a sand dune (heap) of a million grains of sand. Agreeing that a sand dune minus just one grain of sand is still a sand dune (hey, it looks the same, and with no discernible difference!), then we can repeatedly apply this second premise until we have no grains, or even a negative number of grains and we would still have a sand dune. There is no definite point where we would say that the dune goes from "dune" to "not-dune". Such labels are arbitrarily and generally assigned so there is no precision with regards to exactly how many grains of sand a dune should have. And yet you would look at a dune and say, "That is a dune" but look at a bowl of sand and say, "That is not a dune".

Language is simultaneously pragmatic and fuzzy. We could agree by consensus that X number of grains is the legal constitution of a sand dune, codifying it in an encyclopaedia or set of laws. Indeed, this is what we do when countries and states disagree over laws and morals – we always have and probably always will disagree. This is what you would expect given the subjective nature of the exercise. Where does personal responsibility start or finish, exactly, along some continuum of causality? Where does ~X (not-X) become X? The world of abstract entities is not neatly carved into reality like some ancient legal code into a stone stele. Abstract ideas are constructed in our minds, and our minds can differ (given our heritages, backgrounds, histories, and biologies can differ) enough to produce disagreements over definitions and demarcations.

Hence philosophy.

The Evidence

The simple evidence of the world around us supports conceptual nominalism over realism or essentialism. Most everything exists on continua, and we argue about definitions and categorisations of everything. From morality to language, we argue. There is, descriptively speaking, inarguable subjectivity. The fact that morality broadly changes around the world (and over time) and that we can see it in evolved forms throughout the animal world points towards this being a construct of the natural world and not some objectively existing Platonic form.

Caveat

Although I have set out a very simplistic set of arguments here, this is actually a very complex area of philosophy that requires a lot more spadework. There are very many areas and ideas that I am not looking at here, such as trope theory, natural kinds, particulars, instantiation, relations, Bradley's Regress and so on. Feel free to indulge in the many rabbit holes with their twisting tunnels that criss-cross the philosophical landscape.

What Are the Ramifications?

The ramifications of this are far-reaching. It affects any argument that involves moral dimensions. And, let's face it, most philosophical arguments devolve to ones about morality.

Let's look at the abortion debate. Most pro-lifers will take one of two arguments: a) that personhood starts at conception, or b) that a human being is *essentially* created at conception. And this means that aborting a foetus is tantamount to killing a fully-fledged human being, because either that blastocyst has personhood or it has the essence of a human being.

These arguments don't really get off the ground under conceptual nominalism because, under this view, there is no objective category or essence of "personhood". There is no objective category or essence of "human being". We construct them.

However, there are the properties that underwrite them. You *may* argue that personhood is one of six properties, for example (and as some philosophers have):

A person must…

(1) Be a rational being
(2) Be a being to which psychological predicates can be ascribed
(3) Have others treat them in a person-like way
(4) Be able to reciprocate that same person-like treatment back onto others
(5) Be capable of verbal communication
(6) Be distinguishable from other entities by being conscious in a special way

It doesn't matter, for this discussion, whether these specific points work or not. The point is that this argument is a human construction. "Personhood" as an idea is constructed in the human mind and consists of any number of properties. Some will argue for those above, others will argue different properties.

Personhood means whatever we agree it to mean. The problem is that so many philosophers, politicians and laypeople thoroughly disagree on what constitutes personhood. And that disagreement, as with any other term (including morality), reflects the lack of objective facticity.

Can we find agreement? Undoubtedly not, because it is wrapped up with so many other things such as abortion, euthanasia, the afterlife and other ideas that have such strong cultural, religious and contextual influences. That means you cannot separate it from these other frameworks in which it is set. Thus, it is almost impossible for many people to objectively (as in *neutrally*) assess its meaning.

If we all miraculously agree, then we reach a consensus. This doesn't make it objective, but more like universally subjective. Additionally, when we agree on ideas, we like to codify them into dictionaries, encyclopaedias and statues of law. These can all, of course, be changed in the future.

What we agree is a human being, is personhood, or is a human right, is open to debate. And that is philosophy. Whether people like it or not, philosophy underwrites everything.

For another example, take human rights. It is controversial, but human rights do not exist other than in our minds. But without human rights, society becomes a pretty horrible place to live in with persecution around every corner. As a result, we invent them. We do some philosophy and conceptually construct them. But, these aren't very useful, sitting in the minds of philosophers in dusty faculty offices. Therefore, the philosophical venture of conceptually constructing human rights is only meaningful when they are codified into law and then enacted and defended. An idea on its own cannot put someone in prison. Nor can a piece of paper. But a justice system full of people enacting those ideas written on pieces of paper – that's a different matter.

Functioning democracies work when they start with benevolent and constructive philosophy that is then enshrined into law. But as societies change, so do their laws. We used to enslave people. Then we became enlightened and realised we were wrong and changed the laws. Moral laws do not exist objectively, immutable and unchangeable.

There is no reason in the US (for example), that one (the government) cannot change the documentation surrounding the right to carry arms. It was an *amendment*, after all, to the Constitution itself. As a document, the Constitution is a perfect example of a conceptually constructed framework codified into a piece of parchment. The job of a functioning democracy is to constantly assess its suitability and practical use, and to create the legal and societal frameworks about it, changing as necessary. As good as the document may or may not be (and there are a good many Americans who treat the document as a sacred holy text), it is a document that can be and has been changed.

The point is, once we understand the transient nature of abstract objects and ideas, we are more able to shake off the shackles of dogma and make the world a better place for us all. Things can change, and things *should change*, in light of good rational argument.

Okay, I Concede This

In conclusion, I concede that arguing over abstract objects isn't the only argument in town. But it certainly should be the first argument in town. Right at the entrance sign labelling the town.

And no, I'm not going to sit here and debate where the town starts and the countryside ends. It's up to you to decide and convince others. Although most people just stick a sign in the ground and don't think about it anymore. Shame.

So Where Are We Now?

Having hopefully established (at least to the point of further research) the nature of abstract objects, I would ask you to go back and reread the opening quote to this section on ontology. It should now make more sense to you. Furthermore, the initial pieces on labelling and definitions should also have a greater clarity. There should now be no surprise that "True Christianity" is whatever we make it and agree upon, because there is no objective definition "out there" in the aether, especially absent the mind of a god. The question now becomes, "How does this affect other areas of philosophy?" Given that we are attempting a bottom-up approach and that this is a foundational brick or two, the answer to this question is something like, "Quite a lot!" as we shall now see.

The Argument from Format

Or...

How the Cartesian Soul Cannot Be the Originator of Free Will

I have just told you that there is only one argument in town. I guess I lied: here's another. Followed by a lot more throughout the book.

This essay sets out to dispel the myth that the soul can be the originator for free will. I will start the essay by establishing the Cartesian idea of what the body is and showing that Descartes and modern biology indicate that the body is a biological machine. After indicating how Descartes (and others) use the soul as the originator for free will, I will show that in order for the soul to be identified as a soul, it must have the format and properties of a soul. These must be adhered to in order to designate the soul with coherent and consistent properties. To conclude, I will maintain that if a soul must adhere to rules and laws to remain being a soul, then it must operate within a deterministic framework. Indeed, the ramifications of this argument are far-reaching in that in order for anything to meaningfully exist, regularity qua determinism must hold.

It is this second point that, interwoven with the first, means that not only do we not have libertarian free will, but that our existence must *necessarily* be determined. Let us see how we get on...

René Descartes (1596-1650) had profound effects on modern philosophy, so much so that he is often labelled the "Father of Modern Philosophy". This is no more evident than with his ruminations over the mind and the body as he sought to differentiate the two, seeking to prove their separate identity and philosophy.

Descartes established his dualism in his works *Passions of the Soul* and *The Description of the Human Body*, amongst others. In these works, he proposed that the human body, in its physicality, juxtaposes the nonmaterial existence of the soul. The two entities come together in the pineal gland, in the brain, where they interact.[1] Thus Descartes posited a mind-body dualism that still pervades today and provides a hotbed for philosophical debate. Though his knowledge of physiology, whilst being pioneering for the time, is

---

[1] On the point of interactionism, I will stay clear of the problems of this theory (the nonmaterial causally interacting with the material), though I have dealt with this in Pearce (2016).

41

now outdated, much of the core philosophy is still relevant and worthy of analysis.

Let us look briefly at what Descartes saw as the body before looking at his ideas about the soul. Firstly, though, it might be a good idea to look at how Descartes separated the two.

It is important to note that Descartes, in his rationalist approach to finding out what we can know indubitably, came by his *cogito ergo sum* (I think; therefore, I am) by recognising that everything of the body (the senses and its very existence) can be doubted. They could even be the product of an evil genius/demon (as he proposed in his 1641 *Meditations on First Philosophy*), fooling the "I" (whatever that may be) in the style of *The Matrix* films. In order to doubt our own bodies, we must have a mind (again...whatever that may be!).

Thus Descartes, in searching out an epistemological theory of reality, came to see a fundamental, philosophical difference between mind and body. Though this does not necessarily prove that they are separate, since a mind may still necessitate a body to function or even exist, it formed an intuitive belief that the mind and body are categorically separate. However, merely being able to doubt the existence of things does not necessitate that these things are thereby do not exist.

Secondly, Descartes appealed to the imagination by describing how one can imagine themselves without a body, as just a mind. This shows the distinctness of the mind from the body. However, simply imagining that something is the case in no way means that it is the case in reality. Descartes seems to imply that the mind and body being one is somehow a logical impossibility. I could draw a crow without wings, but this does not necessarily mean that the animal drawn exists. Although any such arguments will always boil down to the epistemological certainty of *cogito ergo sum*, there is no knowing that the mind exists apart from the body. This simply begs the question.[1]

Thirdly, Descartes looked at divisibility. Since, he claimed, the body can be divided up (two legs, a single leg, a shin, an ankle...), and the mind cannot be divided up, then this shows a simple differentiation between the two. However, this is not so straightforward either. For example, the shape of a sculpture and the sculpture itself are separate entities, but can hardly be separated in any meaningful sense. Moreover, there *is* a sense in which the mind can be separated. Schizophrenics suffer multiple personalities where different characters can be compartmentalised. We could say that our memories can be separated from our emotions. Certain brain malfunctions or

---

[1] Such arguments bear close resemblance to ontological arguments for God.

injuries can result in distinct parts of the mind being affected, such as a loss of long or short-term memory, the loss of emotion, the inability to perceive certain things in certain ways and so on. These examples blur the line between brain and mind. Descartes himself, in *The Passions of the Soul* (paragraph 47), declares that there are lower and higher, rational and sensitive parts of the soul, potentially invalidating his own theory.

The Supervenience of the Mental on the Physical

For the purposes of this essay, I have not investigated all of Descartes' ideas of separating mind from body. Descartes has employed some logic and arguments that do not particularly stand up to close scrutiny. After all, if I cut off my head, there is nothing short of blind faith that would indicate that my mind or soul would continue living separately from my body. I dare you to do it. No, on second thoughts, just take my word on it. In all honesty, sticking a fork in one's eye is a sure-fire way to establish a supervenience (dependence) of the mind on the brain: doing so would surely affect the conscious mind. The same goes for drugs or any brain injury/malfunction/condition. The mind certainly appears to supervene (depend) on the brain, the mental on the physical.

There are many problem as to how Descartes argues the separateness of the mind from the body. Let me quickly summarise them as follows:

(1) **The evolution of species** demonstrates that development of the brain correlates to mental development. For example: "We find that the greater the size of the brain and its cerebral cortex in relation to the animal body and the greater their complexity, the higher and more versatile the form of life".[1]

(2) **Brain growth in individual organisms**: "Secondly, the developmental evidence for mind-brain dependence is that mental abilities emerge with the development of the brain. The failure in brain development prevents mental development."[2]

(3) **Brain damage destroys mental capacities**: "Third, clinical evidence consists of cases of brain damage that result from accidents,

---

[1] (Lamont 1990), p.63.
[2] (Beyerstein 1991), p. 45.

toxins, diseases, and malnutrition that often result in irreversible losses of mental functioning.[1] If the mind could exist independently of the brain, why couldn't the mind compensate for lost faculties when brain cells die after brain damage?"[2] See the case of Phineas Gage for the landmark example of this. Gage was in an accident where his brain was impaled by a rod. He survived, but his mental function for the rest of his life was affected.

(4) EEG and similar mechanisms used in experiments and measurements on the brain indicate **a correspondence between brain activity and mental activity**: "Fourth, the strongest empirical evidence for mind-brain dependence is derived from experiments in neuroscience. Mental states are correlated with brain states; electrical or chemical stimulation of the human brain invokes perceptions, memories, desires, and other mental states."[3]

(5) **The effects of drugs** and other (physical) stimulants on the brain affect consciousness and conscious experience. E.g., coffee, cocaine, alcohol and paracetamol.

(6) **Synaesthesia and brain asymbolia**. These are genetic/biological variations that have interesting knock-on effects for mental qualia – the subjective experience of the agent. Synaesthesia is a neurological condition that givers synesthetes combinations or variations of sensory experiences across stimuli (for example, numbers having sensations of colour/smell etc.). Pain asymbolia is a condition whereby an agent feels pain without "feeling" and pain. They are well worth looking into further in this context.

This list is not exhaustive but should go some way to showing the problems with a Cartesian, dualist approach to mind and body.

Given that the mind and the body *are* different in some way (perhaps only in a definitional sense such as the shape of the sculpture and the sculpture itself), what does Descartes make of the body?

---

[1] Ibid, p. 45.
[2] Ibid, p. 46.
[3] Ibid, p. 45.

Looking at Descartes' Body

Whilst there is some confusion and changing of mind as to whether the body makes up part of the "I", or whether the "I" is merely the mind, Descartes is clearly at pains to differentiate the two. As he says in *Meditations* (p.10), "The mind is proved to be really distinct from the body, even though the mind is shown to be so closely joined to the body that it forms a single unit with it". The body, in its material existence, is likened to a machine – the soul is seen as the helmsman to 'the Good Ship Body'. As Descartes proclaims:

> I suppose the body to be nothing but a statue or machine made of earth... We see clocks, artificial fountains, mills, and other such machines which, although only man-made, have the power to move of their own accord in many different ways.[1]

This is a sentiment that he repeats elsewhere:

> This will not seem at all strange to those who know of many kinds of automatons, or moving machines, the skill of man can construct with the use of very few parts, in comparison with the great multitude of bones, muscles, nerves, arteries, veins and all the other parts that are in the body of any animal. For they will regard this body as a machine which, having been made by the hands of God, is incomparably better ordered than any machine that can be devised by man, and contains in itself movements more wonderful than those in any such machine.[2]

The mechanistic language makes things quite clear – the mechanisms of the body are deterministic. But bodies are not entirely the result of deterministic mechanisms, according to Descartes, since the immaterial soul is causally linked further up the chain. He also concedes that many actions of the body do not take place as a result of the volition of the soul; in other words, there is a larger range of actions that are automatic. Here Descartes gives the example of defensively putting your hand in front of your eyes when a friend only jokingly goes to hit you:

---

[1] Descartes, *Treatise on Man*, p.1
[2] Descartes, *Discourse on the Method; The Philosophical Writings Of Descartes* I: 139

> ... [all the objects of our external senses and of our internal appetites] Besides causing our soul to have various different sensations, these various movements in the brain can also act without the soul, causing the spirits to make their way to certain muscles rather than others, and so causing them to move our limbs... This shows that it is not through the mediation of our soul that they close, since this action is contrary to our volition, which is the soul's only activity, or at least its main one. They close rather because the mechanism of our body is so composed that the movement of the hand towards our eyes produces another movement in our brain, which directs the animal spirits into the muscles that make our eyelids drop.[1]

He also maintains that there are many mechanistic movements of the body that we do not consciously will, and are thus automatic (without "mental volition"), such as "heartbeat, digestion, nutrition, respiration, when we are asleep, and also such waking actions as walking, singing and the like"[2]. Furthermore, the modes of the body can causally interact with the mind. The body, as well as being able to be influenced by the mind, can influence the mind too. It is a two-way street.

I take issue with Descartes and insist that *all* actions of the body, and even thoughts, take place in a deterministic and mechanistic manner. This is espoused by epiphenomenalists,[3] for there is some good philosophical evidence to defend such a position.[4] I have written voluminously in books, chapters and on my blog about how libertarian free will (the real and conscious ability to rationally choose otherwise in a given scenario) is philosophically incoherent. I will, though (for the sake of argument in this essay), take Descartes' position that the body is, indeed, mechanistic and that the mind/soul can interact with the body, causally and volitionally, to produce bodily effects. Therefore, I will ignore the issues concerning how

---

[1] Descartes, *The Passions of the Soul*, paragraph 13
[2] Descartes, *Reply to Fourth Set of Objections*
[3] Epiphenomenalism is the belief that consciousness is the natural by-product of the mechanistic brain / physical body in the same way that steam is the by-product of boiling water. However, the mind cannot causally interact with the physical world, even though it may seem to do just that.
[4] See Pearce (2010) and Wegner (2002), though it must be said that this position is hotly contested.

interactionism works (how the physical dimension can causally affect the immaterial dimension and vice-versa[1]).

Looking into Descartes' Soul

Whilst we have seen how Descartes viewed the body, his view of the soul is more complex. The mind (and I will use the terms "mind" and "soul" interchangeably, for they are synonymous as far as Descartes was concerned), for Descartes, was very difficult to pin down in any kind of definitional sense. This is because the mind, as described by him, has very few positive qualities. It is easy to say what the mind is not (e.g., material, determined...), but not so easy to define what it *is*. It is claimed to be invisible, without dimensions, unitary, without limit and so on.

We cannot conceive, so Descartes would say, of half a soul. Furthermore, it is not affected if we cut off some part of the body (apart from the head, one could surmise, and there will be much subjective, mind-experienced pain!) though it is joined to the whole body[2] through, as mentioned, the pineal gland in the brain. This is the conduit through which the soul enjoys some degree of control over the body (and vice versa on occasion).

Descartes claims that he is a "thing that doubts, understands, affirms, denies, is willing, is unwilling, and also imagines and has sensory perceptions"[3]. Since he claims that it is nonsensical to ascribe such emotions to material, non-thinking objects such as stones, then only the mind can have such abilities. I must also advise that Descartes was not immutable in his

---

[1] To which Descartes tried to eliminate the problem, "These questions presuppose amongst other things an explanation of the union between the soul and the body, which I have not yet dealt with at all. But I will say, for your benefit at least, that the whole problem contained in such questions arises simply from a supposition that is false and cannot in any way be proved, namely that, if the soul and the body are two substances whose nature is different, this prevents them from being able to act on each other." *Ouevres de Descartes*, 11 vols., eds. Charles Adam and Paul Tannery, Paris: Vrin, 1974-1989,VII 213:

[2] Building on the ideas of Thomas Aquinas who said, "In each body the whole soul is in the whole body, and whole in each part of it" (Aquinas quoting Augustine's *On the Trinity*, book 6, ch. 6 in *Summa Theologica*).

[3] Ibid., VII 28

philosophy and in different works we can see edited and refined ideas, or changes, or, indeed, entirely different philosophies.[1]

Essentially, the soul is mainly a thinking entity. Descartes says, "Thus, because we have no conception of the body as thinking in any way at all, we have reason to believe that every kind of thought present in us belongs to the soul."[2] He also indicates that the soul seems to access memory by making the pineal gland behave in such a way that it can access the memory from the brain. This is problematic since the soul will need to remember what (or that) it needs to remember, thus starting an infinite regression:

> Thus, when the soul wants to remember something, this volition makes the gland lean first to one side and then to another, thus driving the spirits towards different regions of the brain until they come upon the one containing traces left by the object we want to remember. These traces consist simply in the fact that the pores of the brain through which the spirits previously made their way owing to the presence of this object have thereby become more apt than the others to be opened in the same way when the spirits again flow towards them. And so the spirits enter into these pores more easily when they come upon them, thereby producing in the gland that special movement which represents the same object to the soul, and makes it recognize the object as the one it wanted to remember.[3]

The key to the mind-body philosophy of Descartes comes with his interactionist view. Rather than explain how, he simply asserts that the volitional soul has control over the body of the agent, such that:

> ... the activity of the soul consists entirely in the fact that simply by willing something it brings it about that the little gland to which it is closely joined moves in the

---

[1] At times Scholastic-Aristotelian hylomorphist, a gradually more extreme Platonist, idealist, materialist, epiphenomenalist, parallelist, non-parallelist and so on. See Lokhorst (2005).
[2] Descartes, (1974-1989), XI, p.329.

[3] Ibid., XI:360.

manner required to produce the effect corresponding to this volition.[1]

Descartes also declares that there are different types of souls amongst different people insofar as some have strong souls whilst other people have weak souls:

> For the strongest souls, clearly, belong to people in whom the will can by nature most easily conquer the passions and stop the bodily movements that go with them. But some people never get to test the strength of their souls because they never let their will fight with the soul's proper weapons, instead letting it use only the 'weapons' that some passions provide for resisting some other passions.[2]

This is remarkable language, since it leaves a gaping hole in the philosophy of causality that speaks volumes against theories of free will. Too often, proponents of free will do not regress their thinking far enough, but somewhat hastily end the chain of causality with a magic origination of free will (either in some amorphous idea of an agent or soul). What should be asked here is "why do people never let their will do X, Y or Z?" Descartes is saying something almost nonsensical and circular in saying "let their will" since this effectively means "will their will". And who decides who gets a stronger soul? How does this happen? Is the journey to a stronger or weaker will determined by things outside of the agent's control, thus employing determinism?

Putting these issues aside, let us sum up what we can find from Descartes' writings on what the body and soul are. The body is a mechanistic and material entity which can have causal influence over the soul, but is more often controlled by the volitional soul. This interaction takes place in the pineal gland. The soul, on the other hand, is more difficult to define, being immaterial, dimensionless, lacking in extension and so on. It is also the seat of thinking. And these thoughts can, through the pineal gland, will (the brain and) body to its own ends.

Therefore, we can see that at least some of the time, the soul is in control in a freely volitional sense. Remember, Descartes has already told us that the main activity of the soul is the utilisation of free will: "since this action is contrary to our volition, which is the soul's only activity, or at least

---

[1] Ibid., XI:359.
[2] Descartes (1649), Paragraph 48.

its main one". It is from here that I want to investigate whether the immaterial soul can be the originator of free will. Let us first, though, look at free will, and the term *originator*.

Descartes and Free Will

The idea of free will in its most widely understood form[1] requires the idea that the agent (i.e., you or I) could have acted differently when carrying out an action. This idea is often known as *The Principle of Alternate Possibilities*. I often define libertarian free will (as opposed to more philosophically nuanced versions) as the real and conscious ability to rationally choose and do otherwise in a given scenario.

Descartes declared that "the will is by its nature so free that it can never be constrained",[2] which places his cards nicely on the table. This can even happen "when a very evident reason moves us in one direction".[3] To be the originator of free will, the agent has to have ownership over the action. This means that the causal chain cannot be further regressed to find determining reasons for so doing. This is always difficult to defend, and much ink has been spilt[4] over whether an agent can indeed be the originator of free will in any meaningful way. In my opinion, every agent has a causal circumstance – all the molecules of the universe acting on or with the agent at the time of the action, the history and learning of the agent up until that moment, and the genes of the agent themselves – indeed, every single variable that you could possibly imagine.

If you take all of these causally active ingredients away from the equation, then what is there left? Descartes would argue that the immaterial soul can be seen as outside of this causal circumstance and can be the originator of the causal chain itself. Determinists,[5] on the other hand, would argue that the only origination of the causal chain would be the Big Bang, or similar, and that free will (in this basic sense) does not exist.

---

[1] Particularly in the realms of compatibilism, where free will is seen as being compatible with determinism, free will, as a term, is often redefined. This is because determinism can be defined as 'not free will', and free will cannot be compatible with 'not free will'. Logically speaking.

[2] Descartes (1984), V. I, p.343.

[3] Ibid., V. III, p. 245.

[4] Such as in Pearce (2010 & 2016).

[5] One who believes that there is no free will and that every action adheres strictly to a framework of cause and effect.

So, since an effect or event cannot be uncaused, then the volition of will becomes the uncaused cause for the beginning of the causal chain. This, controversially and as I hinted at earlier, denies the existence of motives and other causal influences on the agent. To parse this down, if the agent is said to have free will and chooses to do something (X) using her will V, then there must be no antecedent causality for V, since this then accepts determinism and determining factors for V. Causal determinism theorises that causality runs back from X and through V, either infinitely regressing or back to some other beginning point (say, the Big Bang). The person who believes in libertarian free will has to believe that V (the will) is uncaused in the sense it is the originator of the causal chain. It is an uncaused cause.

Incidentally, this also creates some real headaches for those who argue that only God can be a *prime mover* – an uncaused cause or an originator of a causal chain. This means that the Kalam Cosmological Argument[1] or similar prime mover arguments are mutually exclusive with libertarian free will. But you can read about this elsewhere in my writing, particularly in my book *Did God Create the Universe from Nothing: Countering William Lane Craig's Kalam Cosmological Argument.*[2]

Let us assume for now that the soul or mind in its immaterial form *can* be the originator of free will. Let us assume that the causal chain *can* start with the freely willing soul and that this *can* then affect the mechanistic body to allow material effects based on the notion of free will. I will now look to illustrate that the soul, while it may be the originator of the causal chain, may be no freer than the mechanistic and physical body it purportedly controls.

Identity and Properties

The first idea that I want to deal with is the notion of identity and property. In order for the soul to be an existent entity, it must have properties that distinguish it as a soul. Even if the soul was the only thing within the immaterial dimension, then it must still have properties that distinguish it from other things outside that dimension. In simple terms, a soul must, like any existent entity, have properties that define it as being a soul and not a "not-soul". Any label, as we established in the first essay in this collection, is an identifier of a given set of properties.

---

[1] P1 – Everything that begins to exist has a cause
P2 – The universe began to exist
P3 – Therefore, the universe had a cause
[2] See Pearce (2010 & 2016).

These properties might well be abstracts or universals. As is understood by the definition of abstracts and universals, it is generally accepted that they are causally inert – incapable of affecting a causal chain. As philosopher Gideon Rosen says, "abstract objects are normally supposed to be causally inert in every sense."[1] In other words, if the properties of the soul are themselves causally inert, they will be unable to affect the causal chain.

However, the properties themselves would have to be reflective of the actual soul. In the physical dimension, we could take the example of, say, a chair. Although the label "chair" is an abstraction of the actual matter itself, the chair can be said to have certain properties that enable it to be recognised and defined as a "chair". This may be the physical arrangement of molecules to take the form of a platform with four legs and a back (these now being labels themselves, but you get the picture!). These properties are different to the properties of, say, a stone. These two entities have recognisable and definable properties that allow them to be somewhat clearly differentiated and described as different to each other.

In the same way, a soul must have specific properties so that it cannot be confused with something else. These properties enable you to recognise it and say "that is a soul" or "this is what a soul does". Although the properties of the soul might not be reflective of the sorts of properties existing in the physical dimension, they must still be properties of some description.

Obviously, we do not know exactly how the soul is "constructed" due to our lack of knowledge of exactly what the soul is. This makes it very hard to second guess the philosophy of its properties. The philosophical area of *properties,* as it pertains very much to the discussion of abstracts and universals, is a notoriously difficult and complicated subject, and one that I have given only the lightest of skimmings.

Regularity

Let us look to see whether talk of the physical dimension can lead us to infer theories and conclusions about the non-physical dimension of the soul. First, we must ask ourselves, "what stops the chair becoming a stone?" The properties of the chair, with no other forces or entity acting on them, would remain constant. This constancy is due to the laws acting within the physical world. However, common-sense understanding of laws is often misleading. This is because scientific laws are *descriptive* as opposed to being *prescriptive.*

---

[1] Rosen (2001).

"[S]cientific laws are descriptive; they state how phenomena in nature do in fact always behave."[1]

For example, if you took evolution by natural selection as a scientific theory or perhaps law,[2] then genes in organisms do not mutate because they *have to* (i.e., evolution is not prescriptive), and new organisms (in simple terms) do not originate because by following a prescribed theory/law that has been objectively set out for all the molecules to strictly adhere to. What actually happens is that biological matter behaves in a cause-and-effect framework in dependable and consistent ways, and in combination with environmental factors achieves certain observable ends. This consistency of behaviour is empirically observed and is formulated by man into a theory or a law that simply *describes* this regular behaviour. This human-created law does not *dictate* the behaviour.[3]

Scientific laws describe the myriad behaviours of matter in the universe, mathematical and otherwise, and have properties such as being universal (happening everywhere in the universe), simple, absolute (nothing in the universe can affect them), omnipotent (everything in the universe applies to them) and so on.[4] Thus, for the chair to turn into the stone, we would have to observe a process that strictly adhered to the laws of the universe. What keeps the chair from being or becoming a stone is the behaviour of the matter of the chair that acts in predictable and "law-abiding" ways.

For the chair not to adhere to the laws of the universe, i.e., to behave in an unpredictable manner, then we would have something that would have the characteristic of being random or uncaused. But matter does not behave randomly. If it did, material existence would entirely break down. There would be no coherence, no matter and no life. The universe, matter and life *need* consistency of behaviour in order for there to be complexity.

Just a short discussion about quantum mechanics here. Much can be said about the sort of indeterminism at that level. There are many different theories whereby the seemingly random behaviour at quantum level is simply not fully understood, though matter is still theorised to be determined (such as with "hidden variables" theories). Then there are outright deterministic models, and still other approaches. I do not want to bog this essay down with

---

[1] Harris, C. E. (1956).
[2] There is much debate as to whether evolution is a theory, principle, law or fact. Much can also be made of the different definitions of the term "theory" (applying also to the other terms).
[3] See Pearce (2020) where I discuss this ides – that of Humean or non-Humean Laws of Nature.
[4] See, for example, Davies (1993).

talk of stochastic probabilities and suchlike; however, even at the quantum level, I do expect there to be an underlying deterministic layer to reality for exactly the point I am making. Laws of large numbers still have probability distributions that define different scenarios, dependant on *something*.

The idea for indeterminism is that you can't know with certainty the behaviour of a small *individual* particle but prediction is possible over large numbers (the Law of Large Numbers). My point to tackle this is that if a photon of light, say, is reflected 84% of the time and is absorbed 16% of the time in a large number of samples, but you can't know each the states of each photon *individually*, there must be *something* that is determining that probability. It's almost as if the determination is set one level back.

So, we can see that laws, or predictable consistency of behaviour, are absolutely essential to the existence of everything in the universe. The term "everything in the universe" means anything with a definable identity and that has properties. What stops the chair becoming a "not-chair", ceteris paribus, then, are the laws of nature – the predictable behaviours of the matter of the chair. Of course, the chair can become a "not-chair", but within the predictable framework of nature, as a result of other causes. For example, it could rot in the damp, or be broken into pieces. But this is predictable and adheres to law-like behaviour (the process of rot or a rock falling on the chair).

Now let us return to the subject of the immaterial soul. Although the soul is not physical and is not defined by the physical behaviour of matter in the material universe, we can draw parallels. The properties of laws themselves (that may well be incorrectly, roughly or correctly understood in terms of our *theories* that we often call *laws*), of behaviours and of the philosophy of science are abstractions. They are not defined by the laws for physics, for example, but by the laws of logic, of reasoning in the abstract.

There are many different types of logic and logical systems. Here I will be dealing with a more simplistic and everyday understanding of an appraisal of arguments through an analysis of the relations between propositions. This informal, natural language knowledge distills to a more fundamental, formal logic such that language becomes a syllogism that can then be formulated into a group of symbols. This is then a hop, skip and a jump away from mathematics.

Logic is a set of laws that works in the abstract, immaterial world of thought (this is assuming a properly dualistic, Cartesian sense of thought). The world seems to be occupied by the Cartesian soul, whereby some argue logic is a function that the soul carries out. There are laws to logic; there are behaviours and statements that adhere to logic and those that do not. The rational and the irrational (I am being simplistic here as there is much to be said about different logics and logical frameworks). We make sense of the world by more consistently acting within the confines of logic and rationality. It has contributed to how humans have succeeded in socialising, making connections about the world around us and doing science. Without logical consistency, there would be chaos. For example:

P1) All writers use pens

P2) Jim is a writer

C) Therefore, Jim uses a pen.

This logic is universal. It is always true, given a consistent use of language that underpins the premises that we all agree on. Without this consistency of logic, if *in only some cases of the argument being applied* Jim uses a pen, then logic is rendered impotent and meaningless. Admittedly, we are close to talking about semantics and language here. Propositions cannot be deductively logical if they worked *some* of the time; logic itself cannot be inconsistent as it has to be universal. Therefore, it seems, even in mental abstractions, there is order created by rules and consistency.

What, then, stops the soul from becoming a not-soul? This question is equally relevant to the immaterial world of the soul as it is to the physical world of the chair. Even if the soul is entirely unitary, as Descartes believed, then this is still a problem. A single entity, or an entity made up of constituent parts, still has to behave as that entity in order to be labelled with that identity. Thus the soul must act like a soul, and must have the many different properties of a soul, in order to be called (or *to be*) a soul. Therefore, the soul must adhere to strict soul-like behaviours for it to remain a soul and to be labelled as a soul. These behaviours, I posit, must be predictable and law-like in order for the soul not to have aspects of randomness, or to descend into chaos and non-soulness.

As discussed, random does not give the agent control in any way. Volition or free will are not good bedfellows with random. So for the soul to exist, it must exist within an entirely predictable framework. In other words, the soul must be entirely determined as things are in the physical universe.[1] What I am suggesting is that anything with identifiable and consistent properties must be set within a deterministic framework. That determinism (the basis for regularity) is not only a defining factor of physical reality but a

---

[1] I don't want to get into asides on quantum indeterminacy of which there are many different interpretations, deterministic and otherwise. Interestingly, there is some research, such as the work of Kocsis et al (2011), that seem to cast doubt on aspects of the Heisenberg Uncertainty Principle.

non-physical reality (if there is one). In this way, the soul cannot be the originator of free will, or if it is, it is so within a deterministic framework such that free will is not, indeed, free.

One could posit another entity beyond the soul, or parallel to the soul, that provides the volition to the soul (i.e., God). In order to say there must be some non-determined entity in control of the soul, if one surmises that the soul is itself determined, then we are prone to an infinite regress of looking for originators that are themselves non-determined.

As hinted at earlier, a further problem is that in order for the soul to be the originator of volition, the part that decides to do X rather than Y, it must not be constrained by rules, laws or universally consistent behaviour. Otherwise the decision will always be one way or the other. It makes no sense for there to be any random involvement in the decision (which would allow free will to work). But it seems that the soul cannot have any kind of non-determined property.

As philosopher Daniel Dennett has often espoused (such as in his book *Freedom Evolves*), free will *needs* determinism to make any sense.

As a result, it would seem to me that we are left with an argument that can be formulated as follows (and that I call the Argument from Format):

P1 – An entity that exists has properties and identity.

P2 – In order for the entity to be recognised with such properties and identity, it must have a format that exists within a framework of deterministic laws/behaviours.

P3 – The soul, if it exists, is the originator of free will (à la Descartes).

P4 - If the soul exists, it must have a format and a framework of deterministic laws/behaviours to enable it to be identified as such.

C – Therefore, either the soul does not exist, or it is not the originator of free will (it is deterministic, or something else causes free will and will suffer from the same argument).

If any weaknesses exist in the argument, I feel they would be found in P2. The one criticism that I could see levelled at the argument is that it is inductive – the application of laws to the identity of the soul to retain its identity is invoking past uniformities. I am using examples of identity and properties from other entities and applying their rules of format to the soul.

Here, we might enter into the realms of Hume's Problem of Induction (much more on this later). Can we indubitably say that gravity will always send the ball downwards when I drop it? Well, deductively, we cannot. However, that does not mean that the theory of gravity is not true, or a highly plausible and probable outcome based on past observations. Likewise, it is highly probabilistic and plausible that the soul is determined. In fact, it seems to me that it would be nonsensical if it was not.

What would a soul look like if it was free from any constraining framework? There would be nothing bonding it together, nothing defining its properties, nothing about it that kept it regular. I can make no sense of a thing, whether physical or metaphysical, existing as an entity (that had the capacities that a soul supposedly has) devoid of any constraining framework. I imagine a wisp of smoke dissipating into nothingness.

Perhaps this is a limit to my imagination, to my ken. Perhaps.

The nonsensicality of it comes partly as a result of there being an uncaused cause. Claiming the soul is the originator of free will is saying there is an uncaused cause for the decision at the beginning of the causal chain. In other words, the decision cannot be causally regressed further back from the soul, which sounds awfully similar to saying that there was no reason for the decision. It's just "because the soul". This is somewhat of an aside to my central argument but it seems pertinent to mention that every decision warrants a reason (otherwise it is random). And as soon as reasons are given, we question the determining factors for the rationality employed by the agent. Rationality is based on our education and learning, our genetic makeup and neurological status, and the variables at hand. Therefore, on several levels, positing that the soul is the originator of free will is a hard sell. There is always a context to reason and rationality that cannot be ignored in any discussion about free will and determinism. I sometimes label this the "Soul of the Gaps Argument" where the soul magically plugs the free will origination hole without any kind of proper explanation.[1]

To conclude, in this essay I have looked to agree with Descartes in his theories about the mechanistic qualities of the body. I have posited that these qualities are evident ubiquitously across the material universe. I have looked at what Descartes said about the soul, concluding that we simply don't know what it is and does but assume it to be entirely non-physical in format. However, since it must have properties and identity to be labelled and recognised as a soul, I posited that the soul must adhere to a framework of deterministic laws and behaviours. As a result, the soul cannot be the originator of free will, since it is a determined entity.

The ramifications of this argument are that nothing (whether physical or non-physical) can exist without a framework of consistent regularity – a deterministic   framework.

---

[1] For reference, it might also be useful to see naturalist and physicist Sean Carroll's piece "Physics and the Immortality of the Soul" – Carroll (2011).

What Is a Soul and What Does it Do?

We have just looked into the idea of a soul in the context of Descartes and mind/body dualism. But, really, I granted him and other proponents of a soul far too much.

The idea of a soul permeates popular culture, from soul music to feeling things in your soul, to having soul, to this and, indeed, that. Beyond that, souls are a really important part of many theists' theological frameworks.

But what *is* a soul? And what does a soul *do*?

The answers to these questions are harder to nail down than you might think for something so commonly invoked. Let me build on some of the ideas from the previous chapter.

Catholic doctrine states what a soul is:[1]

> 363 In Sacred Scripture the term "soul" often refers to human life or the entire human person. But "soul" also refers to the innermost aspect of man, that which is of greatest value in him, that by which he is most especially in God's image: "soul" signifies the spiritual principle in man.

That seems a bit nebulous. Let's go to a fairly well respected (by Catholics, at any rate) theological source: *The Catholic Encyclopedia*. The opening section says it all:[2]

> The question of the reality of the soul and its distinction from the body is among the most important problems of philosophy, for with it is bound up the doctrine of a future life. Various theories as to the nature of the soul have claimed to be reconcilable with the tenet of immortality, but it is a sure instinct that leads us to suspect every attack on the substantiality or spirituality of the soul as an assault on the belief in existence after death.

---

[1] "The Catechism of the Catholic Church",
https://www.vatican.va/archive/ENG0015/__P1B.HTM (retrieved 06/01/2021)
[2] Maher & Bolland (1912).

Evidently, we (or, they) are not really sure what it is. However, Christians (in particular) really need it as the basis for immortality, and thus heaven and hell. Therefore, the soul is pretty darned important, but also pretty darned mysterious or incoherent.

St Thomas Aquinas thought as follows, upon which Catholic doctrine is largely built:[1]

- the rational soul, which is one with the sensitive and vegetative principle, is the form of the body. This was defined as of faith by the Council of Vienne of 1311;

- the soul is a substance, but an incomplete substance, i.e., it has a natural aptitude and exigency for existence in the body, in conjunction with which it makes up the substantial unity of human nature;

- though connaturally related to the body, it is itself absolutely simple, i.e., of an unextended and spiritual nature. It is not wholly immersed in matter, its higher operations being intrinsically independent of the organism;

- the rational soul is produced by special creation at the moment when the organism is sufficiently developed to receive it. In the first stage of embryonic development, the vital principle has merely vegetative powers; then a sensitive soul comes into being, educed from the evolving potencies of the organism — later yet, this is replaced by the perfect rational soul, which is essentially immaterial and so postulates a special creative act. Many modern theologians have abandoned this last point of St. Thomas's teaching, and maintain that a fully rational soul is infused into the embryo at the first moment of its existence.

The important takeaways here are that the soul is *rational* and that it is *substantially separated from the body*, though related and deriving properties from it. These ideas are not made easy by various authors within the Bible using the term (or a given term to mean the soul) rather ambiguously (at times meaning the whole body or person; e.g., Ezekiel).

Descartes famously concluded that the soul was connected to the pineal gland, as we previously saw:[2]

---

[1] Ibid.
[2] Ibid.

Descartes conceived the soul as essentially thinking (i.e., conscious) substance, and body as essentially extended substance. The two are thus simply disparate realities, with no vital connection between them. This is significantly marked by his theory of the soul's location in the body. Unlike the Scholastics he confines it to a single point — the pineal gland — from which it is supposed to control the various organs and muscles through the medium of the "animal spirits", a kind of fluid circulating through the body. Thus, to say the least, the soul's biological functions are made very remote and indirect, and were in fact later on reduced almost to a nullity: the lower life was violently severed from the higher, and regarded as a simple mechanism. In the Cartesian theory animals are mere automata. It is only by the Divine assistance that action between soul and body is possible.

The *Catholic Encyclopedia* confusingly concludes, however:[1]

As regards monistic systems generally, it belongs rather to cosmology to discuss them. We take our stand on the consciousness of individual personality, which consciousness is a distinct deliverance of our very highest faculties, growing more and more explicit with the strengthening of our moral and intellectual being. This consciousness is emphatic, as against the figments of a fallaciously abstract reason, in asserting the self-subsistence (and at the same time the finitude) of our being, i.e., it declares that we are *independent* inasmuch as we are truly persons or selves, not mere attributes or adjectives, while at the same time, by exhibiting our manifold limitations, it directs us to a higher Cause on which our being depends.

Such is the Catholic doctrine on the nature, unity, substantiality, spirituality, and origin of the soul. It is the only system consistent with Christian faith, and, we may add, morals, for both Materialism and Monism logically cut away the foundations of these. The foregoing historical sketch will have served also to show another advantage it possesses — namely, that it is by far the most comprehensive, and at the same time

---

[1] Ibid.

> discriminating, synthesis of whatever is best in rival systems. It recognizes the physical conditions of the soul's activity with the Materialist, and its spiritual aspect with the Idealist, while with the Monist it insists on the vital unity of human life. It enshrines the principles of ancient speculation, and is ready to receive and assimilate the fruits of modern research.

This is wholly unsatisfying. Indeed, reading the entry, one comes away thinking it is just a ruse to confuse the reader so much that they forget why they were coming to read the piece in the first place. There is no real, easily discernible definition of what a soul is or does, merely lots of discussion of the idea of it over history.

Perhaps Richard Swinburne can help (in *The Evolution of the Soul*):[1]

> It is a frequent criticism of substance dualism that dualists cannot say what souls are. Souls are immaterial subjects of mental properties. They have sensations and thoughts, desires and beliefs, and perform intentional actions. Souls are essential parts of human beings.

But here we have the soul doing exactly what the physical body and emergent mind do.

The problem with any claims about the soul is that they end up being theological assertions: mere assertions. Because, if we could provide evidence of what souls were, we would *know* what souls were. It is pretty obvious. So a soul ends up becoming something that is unevidenced, and this is why there is disagreement (amongst Christians, for example) over what it really is.

Criticism

Souls as Rational Entities

If souls are to be rational, what really differentiates them from consciousness? Though we don't fully understand consciousness, we know it supervenes on the brain (as seen in the last chapter). Without the brain, we

---

[1] Swinburne (1997).

are not conscious. Moreover, if you take drugs, are tired or hungry, or stick a fork into your eye socket and into your brain, your consciousness *will* be affected. These are all physical and easily evidenced things.

In order to be rational, and yet be separate from the brain and consciousness, I am not sure what the soul can be. If it *is* consciousness, then it is...consciousness, and it will die with your brain's death.

If it is rational, then what part does it play in your life throughout your living years, if separate from your consciousness? What does it do that your consciousness does not? If we are judged either at death or contemporaneously for the decisions our conscious brains take, then what is the soul in this context? What responsibility or part in those actions does it have or play? Is it just a carbon copy or reflection of the consciousness that can continue after brain death? If so, it would have to be invisibly connected to the body in some mysterious way. And if this were the case, then it would play no causal role in your actual life, being merely a photocopy of that which does.

We understand the parts of the brain involved in rational processes. And so making the same claims about the soul is to special plead this can happen without the physical matter of the brain.

Death

A real problem for the soul is the very thing it is supposed to function for: carrying on after death. When we die, it is generally assumed by theists that the soul is the immortal entity that continues our existence into whatever realm we are deemed justified in inhabiting.[1] If we go to heaven, however, if the soul looks like consciousness, then what part of our life is the soul supposed to represent?

Imagine I am an eighty-year-old person who has severe dementia and I go to heaven. Do I take that dementia with me as that was "me" at death? Or do we get some kind of cherry-picking of representation throughout my life? Is it "me" five years before death, ten, or at what point? If the soul is a photocopy, when is that photocopy made? Or is it an amalgam, an average of properties that you have throughout life?

We can try to get around this problem. But not successfully. If the soul is connected to my conscious self (and thus all my memories and sense of

---

[1] Unless the theist is an annihilationist that believes that the soul is destroyed at death.

self), then it ends up being essentially unrelated to "me" – the entity being judged in the first place.

These are fundamental and rather terminal problems for the soul (I set many of these out in my book *The Little Book of Unholy Questions*).

If the soul is rational, but not connected to or reflective of lived consciousness, then in what state is the soul representing me in heaven? How is it rational such that it is in any way reflective of my everyday conscious rationality? This is a veritable two-horned dilemma.

Either the soul is my consciousness at death (a copy or reflection), and I live out eternity in that state (in dementia or whatever mental state at death), or it has no connection to my consciousness at death, in which case it has no substantive connection to me, who I feel I am, and how I operate in the mental realm!

Perhaps God just chooses the best version of me, and that's the "me" that gets into heaven (or hell, or whatever afterlife one claims to exist) to live out for eternity. But that itself is riddled with issues.

Ensoulment and In Vitro Fertilisation (IVF)

The other end of the human timeline is equally fraught with problems. When do humans become ensouled? If it is at conception, then there are some pretty big hurdles for the soul thesis. For example, certain twin embryos don't develop until some time after conception. So this model cannot work, or must be radically altered ad hoc.

Another hurdle is IVF. Fertilised embryos, arguably ensouled with supposedly rational properties and identity, are frozen, possibly for eternity. What happens to the soul of this rational entity if the embryo – that early human physical form – is frozen indefinitely? Is there some soul bar in the netherworld where they hang out until they are summoned back?

It is interesting to wonder how a one-day-old embryo can have any rational properties (or the soul). If the soul has rational properties at this stage, then that rationalism has nothing to do with the developed rationalism (dependent on the brain and life of the later individual) that is created over time by that (what eventually becomes a) person.

Conclusion

The soul is incoherent as an idea, and yet pervades in theological thought. It is an assertion, and one that doesn't work. I can see no function that the soul has that isn't already explained by some other aspect of human existence in body and/or mind. The soul is an utterly redundant concept. And this has grave impacts on concepts of heaven and hell.

EPISTEMOLOGY

The term "epistemology" comes from the Greek words "episteme" and "logos". "Episteme" can be translated as "knowledge" or "understanding" or "acquaintance", while "logos" can be translated as "account" or "argument" or "reason". Just as each of these different translations captures some facet of the meaning of these Greek terms, so too does each translation capture a different facet of epistemology itself. Although the term "epistemology" is no more than a couple of centuries old, the field of epistemology is at least as old as any in philosophy. In different parts of its extensive history, different facets of epistemology have attracted attention. Plato's epistemology was an attempt to understand what it was to know, and how knowledge (unlike mere true opinion) is good for the knower. Locke's epistemology was an attempt to understand the operations of human understanding, Kant's epistemology was an attempt to understand the conditions of the possibility of human understanding, and Russell's epistemology was an attempt to understand how modern science could be justified by appeal to sensory experience. Much recent work in formal epistemology is an attempt to understand how our degrees of confidence are rationally constrained by our evidence, and much recent work in feminist epistemology is an attempt to understand the ways in which interests affect our evidence, and affect our rational constraints more generally. In all these cases, epistemology seeks to understand one or another kind of *cognitive* success (or, correspondingly, cognitive *failure*).

Matthias Steup and Ram Neta, "Epistemology", *The Stanford Encyclopedia of Philosophy*

Can There Be Very Strong Reasons for Believing Something Although It Is False?

The soul. Heaven. Hell.

This is an interesting question partly because it is a complex query dressed up in a simple manner. There are many terms here that require a great deal of unpacking before we are able to arrive at any sort of warranted conclusion. As a result, there are some assumptions that we have to be make in order to analyse these concepts in a concise framework. In the title here, we have terms like "reason" (qualified as "very strong"), "belief" and "false", all of which I have included for a good excuse to discuss them.

This essay is primarily an epistemological investigation into reason, belief and truth. I will first briefly define what I feel qualifies as truth before looking at what it would take to have a warranted belief in a false proposition. My approach after this will take on a twofold tack. To begin, I will attempt to establish a reliable method of arriving at a truth. Specifically, if we use an unreliable epistemological method, then we will not have very strong reasons for believing a proposition. This is especially problematic if someone else can reliably deem this proposition as being false. Second, I will look at whether we can have a defensible epistemological method that arrives at a belief in a proposition that is untestable. Thus both prongs assume that the agent (you or me) is not aware that the proposition is false and may not, in some instances, even have any way of knowing this. Finally, I will explain that reason can take on two different senses, one of causality and one of rationality. This will enable us to conclude that if we use an unreliable epistemological method, or one that leads to an untestable belief in a proposition, we cannot have very strong reasons for believing in something that is false.

It is important to build epistemologies up from their foundations. Remember the talk of bottom up rather than top down earlier in this collection. When investigating epistemological issues, it is crucial to explain our foundations. There is no better place to start than with our friend, the Rationalist René Descartes and his *cogito ergo sum*. Descartes was very much a skeptic in believing that we couldn't necessarily trust our senses. He wanted to work out exactly what knowledge we *could know* indubitably.

"I think, therefore I am" is a declaration of the extent of indubitable knowledge. That is to say, we can only be sure that a thinking entity exists by point of fact *that* it thinks (even if it be doubting, and even if we can define exactly what such a thinking entity might ontologically be). Further, if I were a Pyrrhonian Skeptic, a skeptic who is defined by such a degree of doubt so as to remain effectively agnostic over everything (even their own position), then I would rationally be able to assert this mantra as confirming the limits to my knowledge.

However, this, as a scope for an epistemology, is not very *useful*; it is not entirely *pragmatic*. As a result, it is necessary, in order to form a *usable* epistemology, to build up from this. Yet to do so, one has to make certain leaps of faith. Or to put it another way, we must make claims concerning knowledge that are not indubitable.

For us to make sense of this question, let us first look at notions of truth. Within the framework of this essay, I will adopt the *correspondence theory* of truth, which is defined as follows:[1]

> The basic idea of the correspondence theory is that what we believe or say is true if it corresponds to the way things actually are—to the facts...

> The correspondence theory of truth is at its core an ontological thesis: a belief is true if there exists an appropriate entity—a fact—to which it corresponds. If there is no such entity, the belief is false.

In the realms of philosophy (and elsewhere!), everything can be critiqued, and every theory has its criticisers. In order to fully establish this correspondence theory of truth, I would have a very long regress of having to prove certain positions that hinge on other positions still, so on and so forth. But I *do* believe there to be an objective reality of entities and objects. And we can ascribe human beliefs and claims to these entities. I am not a brain in a vat or a body in an experience machine as seen in *The Matrix*, or, indeed, a victim of Descartes' Evil Daemon, inputting sensations into my mind. I can think on my own.

However, any truth claim surely needs to be grounded *somehow* – in *something*. So this might be a good time to introduce the construct known as the Münchhausen Trilemma that looks to lay out the various options for grounding a claim.

---

[1] Glanzberg (2006).

The Münchhausen Trilemma

The Münchhausen Trilemma is a useful mechanism for understanding how to ground a claim. A simple Wikipedia definition will suffice here:[1]

> The Münchhausen trilemma (after Baron Münchhausen, who allegedly pulled himself and the horse on which he was sitting out of a swamp by his own hair), also called Agrippa's trilemma (after Agrippa the Skeptic), is a philosophical term coined to stress the purported impossibility to prove any truth even in the fields of logic and mathematics, without appealing to accepted assumptions. It is the name of an argument in the theory of knowledge going back to the German philosopher Hans Albert, and more traditionally, in the name of Agrippa....
>
> If we ask of any knowledge: "How do I know that it's true?", we may provide proof; yet that same question can be asked of the proof, and any subsequent proof. The Münchhausen trilemma is that we have only three options when providing proof in this situation:
>
> - The circular argument, in which theory and proof support each other (i.e. we repeat ourselves at ssome point)
>
> - The regressive argument, in which each proof requires a further proof, *ad infinitum* (i.e. we just keep giving proofs, presumably forever)
>
> - The axiomatic argument, which rests on accepted precepts (i.e. we reach some bedrock assumption or certainty)
>
> The first two methods of reasoning are fundamentally weak, and because the Greek skeptics advocated deep questioning of all accepted values they refused to accept

---

[1] "Münchhausen Trilemma", *Wikipedia*, https://en.wikipedia.org/wiki/M%C3%BCnchhausen_trilemma (retrieved 17/08/2017).

71

proofs of the third sort. The trilemma, then, is the decision among the three equally unsatisfying options.

In contemporary epistemology, advocates of coherentism are supposed to be accepting the "circular" horn of the trilemma; foundationalists are relying on the axiomatic argument. Views that accept the infinite regress are branded infinitism.

For the purposes of this piece, let me exemplify using morality – happiness and the good. Imagine this conversation:

Peter: Why bother doing X?
Jane: Because it leads to A.
Peter: Why do you want A?
Jane: Because it leads to B.

This conversation could go on, as Jane keeps deriving her answers. This would be an infinite regress. So she might prefer to ground her answers at some point, but her grounding should be non-derivative. A foundational block – a self-evident truth. For example:

Peter: Why do you want E?
Jane: Because it makes me (us, humanity etc.) happy.
Peter: Why do you want to be happy?
Jane: In order to be happy/because it is self-evidently "good" to be happy.

The idea for Jane is that being happy is self-evidently good, and desired. And there is no further reasoning to be done. She can derive this answer no further and here is her axiomatic grounding. This is why happiness/pleasure/wellbeing is such a powerful moral currency in this kind of debate – it appears non-derivative and axiomatic. Of course, as with all such claims, we can further debate this. But hopefully the point about grounding claims is made here. The open question about happiness being a non-derivative value is something to which we will return later in this collection.

Phenomenology

If any given claim corresponds accurately to actual properties of the world, then we deem it as being true or factual. This is the theme of this essay. However, the axiom here is that such entities (with properties) exist and that our claims can correspond to them. As I cautioned before, this is my first leap of faith, if you will. Knowledge is knowing that one's claims correspond to actual properties. We can define knowledge as a true belief we have about a proposition. The problem is in establishing what is true – the correct correlation between a belief of the external world, and the reality of the external world.

Philosophers will define "truth", "fact" and "knowledge" differently. For me, knowledge is a true belief we have about a proposition. The problem is in establishing truth – the correct correlation between a belief of the external world, and the reality of the external world.

With this in mind, it is worth quickly covering some terms pertinent to phenomenology (the study of the structures of experience, consciousness and the mental world).

Idealism: The belief that the mind and ideas are the primary source of existence; that the physical realm is either secondary or, in the extreme, doesn't exist.

Materialism: The belief that matter is primary and the mental realm is a product of the material realm.

Rationalism: The belief that the rational mind is the best way of knowing things – the mind is more trustworthy than the senses.

Empiricism: The belief, opposing rationalism, that the senses are the best way of knowing things, such as observing the external world. Truth is confirmed by sense data.

We have already touched on realism and nominalism, dualism and monism.

Returning to Descartes, let me bring into play his idea of the Evil Daemon (from his 1641 *Meditations on First Philosophy*). The Daemon (or Demon) is analogous to the modern thought experiment that we are all simply comprised of brains in a vats, or participants in a virtual reality or simulation like the movie *The Matrix*, with all of their implications.

All of these thought experiments (or movies… or maybe realities) state that we could be existing in a world controlled by an evil demon (or hooked into a machine, or be brains in vats, or even have a non-cynically designed faulty set of senses). This would mean that all of our experiences are actually false and do not correspond to an objective reality. This is what the assumption (or leap) above is attempting to overcome.

However, even if we are brains in vats, we make sense of the reality that we experience, even if it does not correlate to an objective reality outside of our experiences. Consequently, it does not matter either way whether we are indeed real humans experiencing real objects, or whether we are brains in vats experiencing simulations. In the context of our experiences, the epistemological methods we build up are pragmatically useful.

Can I prove that I am not a brain in a vat, or a body in a *Matrix* machine? Not indubitably. But it is not *useful* to believe that I am in a vat or experience machine, and there is no *good* reason or *positive* evidence to think that I am. Therefore, I think I am justified in taking that leap to believe that I am not a body in a *Matrix* machine.[1] This scenario is a direct analogy of idealism.

Having made this assumption (that an objective reality exists, and that claims *can* correspond to that reality), let us move on in building up an epistemology. Before we do this, it is worth spending some time discussing the positions of realism and idealism to establish our foundations.

We start with our own minds (Descartes' *cogito*). Our minds have experiences, and experiences of other things we call objects. Knowing these objects is a subjective ideal, contingent upon both the conscious mind and the object itself. Immanuel Kant recognised that there was a limit to our subjective minds knowing these objects. In his *Critique of Pure Reason,* he delineated a difference between what he called *phenomena* and *noumena.* Phenomena are objects that are interpreted through the subjective mechanisms of human consciousness and senses. Noumena are what he called "things-in-themselves". Kant declared that humans are unable to access this noumenal knowledge, since it is only interpretable through our subjective senses. In this way, Kant synthesises both empiricism and rationalism (some call him an empirical realist).

Let me use an analogy. Imagine a human and a bat looking at or sensing a moth. Each has our own subjective senses, and each experiences the moth in very different ways. Even our sense of colour will be different. Neither know the thing-in-itself, only their own representation of it (the moth).

We can extrapolate this sensory and experiential difference onto two different humans. The two individuals will likely have similar subjective

---

[1] This is also analogous to the Simulation Hypothesis – that we are all living in a simulation – as argued by philosophers like Nick Bostrom. See Sabine Hossenfelder's arguments against this position, for example (i.e., Hossenfelder 2021).

experiences of a moth, but they will not be identical. Our knowledge of all things will be different and contingent upon our individual cognitive faculties, our senses and our consciousnesses. None of these agents (the humans or the bat) *know* the *thing-in-itself* (what Kant called the *Ding an sich*), all have different "knowledges" of the same object or thing. Kant saw humans as making sense out of the world around us – out of the phenomena – by using reason and our conscious deliberations in a process he described as transcending the observations. However, to truly *know* these objects, these noumena, is beyond the capability of such transcendental analysis. Therefore, these objects (our universe) remain fundamentally unknown and unknowable.

Kant's view inspired a torrent of idealist philosophies and it is worth seeing if we can defend his view on objects since this will have some bearing on how we progress. German philosopher Georg Hegel (1770–1831) moving things on a great deal (through other philosophers like Johann Fichte and Friedrich Schelling), claimed that Kant assumed (through his phenomenology) that the human was one step removed from the objects of the world (things, perceptions, ideas, feelings), confined by our limits of human experience.

Kant believed that mental structures – *categories* (including the concepts of *cause, substance, existence* and *reality*) – were a priori, which is to say they exist prior to experience. They are independent of historical development. Our experience cannot quite give us knowledge of that outside world.

Hegel, in contrast to Kant, asserted that the categories that we bring to bear on the world can indeed constitute actual knowledge. This was based on Hegel's criticism that the search for knowledge entails first being able to set out what knowledge ontologically is before actually making claims of knowing anything. However, this sequence, Hegel believed, goes down the path of an infinite regress (remember our trilemma) making its foundations self-contradictory. His phenomenology attempts to dissolve this problem by seeing the mind and the object as, in some sense, unified. He found Kant's "world in itself" as somewhat meaningless. As Paul Redding in the *Stanford Encyclopedia of Philosophy* states:[1]

> Like Kant, Hegel thinks that one's capacity to be "conscious" of some external object as something distinct from oneself requires the reflexivity of "self-consciousness," that is, it requires one's awareness of oneself as a subject for whom something distinct, the object, is presented as known. Hegel goes beyond Kant, however, and expanding on an idea found

---

[1] Redding (2010).

in Fichte, makes this requirement dependent on one's recognition... of other self-conscious subjects as self-conscious subjects, and, moreover, on one's recognition of them as similarly recognizing oneself as a self-conscious subject. Such patterns of mutual recognition constituting "objective spirit" thereby provide the matrix within which individual self-consciousnesses can exist as such...

Hegel rejected Kant's thing-in-itself as being self-contradictory because a thing must be an object of our consciousness if it is to be an object at all. As Fichte and Hegel believed, a thing is only a thing when it is something *for us*. The thing-in-itself is actually a *product of our thought*. This new kind of German Idealism (where idealism is the belief that fundamental reality is intellectual rather than material) moved idealistic thinking along since Hegel and his contemporaries were willing to dissolve the distinction between *being* and *thinking*.

Kant believed objects were independent of the mind, and that we could not truly know them. This new wave of idealists, on the other hand, saw a universality to conscious thought, that did not necessitate a distinction between the mind and the object.

Hegel, in believing that the Whole Truth could be known, set out to show that the "I" was absolute, not contingent upon nature (it was something *real*). If the "I" were dependent upon nature, it would thus adhere to a form of duality that he saw as contradictory. Kant says we cannot know the object in itself. Hegel says the object exists in our conception: the nuomenal world beyond thought is actually *dependent* upon thought.

For idealists, such as Hegel, there are no things-in-themselves (in a material realm). What we call objects and events are actually constellations of perceptions so that there exist only two things: perceptions and perceivers.

The discussion of idealism is similar to Descartes' cogito, where in order to doubt one's existence, one must exist. The idealist says that object cannot "exist" independent of the mind because, in order to consider it, we are using our minds. This is rather similar to the idea that there is no sound of a tree falling in a forest if there is no one to hear the sound. There is no tree at all if it is not in anyone's conception.

Kant's philosophy is incredibly complicated; Hegel takes that complexity and raises it a good few levels. For Hegel, there was a great connection between his concept of idealism history. Two people thinking at different historical epochs would not only be thinking about different things, but would be thinking differently. Different consciousnesses would represent historical stages in the development of thought and consciousness.

Everything about humanity is about change and history, in a non-random *dialectical* process towards an end point, implying an unfolding in time of an inner spiritual principle.

Hegel's idealism concerned God, in the form of the "Absolute (Spirit)" – a pure consciousness. The subject and the object – the mind and the thing – are both manifestations of the same thing. Where Kant was more of an empiricist realist, Hegel was an idealist – reality is indistinguishable from perception, or understanding, in the mental realm. Strict naturalist/nontheistic idealism exists on a continuum. At one end is solipsism, where the world is a figment of our own mind. At the other end is some kind of panpsychism, where there is an uber-consciousness, or that everything is participating in some aspect of a "unifying" or universal consciousness.

I mentioned earlier of having a "faith" in the Correspondence Theory ("true" propositions correspond to the facts of an objective reality) in order to move on with my arguments. But Hegel's idealistic outlook makes it unnecessary to have to make this leap of "faith". This is because the world is arguably metaphysically one single unity of conscious thought. An individual person is not a separate part of reality, but an aspect of the Spirit in development. If this were the case, *my pragmatic approach would still apply*. We do not necessarily have to dismiss Kant in constructing a reliable and practical epistemology to navigate our daily existences.

Despite a number of arguments supporting idealism, this approach creates a mystery for why we *appear* to live in a world of things that exist outside of our perceptual minds. If I hide a ball under a blanket, we all assume (even toddlers) that the ball is still there, even though you cannot perceive it. And it is, which makes sense when I lift the blanket. Bishop Berkeley, a famous idealist, tried to solve this intuitive problem (object impermanence) for idealism by saying that the external world *does* exist in the mind of the Great Perceiver: God. As you may have guessed, I'm not all that sure of the God concept, so I don't buy into this philosophical conclusion.

Idealism vs realism. There is something to be said for our own minds being evidence of realism (the idea that reality exists independent of our thoughts). Since we struggle to control our realities and our own minds, I find it difficult to give full credence to idealism. Not only can I not control everything, I also don't know everything. What is limiting my mind? It seems, to me at any rate, that the external world is the best explanation for this.

Other minds also present a problem for idealism. As an ontological realist, I assume that other minds result from other brains. And I communicate with them on the basis that they are similar to my brain and mind. I don't go about my daily business assuming that other minds are merely a figment of my perception. But modern idealist philosophers do have answers for this along the lines of each mind being an "alter" with dissociative boundaries in the non-material realm. I'm not sure what evidence would look like to either confirm this or disconfirm it. Perhaps it comes down to intuition and common sense.

As philosopher Arthur Schopenhauer observed that idealism runs counter to common sense:[1]

> In spite of that one may say, nothing is so persistently and ever anew misunderstood as Idealism, because it is interpreted as meaning that one denies the empirical reality of the external world. Upon this rests the perpetual return to the appeal to common sense, which appears in many forms and guises; for example, as an "irresistible conviction" in the Scotch school, or as Jacobi's faith in the reality of the external world. The external world by no means presents itself, as Jacobi declares, upon credit, and is accepted by us upon trust and faith. It presents itself as that which it is, and performs directly what it promises

We might all be our own separate mental representations of a single mental existence, or something similar. But this is unfalsifiable, just like the idealists claim materialism or realism is. A materialist or realist has to make that jump of faith from the mind to an external world without being able to either prove or disprove it; it is unfalsifiable. Equally, the idealist who denies the external world must also make an unfalsifiable claim that the external world doesn't exist – she can neither prove or disprove it.

This is something of an impasse.

So much more could be said of idealism and the many idealist thinkers, arguably most notably with one of the founders of phenomenology (partly by later coining the term), Edmund Husserl (1859-1938).[2] Much of his philosophy was influenced by the fact that he started off as a mathematician and that sense of mathematical certainty took centre stage. His desire was to find a priori foundations for the sciences. He believed that, despite all the methodological and technological sophistication of modern science, there was still a failure to account for the basic epistemic foundation on which

---

[1] Schopenhauer (2015), Chapter I, The Standpoint of Idealism.
[2] Although I think the most interesting view of idealism is from modern philosopher Bernardo Kastrup. He is well worth looking into.

science relies. Husserl thought that this foundation may be discerned in consciousness.

Rather like Descartes, he wanted to cast aside (or "bracket out" as he called it) assumptions and see what we could build up from secure foundations. He felt that the sciences could not be built on firm foundations if those foundations included experience. Husserl decreed that we must remain agnostic, that we should (as with Pyrrhonian skepticism) suspend judgement over whether we can or cannot have knowledge over our subjective sensations.

Husserl thought that our consciousnesses are products of their times and environments and so should be analysed from that perspective. The difficulty in that approach is that nature is fundamental to shaping the consciousness (the "I"), making it very subjective. Husserl saw it as impossible to derive certainty from our external world, much like Descartes. He was looking at philosophy in terms of finding a foundation for mathematical and scientific truths. However, he did see truths in sense impressions (sensory experiences) making his epistemology more wide-ranging than that of Descartes (he was opposed to such a form of skepticism).

Husserl set out to describe the whole array of complex and interconnected cognitive mechanisms that we employ when sensing or observing something. Things aren't just what they appear as a snapshot since our consciousness is able to create a complicated "picture" full of nuance of what that object might be. For example, when I look at a mobile phone on my table, I do not just see the outer case facing me, but I can envision its rear casing, what is inside it, its weight, the screen and its capabilities. There is a more holistic experience to the phenomenology of the phone. It is not just what the phenomena bring to me as a conscious entity but what I, as the experiencing entity, bring to the table, too, so to speak. Our judgements, according to Husserl, are confined to judgements about the phenomena only, not about anything external to them. Husserl "brackets" any such judgements on this external world:[1]

> Whereas Descartes took his own conscious awareness to be epistemically basic and then immediately tried to infer, based on his knowledge of this awareness, the existence of a God, an external world, and other knowledge, Husserl takes first-person conscious awareness as epistemically basic and then proposes the systematic

---

[1] Spear (n.d.).

> study of this consciousness itself as a fundamental philosophical task....
>
> The idea behind this is that most people most of the time do not focus their attention on the structure of their experience itself but rather look past this experience and focus their attention and interests on objects and events in the world, which they take to be unproblematically real or existent.... A subject who has...adopted the phenomenological attitude is in a position to objectively describe the features of her experience as she experiences them, the phenomena. Questions of the real existence of particular objects of experience and even of the world or universe themselves are thus set aside in order to make way for the systematic study of first person conscious experience

Personally, I think Husserl's work is useful in pointing out the problems inherent with the mind – our experiences and senses – in trying to create an accurate, a priori epistemological picture. Indeed, psychology and the idea of hermeneutics (interpretation) have a lot to thank Husserl for. When one suspends judgement, it is perhaps the safest option – but it seems to restrict the scope of an epistemology.

What is important for *me* is what is *useful* to *me*, and is *reliable* for me navigating the world. By extension, I assume that this is also what at least appears (and if not *is*) useful for those around me and for the world that I assume exists in some form. I am not sure that idealism is particularly *useful* in any great way, though I am happy to be shown otherwise (although I am at some deeper ontological level rather ambivalent about it). I get the sense that we would not get a lot of science done, building that dam or that wind turbine, if we adopted a strict idealism on a daily basis.

Personally, I favour a Kantian view that there is an objective reality that we cannot "know" in and of itself, but about which we can have some sort of transcendental knowledge. I am a realist about the world in that it is largely mind-independent. I cannot prove this, since this is the very nature of the thing itself! Thus, the axiomatic faith in the Correspondence Theory of truth is one that implies a Kantian view of the world. A Hegelian one would imbue its truth through the very mechanism of consciousness itself.

In fact, my position of *indirect realism* is perfectly defined in this explanation:[1]

---

[1] LK (2014).

This states that it is highly probable that there is an external physical world of objects or things/events that corresponds indirectly to some objects of perception in the sense that some objects of perception are causally dependent on real objects.

But we do not have direct access to the external objects of reality, but only to some conscious "objects of perception" that are causally dependent on them. That is to say, the objects and events of the world of matter and energy described by science are not objects of immediate experience/"objects of perception".

So the indirect realist/materialist's inductive argument does not say that the external object and the internal "objects of perception" are absolutely equivalent....

The human mind's "objects of perception" are representations (with colour sensations, shapes and so on) of sense data from the external world such as, for example, from the swarm of particles called a tree, and this system of internal representation is the product of Darwinian evolution, and one could conceive of a mind capable of representing the same tree in different ways from different data beyond the visible spectrum (e.g., infrared or x-rays).

Furthermore, the actual qualities we perceive in our minds like green and red are not qualities of the actual object existing in material reality, but are merely causally dependent on them to some extent (e.g., light waves reflected off the object are the causal factor for perception of colours).

So we see that the indirect realist makes a crucial distinction between (1) "objects of perception" and (2) external objects that we do not experience directly. Our argument for the existence of an external world of events/objects is an inductive one based on empirical evidence. Its truth is at most very probable, not certain.

I would disagree somewhat with the last two sentences. Empiricism will not provide evidence for the external world; or, it only figures after we make that "leap of faith" to the existence of an external world. Indeed, the faith in matter is equivalent to an idealist's faith in other minds, or faith that the non-material world is all there is.

From here, however, from this realist foundation, I will look to propose an evidentialist (empiricist) progression. This is, in some sense, even in line with Hegel himself, who stated:[1]

> Every philosophy is essentially an idealism or at least has idealism for its principle, and the question then is only how far this principle is actually carried out.

So the "I" experiences phenomena, which, presumably, represent real objects. I use my cognitive faculties of consciousness (mind) to assess such phenomena. It appears to me that other people, other minds, have similar experiences. These other minds might or might not exist. But since I have assumed some kind of realism standing behind such phenomena, then I would be using double standards to assume that these other minds did not exist.

From this, I can build up a coherent picture of the world. As mentioned, this world may or may not exist, *but this doesn't matter*, since pragmatically it might as well exist since I am experiencing it (falsely or otherwise), and I find such a representation helpful.

There are aspects of idealism that are coherent; I think that conceptual nominalism has an exceptionally close relationship to idealism. Here's the point I have already made: If idealism were the case, *my pragmatic approach would still apply*. Whether matter is an abstraction of our minds or our minds are an emergence from matter is irrelevant. We experience. *So what is the best way to use that experience to navigate this reality?*

Therefore, what builds up my knowledge are phenomena and the patterns and properties that they exhibit. Some of these phenomena are other experiencing minds that report back to me, as phenomena, their own experiences. And I form beliefs about the world that are dependent on these phenomena. These beliefs, however, are justified by the phenomena themselves to a greater or lesser degree.

In other words, the phenomena (my experience of external objects) act as evidence for my beliefs. Some of my beliefs may have more evidence to

---

[1] Hegel (1969), p.154-5

support them than other beliefs. As Matthias Steup states in the "Epistemology" entry for the *Stanford Encyclopedia of Philosophy*:[1]

> For example, if the coffee in your cup tastes sweet to you, then you have evidence for believing that the coffee is sweet. If you feel a throbbing pain in your head, you have evidence for believing that you have a headache. If you have a memory of having had cereal for breakfast, then you have evidence for a belief about the past: a belief about what you ate when you had breakfast. And when you clearly "see" or "intuit" that the proposition "If Jack had more than four cups of coffee, then Jack had more than three cups of coffee" is true, then you have evidence for believing that proposition. In this view, evidence consists of perceptual, introspective, memorial, and intuitional experiences, and to possess evidence is to have an experience of that kind. So according to this evidentialism, what makes you justified in believing that p is your having an experience that represents p as being true.

Evidence, then, becomes something we can know through direct experience, and also something that we can use in order to justify a belief.

The Problem of Induction

As an aside here, let me take a short diversion into the realms of Hume and the Problem of Induction. Before I do this, let me establish the difference between *deduction* and *induction*.

A deductive argument is one that is beholden to the rules of logic. For example:

All humans are mortal.
Socrates is human.
Therefore, Socrates is mortal.

The conclusion follows necessarily from the premises. I am leaving it very simple here, and not discussing the finer nuances of deductive logic.

---

[1] Steup (2005).

Induction, on the other hand, is a different kettle of fish.

Hume claimed that we do not have good *reason* to form a belief about a future event based on past uniformities. We cannot be (deductively) sure that the pen I drop won't fall up even though every pen dropped in the past has fallen down. Gravity might be supported by evidence (experience) up until I drop the pen, but it does not *necessarily* follow that the pen will continue to adhere to gravity in the future, or that gravity exists in the manner we understand. However, admitting the logical truth of this, one still has better reason for believing the pen will drop than believing it will not drop (remember our talk about the regularity of the universe). It is a case of probability: If a horse has won a million races up until now, never having lost one, then betting against it in the next race is probabilistically irrational.

In practice, we make interpretations of our senses as they detect, categorise and theorise external phenomena. In this way, we start moving towards the realm of science – a body of techniques for investigating phenomena, acquiring new knowledge, or correcting and integrating previous knowledge.[1]

If we superimpose this previous point (gravity and the pen) onto the discipline of science, we can then make some sense of the term "fact". A scientific fact is one that is recognised as being supported by overwhelming evidence.

Looking at the pen and gravity, we take the Theory of Gravity as being a scientific fact. That is not to say it is indubitable: we may be wrong; the pen could fall up the next time. Or we could be a brain in a vat. However, neither of these alternative explanations appear to be the case. And if we thought like that with every piece of knowledge, we would remain Pyrrhonian Skeptics, intellectually immobilised by eternal doubt. Thus, for pragmatic purposes, in order to live our lives sensibly (involving prediction, estimation and planning), we take certain claims (i.e., gravity) as fact.

The problem is that the term "overwhelming support" is very subjective and open to criticisms of being arbitrary – remember back to the talk of arbitrary lines drawn on continua from the first chapter. Therefore, we need a common-sense approach in order to determine how to employ such facts and non-facts (or theories). For example, if 99.99% of scientists and thousands of peer-reviewed journals defend the law of gravity, then the probability of it being true is greater than the belief that the moon is made of cheese. Thus, I can incorporate this as a true fact, or knowledge, in order to utilise and rely on it (in planning or carrying out actions successfully).

---

[1] Goldhaber and Nieto (2010)

However, if a theory is only supported by 55% of relevant experts, then I should adapt my plans in correlation to the probability of it being true. If the evidence for a claim is severely lacking (such that 3% of scientists in the relevant fields defend it), then relying on it as a fact would be ill-advised. Thus, I can appraise the phenomena of the objects themselves, as well as the scientists (as objects) and journals (as objects) and assess accordingly.

We must also take into account that scientific theories *do* get overturned and new ideas *do* supersede older ones, for various reasons (hopefully, that they are true and better evidenced!).

Of course, we have the danger of cognitive heuristics (mental shortcuts) and biases. For example, confirmation bias may cause one to accord more value to a claim given its provenance from a more (subjectively) respected person, or group, or if it confirms some already-held belief. But, hopefully, if we are honest with ourselves, with the data, and with the methodology, we can start to approach a useful and arguably accurate truth.

If I am not confident in my cognitive faculties to fully understand such phenomena, I can defer to the experts without critically examining the objects and phenomena myself. This process should be based on evidential foundations. If, in the past, I had deferred to experts who almost unanimously defended a truth claim fifty times, and each time the claim had been reliable so that my plans or actions could take place with reliable outcomes, then, probabilistically, deferring to these experts when I do not have the required faculties to investigate the truth claims myself is a reliable mechanism.

Subsequently, we are making a case for evidence, when used this way, to be a reliable mechanism for justifying beliefs. There is an overlap here of *evidentialism* and *reliabilism*. As a follow-up to his last quote in the previous section, philosopher Matthias Steup describes this overlap as follows:[1]

> [Reliabilists] hold that a belief is justified if, and only if, it results from cognitive origin that is reliable: an origin that tends to produce true beliefs and therefore properly
>
> probabilifies the belief. Reliabilists, then, would agree that the beliefs mentioned in the previous paragraph are justified. But according to a standard form of reliabilism, what makes them justified is not the possession of evidence, but the fact that the types of processes in which they originate — perception, introspection, memory, and rational intuition — are reliable.

---

[1] Steup (2005).

The various evidences used here are indeed those phenomenological mechanisms of perception, introspection, memory and rational intuition.

Here we are starting to build an epistemology that is both reliable and coherent to the individual experiencer. And by "coherent", I mean one that fits in with all the other philosophies, knowledge, and maps we use to navigate reality.

Let me recap the discussion so far. We understand that phenomena reflect the real world. These phenomena include other conscious minds who also experience the world. As a result, there is a collection of recorded experiences that constitute a growing body of evidence that can be applied towards finding the truth values of certain propositions. These propositions are ascribed a pragmatic truth if supported by overwhelming evidence.

Additionally, the process of gathering experience (such as data and information), known as the scientific process, refines the data so that it becomes increasingly more accurate. And this process is self-correcting (formally through the peer-review process, but also in how scientific progress works, with scientists analysing each other's work and seeking to confirm or disconfirm it). This is an extremely important idea. What this means is that the experience of those others around me (the data that they or we collect) is testable. One caveat here: the experience should be a claim or observation about the objective world, not merely untestable personal experiences. Therefore, in practice, I have the ability to test the claims or to observe testing (of those claims and data) by another reliable source.

The Scientific Method

It is time to look in more detail at the term "scientific method" – a process by which we gather knowledge of the world. It is also a process that can refine this knowledge. The process should lead to a more and more accurate understanding and knowledge of the world as time passes. The traditional view of science (i.e., the scientific method) can be summed up as follows:[1]

> Science is often distinguished from other domains of human culture by its progressive nature: in contrast to art, religion, philosophy, morality, and politics, there exist clear standards or normative criteria for identifying improvements and advances in science. For example, the historian of science George Sarton argued that "the

---

[1] Niiniluoto (2011).

acquisition and systematization of positive knowledge are the only human activities which are truly cumulative and progressive," and "progress has no definite and unquestionable meaning in other fields than the field of science" (Sarton 1936).

The order of scientific events can be understood as:

(1) Formulate a question
(2) Formulate a hypothesis
(3) Make a prediction
(4) Test the prediction
(5) Analyse the results

This can be a circular and repeating pattern of acquiring knowledge such that the results of one test influence the forming of another question, which can then start the process again. Karl Popper, the famous philosopher of science, espoused the approach of falsifiability. This is the concept that dictates that if a claim is false, then it can be shown to be so by observation or experiment. Popper would state that only falsifiable claims belong in the realms of scientific enquiry. At the heart of this is the notion that truth claims about the universe cannot be verified but only falsified. This refers back to the Problem of Induction discussed earlier. The pen might fall up next time. Therefore, we cannot verify the Theory of Gravity and its effects to be *absolutely* true – there is space for doubt. However, we *can* falsify such claims. If my pen did fall up (ceteris paribus), then the theory would be falsified.

Where does this leave us? Again recapping, we have that internal and absolute truth that we, as thinking entities, exist. Moving on, we rely on a pragmatic approach of analysing phenomena. We can show this to be reliable (whether we are a brain in a vat or not) within our subjective existence. We gather evidence and data of the external world. This data must be verifiable (i.e., testable) in order for us to (reliably) determine whether it is true or not).

We are not alone. Our pragmatic knowledge contains a set of data that we have collected both from our own experience and from the experience of reliable others. A note on this: I would not take a truth claim as factual from a person, who had lied to me before, walking up to me on the street and claiming that a tiger had attacked and eaten someone in the local supermarket. I would, however, take the story as factual if the police told me, or I saw it reported by experts on the television news shown in a nearby shop window. These sources had both proved themselves to be reliable to me before.

So, the claim that if I drop my pen in the living room it will fall downwards, is something that I would believe as a truth, a predicted fact. This is built upon a huge amount of experimental data. It is testable, and it is falsifiable (it could fall up). As a result, given the past uniformities of such an experiment, I would take this as a reliable piece of knowledge, and I would say that I *do* have very strong reasons for believing that my pen will fall down when I drop it.

But, if I had a false truth claim, could I have very strong reasons for believing it? First of all, let me ask this with reference to a truth claim that is falsifiable and testable (a Falsifiable Claim). In this situation, the claim would be an empirically testable claim about the external world. If I had (at t_1) a new tentative hypothesis for a cosmological theory of the way the universe started, would this be taken as a truth? A tentative theory like this that is not defended by overwhelming evidence would not have very strong reasons for believing it, but it would also be seen as a theory and not a fact. It is a hypothesis as opposed to being a truth claim. One could believe it, but it would not have the support of much evidence and would require a large amount of faith to be believed. It might be both coherent (mathematically, etc.) and falsifiable, but it is not established nor is it the consensus among the experts.

On the other hand, one could believe (also at t_1) in the Standard Big Bang model. It is coherent, falsifiable and defended by the consensus of experts in the relevant fields. Thus, one would have very strong reasons for believing it.

The Standard Big Bang model could be proved wrong as different evidence is added into the mix, and as other newer and related theories are expounded (at, say, t_2). However, at t_1, one would indeed have very strong reasons for believing it. Therefore, one could have overwhelming evidence to support a false Falsifiable Claim if the overwhelming evidence (at t_1) supported that claim, and there was incomplete evidence available to the believer to support its falsification. In this way, justified beliefs (beliefs with very strong reasons to believe them) are dependent upon the evidence for them. Incomplete or incorrect evidence can lead to false beliefs.

However, it can be difficult to know whether we *ever* have sufficient or complete information, and to know whether the claims are false. Therefore, the best we can hope for is to make judgements with the most complete information available. This raises the issue that "very strong reasons" cannot be given if the evidence is incomplete. But since we often cannot know whether the evidence is complete or not, we interpret such evidence as being good enough. However, if we *knew* the evidence was largely incomplete (and if there were gaping theoretical holes or issues), then this could invalidate the idea that one has "very strong reasons" for believing the claim.

With regard to positions that are made of unfalsifiable claims, things are a little different. If one cannot falsify a claim, then one cannot have very strong reasons to believe it. One must do so based on faith. Normal, empirical evidence is full of consistent patterns. Without these consistent patterns (i.e., if things were non-deterministic or random), we could not form any hypotheses and likely would not even exist (see my Argument from Format chapter for elucidation of this point)! This framework of evidence is vital for making reliable and falsifiable claims.

Let us look a bit more closely at an unfalsifiable claim. If we take, for example, the truth claim that "God answers prayer" we might be able to more clearly understand this point. This claim is unfalsifiable. It involves both the testable and the untestable. We can test, and have tested, prayer and its effects, using double-blind experiments. However, the experiments have shown no positive results for intercessory prayer (when God intervenes for someone at the behest of someone else). However, defenders of this truth claim move the untestable, unfalsifiable agent (God) outside of the normal causal bounds. For example, a defender might claim "God may decide not to answer those prayers because he doesn't like being tested". This means that the claim is effectively unfalsifiable. We have seemingly empirically falsified the belief that God answers prayer using an evidential procedure. However, since God is not consistent, deterministic and testable in such a manner, one cannot reliably say whether God does or does not answer prayer. Thus, such a belief is not supported by very strong reasons, but by unevidenced faith.

In this way a defender of an unfalsifiable claim can move the causal factors of the claim around like a pea in the shell game, defrauding the tester of any ability to test the agent (in this case, God).

As mentioned, the claim might well be true, but one does not have very strong reasons for believing so. For this epistemic method, reliability is contingent on the ability to test and possibly falsify the claim. Claims that deny one the ability to do this are not supported by very strong reason.

Let me finally recap where we are for reliably finding truth:

(1) The thinking entity exists (cogito ergo sum).
(2) Any other existence (i.e., other people, objects) assumes a grounding in faith in an external reality, combined with a lack of positive knowledge that an external world *doesn't* exist as such.
(3) All phenomena assumed to relate to the outside world count as evidence.

(4) A fact is a piece of knowledge that is a truth claim supported coherently by overwhelming evidence.

(5) A fact must be falsifiable.

(6) A truth claim cannot be supported by very strong reasons if it is unfalsifiable.

(7) An unfalsifiable truth claim cannot be a fact.

(8) In one sense, you can have very strong reasons to believe something if you have incomplete evidence. Therefore, very strong reasons fit within the context of the best available evidence.

The criticisms to this epistemology focus as follows. First, the notion of falsifiability, as previously discussed, can be applied to premise (2). This premise is not falsifiable. Therefore, it is not a fact. This is why I have been careful to label this as a "leap of faith", or similar.

Second, if one has incomplete evidence, then one can claim that one does not have very strong reasons. This criticism can be dismissed on the basis of a paradox of knowledge. One cannot know if one knows everything since, by definition, one does not know something that one does not know. This is the logical incoherency involved with the claim that God is omniscient, since God cannot actually know that he knows everything (along similar lines to the brain in a vat). For example, God cannot indubitably know there isn't another God (or Evil Daemon) sitting behind their reality.

Therefore, one can never really know indubitably that one knows everything about a particular object. In this way, it is safer to judge very strong reasons on the available evidence. What we know about quantum physics is at any moment incomplete. However, it shouldn't stop us from knowing certain pieces of knowledge about quantum mechanics (under the implicit understanding that this could change). We need to adjust our reliance and predictions based on the confidence that we have in our knowledge.

Thus, we cannot *know indubitably* that a truth claim or a fact is true, in a Cartesian sense. So everything defers to a *probability*. And when making some kind of probability analysis, we consider how coherent our analysis is, how coherent our conclusion is, how reliable our metrics have been, and consider the very best evidence and very best reasoning to hand. As ever, we need to be aware of cognitive biases and heuristics that may present obstacles to this project, and mitigate where possible. And finally, if claims are unfalsifiable, we need to thoroughly consider why this might be and what the ramifications are.

Indeed, this all looks rather like the prelude to discussing Bayes' Theorem and a Bayesian probability analysis. I have done this in my books investigating the Nativity and Resurrection claims, and tackle it in the chapter "Extraordinary Claims Require Extraordinary Evidence, and Bayes' Theorem" later in this book.

The Evolutionary Argument Against Naturalism

Famed Christian philosopher Alvin Plantinga has created the Evolutionary Argument Against Naturalism (EAAN) to refute the worldview position of naturalism. Naturalism, as we have discussed, is a difficult concept to define, but it broadly entails that there is no supernatural entity to explain the universe itself, or phenomena within the universe.

I will not spend too much time on Plantinga's argument – it is not for the scope of this book. But, in summary, it tries to show that evolution by natural selection does not select for truth. There are many aspects to the argument, and I am being incredibly simplistic here because I am using it to bring up a point I see as pertinent for this chapter: I posit that evolution *does* select for truth over time in a way that is pragmatic and shows us the relationship between pragmatism and reliability.

Imagine a frog X. It has a "belief" that a fly is at position A. If this belief is true, the frog will successfully catch the fly and eat it and thus survive. Now imagine frog Y; it believes incorrectly that the fly is at B. Frog A catches the fly, frog B goes hungry.

If this situation persists over time and circumstance, frog B will die before reproducing and frog A will survive and reproduce.

Therefore, evolution does have a pragmatic place for truth. If we consistently held false beliefs, our beliefs would not correspond to objective reality. They simply would not offer much use to us at all. Thus, true beliefs are more likely to be reliable in the long run. And reliable beliefs are more useful. Thus, we have a pragmatic and reliable dynamic to our epistemology that has its basis in naturalism.

Or, we don't need God to determine truth and knowledge.

We then recognise that naturalism coheres with the scientific method. Science (with its self-correction) and naturalism are together more likely to represent reality over time, and become (as science so obviously does in our daily lives and global existences) useful to us in multiple ways. In sum, we can see the importance of science and the scientific method to our epistemological outlook.

Religion

We could build a case that religion insulates a false belief (or many). Most religious beliefs are mutually exclusive and so any religious adherent generally believes that all other religions (qua religious claims) are false. (Let us consider that everyone is dogmatic, for the sake of argument.)

The evolutionary psychologist wonders why such false beliefs pervade. Or ponders what the evolutionary benefit is of religion or believing these things.

To approach this, let us assume that all religious claims are false. The evolutionary psychologist might claim something like "religion gives a social benefit and psychological security to those who believe it". What I am uncovering here is that we might be able to posit some good reason to believe something that is false.

But here, I think there is an equivocation over the term "reason" such that it is better seen as a *consequence of* as opposed to a *rational argument towards* a belief. This isn't about believing a religious claim being based on good *reasons* (such as a holy text, or a particular theistic argument), but the beneficial consequences that might come about from believing it over time.

Additionally, religious networks and frameworks of belief have arguably been good at doing this in times and places of ignorance. But once we have a more accurate understanding of the universe around us, and once we are free to start forming positive social networks around these ideals (such that atheists and naturalists can coalesce around their beliefs and form social networks without persecution), then the power of religion in begetting positive consequences to its adherents starts to recede.

As our knowledge of the universe grows, the consequences of holding false beliefs diminishes – the fear of going to hell evaporates if one realises there is no hell. In this way, we can see the very fractious relationship between science and religion.

I claim that we are in that position now. I neither think that there are good reasons for believing in God (religion) nor good consequences from believing in such (or, at the very least, not any more advantageous than atheism in any given context).

Thus, if we are interpreting "good reasons" to believe to be the same as "consequences of" believing, then there might be scenarios where this might hold. But I would posit that this would only really hold in the short term, especially in these days as our knowledge base has grown exponentially.

Before I offer a few final words on this subject, it is worth noting that I really have only sketched out a bare bones framework of my position. I am merely whetting the appetite of the reader to go and think about these matters further.

In conclusion, and to return to the original question (and with particular reference to religious beliefs), I argue that one can only have very strong reasons to believe a falsehood if that claim is a falsifiable claim and the believer has made sincere effort to use the best information and evidence available at the time of believing. Moreover, in using predominantly faith without evidence in believing a claim (whether it is true or not) does not qualify as having very strong reasons.

However, I have also adopted a "position of faith" in accepting that the external world exists. That said, I have also presented reasons to defend this position so that it is not merely blind faith, but a rationally justified, if unfalsifiable position to take.

Hume and Having No Reason for Forming Beliefs about the Future on the Basis of the Past (The Problem of Induction)

Scottish Enlightenment philosopher David Hume has influenced many modern intellectuals with his erudite writings and treatises. One of his most influential works was the 1748 work *An Enquiry Concerning Human Understanding*,[1] a reworking of his early piece, *A Treatise of Human Nature*. There is much to ruminate on in *An Enquiry*, most notably his philosophy concerning epistemological matters, theorising about knowledge and fact.

In this essay, I will explain the terms of the title above. I will then investigate what is entailed in forming beliefs about the future based on the past. The previous essay on minds, beliefs and knowledge should serve to provide some introduction or foundation to this piece.

After the initial discussion, I will argue that we can *reasonably* form beliefs using probability and inductive reasoning. I will also investigate the idea that under metaphysical naturalism, and with perfect knowledge of any given system, we could reasonably "know" future events based on past experiences. Though on true Pyrrhonian skepticism (as already mentioned), we must doubt almost everything – at least to some degree.

I will also show that this form inductive reasoning is not what Hume had in mind and that he was demanding deductive reasoning to validate the movement from past uniformities to future events. This "Problem of Induction", and the logic not being as decisive as deductive reasoning, presented a headache for Hume. I will continue by looking at some attempts to produce deductive arguments using past uniformities before looking briefly at the work of Colin Howson who declared that "there are nevertheless demonstrably sound deductive inferences".[2]

Finally, I will question the meaningfulness of raising the problem of induction itself. I will do this whilst also explaining the terms and positions to allow universal understanding of the debate and giving references for further reading when the subject matter becomes too complex for the scope of this essay. Remember, my writing here is not aimed at being the final word, but the opening salvo.

Let us first look at how Hume sets out ideas in *An Enquiry Concerning Human Understanding* as these form some of the fundamental structure to his

---

[1] I will call his work *An Enquiry* from hereon in.
[2] Howson (2000) p.2.

arguments. Hume differentiates two forms of thought: *impressions* and *ideas*. Impressions are sensations or experiences of the senses. Ideas are memories or imaginings. Hume claims that impressions form the basis for ideas. I would agree with Hume here since every science fiction or fantasy writer would admit that it is impossible to make up a new creature that is not in some way based on entities that have already been experienced in one way or another. In other words, our imagination cannot create ex nihilo, we are always pulling on ideas or experiences that already exist.

Hume exemplifies the way we do this and categorises them into *compounding, transposing, augmenting* and *diminishing*. He then seemingly pokes a hole in his own argument by declaring that one *can hypothetically* imagine a missing colour in a spectrum of blue.

I actually think that this example of the spectrum of blue fits into the augmenting/diminishing category. As another example, instead of claiming that a giant is the idea of a human but that human made bigger, we should see this as an increase or decrease in any given characteristic. In the case of blue, it is simply a diminishing or augmenting of the hue of an already existing hue of blue.

This leads on to Hume's analysis of *relations of ideas* and *matters of fact*. Relations of ideas can be demonstrated and would include geometric, semantic and logical propositions. On the other hand, matters of fact are experiential in nature. This very point here could lead us down several rabbit-holes (language, semantics, logic, conceptualism vs. realism, and so on) but this would only serve to throw us off course.

Hume takes the ideas of matters of fact and inquires as follows:[1]

> When it is asked, *What is the nature of all our reasonings concerning matter of fact?* the proper answer seems to be, that they are founded on the relation of cause and effect. When again it is asked, *What is the foundation of all our reasonings and conclusions concerning that relation?* it may be replied in one word, Experience. But if we still carry on our sifting humour, and ask, *What is the foundation of all conclusions from experience?* this implies a new question, which may be of more difficult solution and explication....
>
> I say then, that, even after we have experience of the operations of cause and effect, our conclusions from that experience are not founded on reasoning, or any process of the understanding.

---

[1] Hume (2006), p.28.

The Problem with Induction

Herein lies the crucial exposition of Hume's argument. Hume is claiming that there is no *reasoning* that can lead from experience to matter of fact. A matter of fact being, for example, that a pebble landing in a lake (A) always causes a splash (B), and this is a cause and effect relationship that is derived and understood through experience. There is no *a priori* reasoning that could lead us, without that experience, to conclude that A would necessitate B. In other words, there is nothing that logically necessitates the causal effect of A to B, such as the definition of the terms, or some kind of abstract mathematical derivation. We find that B results from A; that a splash is caused by a pebble landing in the lake, through experience.

If we threw a pebble into the lake again and again, and it splashed every time, we would start to experience a repeated phenomenon. B consistently results from A. If, after a thousand pebbles, we were to throw another pebble into the lake, it would be imprudent to bet against there being another splash. This wager that there would be a splash on throwing the pebble becomes a *belief* that there would be a splash. Hume sees belief as related to fiction but gives it a certain feeling of confidence that fiction does not imbue. Hume sums up the belief that a future effect will arise from a cause to be provable only from experience as follows:[1]

> ...having found, in many instances, that any two kinds of objects – flame and heat, snow and cold – have always been conjoined together; if flame or snow be presented anew to the senses, the mind is carried by custom to expect heat or cold, and to believe that such a quality does exist, and will discover itself upon a nearer approach. This belief is the necessary result of placing the mind in such circumstances....
>
> But still our curiosity will be pardonable, perhaps commendable, if it carry us on to still farther researches, and make us examine more accurately the nature of this belief, and of the customary conjunction, whence it is derived. By this means we may meet with some explications and analogies that will give satisfaction; at least to such as love the abstract sciences, and can be entertained with speculations, which, however accurate, may still retain a degree of doubt and uncertainty.

---

[1] Hume (2006), p. 38.

Hume claims in this very important quote that what allows the philosopher to arrive at B from A is nothing more than experience and *custom*. It is only that this effect has taken place with such habit that one can guess, probabilistically, that it will happen again. There is no *reason* outside of the reliance on custom that can verify that B will always occur after A. Moreover, this belief in custom, Hume declares, is open to doubt and skepticism even though it may appear to be accurate. This doubt is akin to being certain that the sun will continue to rise tomorrow. The certainty that arises is a different idea of certainty, one that resorts to the plea of uniformity and not of logical verification.

Let us look, then, at how *reason* is defined and then examine what Hume says about it. In philosophical terms (and much ink has been spilt on the topic of "reason"), reason is a way by which one can connect one idea to another related idea, whether by cause and effect, or by asserting the truth values of a proposition, or myriad other relations.

Reason is answerable to the constraints of logic, the axiomatic system of arbitration. Logic (and there are many different logics and an awful lot that could be said of logic and logical systems) is often split up into two divisions: *inductive reasoning* and *deductive reasoning*. My usual caveat applies: I will be dealing with ideas here in a cursory and simplistic manner. Whole books have been written on inductive and deductive logics and reasoning alone.

Inductive reasoning is a form of argument or logic that allows for the possibility that the conclusion is false, even though the premises are true. For example, we could state:

(1) All the penguins we have seen have beaks.
(2) All penguins have beaks.

We can conclude from this simple argument that all penguins have beaks but the conclusion does not *necessarily* follow from the premise. This is inductive reasoning. Deductive reasoning would be more concrete:

(1) All authors write.
(2) Jim is an author.
(3) Therefore, Jim writes.

Now the premises may or may not be true, but the conclusion necessarily follows from the premises.

I mention this because Hume declares that there is no *reasoning* that can lead us to make conclusions about the future; that we can only rely on custom. However, it also appears that the use of custom to connect one idea to another is a form of reasoning. Indeed, custom appears to be a form of inductive reasoning. This would be set out as follows, using our pebble example:

(1) All pebbles that we have observed thrown into a lake cause splashes.
(2) I will throw a pebble at the lake.
(3) Therefore, it will cause a splash.

Inductively, we can "reason" that there will be a splash, but the conclusion does not *necessarily* follow from the premises. The problem with trying to look for an argument that concludes a Uniformity of Nature (UN) is that it must be inductive and have Uniformity of Nature as a premise. This creates an unwanted circularity. Because of this, the above argument would have to have a hidden *a priori* premise that upholds UN (where *a priori* denotes reasoning or knowledge that precedes observation or experience):

(1) All pebbles that we have observed thrown into a lake cause splashes.
(2) All consistently observed phenomena will repeat in accordance with the laws of nature (UN).
(3) I will throw a pebble at the lake
(4) Therefore, it will cause a splash.

Premise (2) must be there in order for the conclusion to necessarily follow. But premise (2) might be what we are trying to conclude, so for it to be there makes the entire argument circular and logically fallacious.

From an epistemological perspective, the only true knowledge that we can hold indubitably is the knowledge that "I exist", as previously discussed. When dropping the pebble in the lake, I might think that I know that if I drop the pebble, it will fall downwards. I may think that I have the "Law"[1] of Gravity to define this circumstance.

Yet even physical laws are prone to Cartesian doubt. René Descartes, the previously mentioned seventeenth-century French philosopher, declared that the only statement that does not lay victim to doubt is "cogito ergo sum": I think, therefore I am. We cannot doubt our own existences, in

---

[1] Thompson (2006), p. 49, states "In common parlance, 'law' is taken to be something which is imposed, a rule that is to be obeyed. But it would be wrong to assume that a scientific law can dictate how things behave. The law simply describes that behaviour, it does not control it (as Hume argued)."

whatever form that may take. The Law of Gravity *may* only be a descriptive law that *may* not work the next time you drop a pebble. There is always an element of doubt even if it is infinitesimal. It could be that we are living in a *Matrix*-style universe where our minds are plugged into a machine and everything else is an illusion. But still "we" exist in some form in order to be able to experience the illusion. Because we are unable to prove absolutely that this either is, or is not, the case, we are resigned to being at least a little skeptical about almost everything in the known cosmos.

Therefore, there can only actually be one true, indubitable piece of knowledge – "I" am. And only the individual experiencing this can have this knowledge; it cannot be transposed onto any other entity. So real knowledge is limited to one fact: that you, as the reader, exist. This leads us to Pyrrhonism.

I have mentioned Pyrrhonism already, but just a few more thoughts…

Greek philosopher Sextus Empiricus first recorded the use of Pyrrhonian skepticism (named after Pyrrho of Elis) in the late second century CE. This position dictates that we cannot know anything, in a Cartesian manner, and thus we must logically adhere to strict agnosticism. This is an approach that even goes as far as stating that one must be skeptical over one's own skepticism to the point that one must remain in perpetual enquiry, making no dogmatic statements about anything. This type of logical skeptic would never achieve anything pragmatic in life and so would rely on custom to navigate through everyday existence.

Within a naturalistic framework, we take knowledge to be an inductive principle based on probability and overwhelming scientific evidence. That was the point of the previous essay. This metaphysical naturalism entails that the only things that exist are natural phenomena, forces, causes and effects. Supernatural entities or causes are ruled out *a priori*. A problem here could be that to reach a conclusion of metaphysical naturalism (that becomes *a priori*) we use an *a posteriori* (or evidentially based) process.

A scientific fact, in the face of Cartesian doubt, can be defined as a claim backed up by overwhelming evidence. This seems rather more subjective and arbitrary than the simple idea of a brute "scientific fact". Probability (assuming there is no such thing as true randomness[1] in the universe) becomes the defining principle that allows one to induce a conclusion from previous experiences. Probability is fundamental to

---

[1] I am intuitively a follower of the narrow frequency interpretation of probability, which asserts that no event can be said to have probability, since there is only one universal outcome (when I am not being entirely Pyrrhonian!).

inductive reasoning. As philosopher Dugald Murdoch[1] said, "not only is this discussion [of probability] essential for a proper understanding of Hume's philosophy of induction, but it is also of great interest in its own right". If I have thrown that pebble a thousand times and received a splash each time, then throwing it again will probably cause a splash. In my opinion, naturalism leads to causal determinism,[2] and these deterministic qualities can lead us to have a much smaller degree of doubt than without determinism. Laplace's Demon, a theoretical entity that knows every single variable in the cosmos, under a deterministic framework, would have the best chance of knowing everything that might come to pass. Does Laplace's Demon have good reason, then, to believe claims about the future? More on that and this second demon later.

Science inextricably linked to inductive reasoning since it is based on observation (experience). Philosopher Mel Thompson connects inductive reasoning to the scientific method as follows:[3]

> It is clear that this process of induction, by which a theory is arrived at by the analysis and testing out of observed data, can yield at most only a high degree of probability. There is always the chance that an additional piece of information will show the original hypothesis is wrong, or that it applies only within a limited field.

Here, we begin to cast doubt on Hume's claim that there is no reasoning that can lead you to conclusions about future events based on past experiences. Inductive reasoning, using probability (especially on a naturalistic foundation that leaves everything to the deterministic machinations of nature), seems to have got us, quite literally, from A to B. However, the induction argument is not so easy. Specifically, Hume appears to believe that induction is not a form of reasoning: that deduction is the benchmark for reasoning. Hume is effectively claiming that there is no deductive reason to get a thinker from A to B.

Hume certainly recognises that inductive reason is vital for humans to function. If we did not induce conclusions from habitual experiences, then we would be very different entities:[4]

---

[1] Murdoch (2002), p.186.
[2] As I have set out in detail in my book *Free Will? An investigation into whether we have free will or whether I was always going to write this book*, Pearce (2010).
[3] Thompson (2006), p.48.
[4] Hume (2006), p. 36.

> Without the influence of custom, we should be entirely
> ignorant of every matter of fact beyond what is
> immediately present to the memory and senses. We
> should never know how to adjust means to ends, or to
> employ our natural powers in the production of any
> effect. There would be an end at once of all action, as well
> as of the chief part of speculation.

But it still remains to be seen whether *deduction* can get us from A to B. Let us reset the pebble argument to weigh it up in a deductive manner:

(1) All pebbles that we have observed thrown at a lake cause splashes.
(2) I will throw a pebble at the lake.
(3) Therefore, it will cause a splash.

This argument is clearly inductive in its opening premise, and one cannot squeeze a deduction out of it. Apples are apples, they are not oranges. But does this mean that there is no form of deductive reasoning that can be employed in defence of the aforementioned argument?

Seeking to Solve the Problem

There have been a number of philosophers and mathematicians who have argued that the Problem of Induction can be solved by employing deduction. Hume did not label propositions inductive or deductive as these are more modern terms. But he argued that one could not defend inductive reasoning by further inductive reasoning, as this would entail using a circular argument, a logical fallacy. In this way, Hume actually showed that if we relied on the probabilistic qualities of induction, such that we could *reliably* infer that a pebble would cause a splash, then there would be no way to deduce that this was any more "reliable" than any other conclusion. As philosopher John Vickers states in the *Stanford Encyclopaedia of Philosophy*:[1]

> Now as concerns inductive inference, it is hardly
> surprising to be told that the epistemological problem is
> insoluble; that there can be no formula or recipe,
> however complex, for ruling out unreliable inductions.

---

[1] Vickers (2009). This has now been replaced by Henderson (2018). However, it is archived as can be seen in the bibliography.

But Hume's arguments, if they are correct, have apparently a much more radical consequence than this: They seem to show that the metaphysical problem for induction is insoluble; that there is no objective difference between reliable and unreliable inductions.

Therefore, it seems necessary to somehow defend inductive reasoning by employing deductive reasoning. As philosopher and logician Bertrand Russell complained:[1]

It is therefore important to discover whether there is any answer to Hume within a framework of philosophy that is wholly or mainly empirical. If not, there is no intellectual difference between sanity and insanity. The lunatic who believes he is a poached egg is to be condemned solely on the ground that he is in a minority, or rather – since we must not assume democracy – on the ground that the government does not agree with him. This is a desperate point of view, and it must be hoped that there is some way of escaping from it.

What Russell is begrudgingly accepting is that inductively derived conclusions have no more epistemological veracity than any other such knowledge. We must, then, find a way, epistemologically speaking, to use experience to derive knowledge *reasonably* otherwise the foundations of science fall away, and science itself becomes arbitrary.

Probability as Based in Natural Law

Some philosophers have argued that there is a logic to inductive reasoning that gives it a greater credence than Hume gives it credit for. The Williams-Stove thesis put forward by philosophers D.C. Williams and D.C. Stove in 1947 (and then corrected some 40 years later) set out to prove that you could get necessary truths from inductive reasoning. This would mean that there were demonstrable (deductive) qualities to inductive logic. The two philosophers proposed that relative frequencies of traits in a population are matched in relative frequencies in large samples of that population. In synopsis, they concluded. As philosopher John Vickers says of their work:[2]

---

[1] Russell (1946;1961), p. 646.
[2] Vickers (2009).

> Williams and Stove, for their part, maintain that, though there may be no demonstrative proof of the principle of the uniformity of nature, there are good demonstrative or deductive proofs that certain inductive methods yield their conclusions with high probability.

However, after several criticisms, it seems that the theory (a complex exposition of modal logic too complex for the scope of this essay) only holds probabilistically and in certain limited instances. As philosopher John Vickers continues:[1]

> It began life as the strong and simple modal assertion that it is a necessary truth that inductions of a quite common sort yield their conclusions with high probability. That thesis is seen to be false. What remains are, at best, certain specific instances of it.

Philosopher D.M. Armstrong took a different tack. Rather than trying to prove that an inductive argument itself was intrinsically rational, in the Humean sense, he looked to prove that the *use* of an inductive argument was rational and necessary. He considers the application of the argument, rather than the actual argument itself. As Armstrong himself declares:[2]

> ...ordinary inference from the observed to the unobserved, is, although *invalid*, nevertheless a rational form of inference. I add that not merely is it the case that induction is rational, but it is a necessary truth that it is so.

Armstrong claims that observed uniformities are best explained by first hypothesising strong laws of nature that are by definition objectively necessary. He then makes conclusions about the unobserved (which in our case is the future predicted event of the pebble making a splash). This would be a testable, verifiable law. One immediate problem: his existence of a "strong law" goes against the descriptive quality of laws that was mentioned earlier. Like the Williams-Stove thesis, Armstrong depends on laws of probability. And this is where he, too, is criticised.

Part of the attractiveness of these theories is that they employ laws of probability, frequency and other mathematical laws. Such laws are themselves

---

[1] Vickers (2009).
[2] Armstrong (1983), p. 52.

mathematical consequences, so we can see them as necessary truths. The idea is that the deductive capacity of the maths involved gives the inductive arguments a deductive foundation and thus a reasonable and reliable dimension. In this way, as Vickers states:[1]

> Of course the application of these laws in any given empirical situation will require contingent assumptions, but the inductive part of the reasoning certainly depends upon the deductively established laws.

The problem for Hume is that he did not have a sophisticated grasp of probabilistic laws and their arguably deductive qualities. Therefore, he might have been a little premature in his conclusion that there was no "reason" to believe that past uniformities could inform us of future events. One can hardly blame him, of course, because such laws depend upon modern logic and the "axiomatisation of probability".[2] Neither of which even existed in the intellectual landscape of Hume's time.

So where does this leave us now? Well, it seems that we can make specific cases for the deductive justification of the inductive method. However, metaphysically speaking, there is still the seemingly insoluble problem: Why should we trust induction? It is here that I want to concentrate the rest of the essay. I hope to answer that question with the response "because it is reasonable". And I think it should give Hume pause to think (if he were currently in a place where thinking is possible; which he is not).

Colin Howson, the late British philosopher and Professor of Philosophy at the University of Toronto, dealt with this very idea in his book *Hume's Problem: Induction and the Justification of Belief.* He claims that:[3]

> The resolution of the paradox is that inductive inference arises as a necessary feature of consistent reasoning, *given* the sorts of initial plausibility assumptions scientists habitually make.

Howson insists that Hume's argument does not say that we are "misguided" in any way in relying on the scientific method of induction. The

---

[1] Vickers (2009).

[2] For the detailed criticisms of his argument, particularly how it falls victim to the vagaries of the laws of probability, see Vickers (2009). The discussion gets fairly heavy in invoking Bayes' Theorem, a probability theory previously referenced in passing and later discussed in more depth.

[3] Howson (2000), p. 2.

inductive method is not wrong simply because it is not deductive. Howson claims that there is a sound logic to be employed in inductive inferences. He combines the work of Hume and F.P. Ramsey. From Hume, he takes the notion that "inductive conclusions may be soundly inferred from inductive premises".[1] Ramsey's influence for Howson is that since evidence-based reasoning is dependent upon probability (as we saw earlier) then it is "nothing but the application of logical principles of consistency".[2] Essentially, Howson's argument is that by using Bayesian probability theory, induction is reliable. Moreover, it appears that the basic axioms of probability (something that Hume would not have known) produce this reliability. Induction, based upon valid assumptions (likely prior probabilities) results in real knowledge. Thus, Howson claims, this probability model of induction has the same qualities as deductive reasoning. Howson gives more credence to his argument by highlighting the probabilistic arguments' deductive characteristics. As philosopher Peter Lipton puts it:[3]

> Howson makes a great deal of the analogy between deductive and probabilistic argument. The principles of deductive logic place constraints on proper deductive reasoning even though they do not specify the premises. Similarly, the principles of probability place constraints on proper inductive reasoning, even though they do not specify the prior probabilities...

I will now move away from the often-confusing world of modern logic and into the often-confusing world of intuition. It seems to me that inductive reasoning yields results that are pragmatically very useful. It is in this way that the reasoning appears sound. Though it may (or may not) have the necessary conviction of deductive logic, there is soundness in achieving a goal. And the more knowledge we have of all the input variables, the more accurate and predictive the probabilistic calculations for the inductive argument will be.

The aforementioned theoretical Laplace's Demon, with its perfect knowledge of all the variables in the cosmos, all its forces and natural laws, could probabilistically calculate all future events, and could have complete certitude over the likelihood of those future events (quantum indeterminacy notwithstanding). Thus, it appears that Laplace's Demon could circumvent Hume's argument, given the adherence of everything to natural laws.

---

[1] Merrill (2003), p. 159.
[2] Howson (2000), p. 4.
[3] Lipton (2002), p. 579.

So What? It's Useful!

With these ideas in mind, could Hume argue that Laplace's Demon is not inducing knowledge from experience, and is not using only past experiences to inform future predictions? If this objection applies to the Demon, then it would surely apply to humanity. With each passing year, our collective intellect and knowledge base grows. Humanity, together with human-designed computing systems (think Big Data), is approaching ever closer to the zenith of Laplace's Demon. Though we may never reach ultimate knowledge, we seem to be getting forever closer. And thus our calculations are becoming ever more accurate. Our abilities for calculating future effects from their causes mean that we are more consistently arriving at the predicted outcome, realising some kind of truth. Are we not becoming more sound in our predictions? In this way, I would argue that, theoretically speaking, Laplace's Demon would have a deductive reason to form beliefs about the future based on past uniformities (given the assumption of determinism). It is only humanity's imperfect knowledge of our system that requires us, from Hume's perspective, to rely on custom.

Statements of knowledge, the common parlance (non-Cartesian) knowledge, should be understood in the light of experience and probability. They are empirically meaningful. On a daily basis, they have meaning to all of us, even to Hume, by his own admission. Induction is very much an integral part of human nature. It does not matter whether our conclusions that turn out to be reliable and correct are deductively derived. What matters is that we have sound mechanisms to predict future events using data and observations garnered from past events. This is the scientific method, and it is inductive. And it works. This is not too far from Hume's own position of accepting the usefulness of everyday pragmatism, though he did concern himself greatly (too greatly?) with the notion of the Problem of Induction.

Therefore, we have ended up in a position that is known as *reliabilism*. This position contends with Hume's claim that inductive reasoning cannot justify inductive reasoning – induction cannot be circular. Reliabilism, with its claims of reliable predictions of future events, and *scientific realism* with its claims of correlating predictions with truth, may not be able to escape the whirlpool of inductive circular reasoning. But I do not think that matters at all. When it comes down to it, pragmatism and reliability are far more useful (a truism if ever there was one), and therefore meaningful, to a person who acts in the real world. Generally, none of us care whether something can be justified deductively or not. Being able to accurately predict, using gathered data from experience and observation, whether or not a certain experiment will result in disaster and death is much more relevant and important than trying to justify the outcome deductively.

Inductive reasoning (as well as the scientific method that uses it) also has self-correcting methods. When the results become unreliable, these observations and calculations get taken into consideration for future calculations. The scientific inductive method is always improving. In this way, it is more likely to bring us closer to the truth than not. Even Hume himself saw the scientific approach as being preferable to one of superstition.

To conclude, it seems pertinent to question the question. Hume's argument against induction is potentially devastating. Yet, whilst it can theoretically undermine the entire rubric of scientific academia, it can also be (and *is* by so many scientists) ignored. The question that really remains is: does Hume's problem matter?

> "We are all convinced by inductive arguments", says Ramsey, "and our conviction is reasonable because the world is so constituted that inductive arguments lead on the whole to true opinions. We are not, therefore, able to help trusting induction, nor, if we could help it do we see any reason why we should" (Ramsey 1931, 197). We can, however, trust selectively and reflectively; we can winnow out the ephemera of experience to find what is fundamental and enduring.[1]

Regarding my own epistemological outlook, I see knowledge as a mixture of that which is pragmatic, coherent, and reliable – all using our sense data and reasoning (and mitigating cognitive biases and problematic heuristics). I use probability to assess the reliability of those claims and beliefs. This is an inductive approach. Moreover, I think I am being reasonable in following this approach.

When claims are unfalsifiable and untestable, we are right to be suspicious of them.

Quite often, these claims involve God; a subject that is drawing ever closer.

---

[1] Vickers (2009).

Extraordinary Claims Require Extraordinary Evidence, and Bayes' Theorem

Since probability has been mentioned already in the previous essay, and will come into play in a proceeding section, let us talk about it here.

Extraordinary Claims Require Extraordinary Evidence

The maxim "extraordinary claims require extraordinary evidence" is often rejected by theists trying to justify incredible claims with very poor evidence to back them up.

This maxim was popularised by Carl Sagan, the popular scientist who died in 1996.[1] But the idea already existed in some form or other since the philosophising of David Hume, the aforementioned Scottish Enlightenment philosopher. This is a self-evidently true maxim, even though (as mentioned) many theists deny its power. This is because they misunderstand its best application.

This statement is most aptly applied to the need for secondary or tertiary evidence. Let me explain what I mean by way of five claims and how most people would assess them (as I used in my Nativity book):

Claim 1: I have a dog.
Nothing more than verbal testimony needed.

Claim 2: I have a dog which is in the bath.
As above, with one eyebrow raised.

Claim 3: I have a dog in the bath wearing a dress.
I would probably need a photo of this to believe you.

Claim 4: I have a dress-wearing dog in the bath with a skunk wearing a SCUBA outfit.
I would need some video evidence at the least.

---

[1] "Encyclopaedia Galactica". Carl Sagan (writer/host). *Cosmos*. PBS. December 14, 1980. No. 12. 01:24 minutes in.

Claim 5: I have the above in the bath, but the bathwater is boiling and the animals are happy.

I would need video and independent attestation that the video was not doctored agreeing that this is what appeared to be happening.

Claim 6: All of the above, but the dog has a fire-breathing dragon on its shoulder and the skunk is dancing with a live unicorn.

Well, I'll be damned. I'll need video, plus video of the video, plus independent attestation from multiple recognisably reliable sources, and assessment and evaluation by technological experts and biological experts, plus a psychological evaluation of the claimant, and so on.

Bayes' Theorem

The exercise above shows that when evaluating evidence that is not first-hand, we have different criteria for assessing its veracity depending on the type of claim. It is actually all about probability: claims that are highly improbable require a great deal of evidence, even if they are physically (naturalistically) possible. The claim that I climbed Mount Everest without using my right arm, and with only one eye, is something that is physically possible but very unlikely. As a result, people would naturally demand more evidence than me merely telling them in a casual conversation. The more improbable my claim, the more incredible. And the more incredible, the higher the demands for evidence. This is intuitive. If we then make a claim that is unlikely as can possibly be (e.g., that a man-God dies and is resurrected, or performs any of his miracles), then these claims defy the laws of nature as we know them. This set of Christian religious claims is most improbable. As a result, they should demand the highest level of evidence, especially when not witnessed first-hand.

The standard of evidence must meet the level of improbability in the claim. This can be mathematically set out and assessed using Bayes' Theorem. Essentially, this theorem involves the idea that if one has to make a decision about believing a hypothesis, then it should be the one most probable. This probability is made up from two different calculations: the *prior probability* and the *likelihood ratio*.

It can be written as follows:[1]

$$P(A \mid B) = \frac{P(B \mid A)P(A)}{P(B)}$$

Don't worry about the notations in the above equation as I will try to explain it in simple terms: the odds that a claim is true equals the prior odds it is true times the likelihood ratio. For the record, the above notations mean the following:

- $P(A \mid B)$ – the probability of event A occurring, given event B has occurred
- $P(B \mid A)$ – the probability of event B occurring, given event A has occurred
- $P(A)$ – the probability of event A
- $P(B)$ – the probability of event B

To arrive at a decision regarding rival hypotheses, we can compare the relative likelihood of two theories for explaining an event after analysing *background knowledge* and *evidence*. We will add to our background knowledge the *prior probability*. The prior probability is the odds on any such claim being true before entertaining any evidence particular to the claim.

The likelihood ratio is a ratio of two probabilities: first, how likely the claim is true based on all the evidence we do and do not have? Second, how likely the claim is false given all this same evidence? And if it is false, then something else happened, but not the original claim. The *posterior probability* is the final probability of the claim being true given all of the above.

It might be interesting to choose an example of this. Let us take the example of the claims that Jesus resurrected into heaven (a claim to which we will return later).

What is the prior probability of a man, even a god-figure, being resurrected after dying?[2] No Christian, and certainly no skeptic, believes any

---

[1] Michael Martin, in his chapter "The Resurrection as Initially Improbable" in *The Empty Tomb: Jesus Beyond the Grave* (Price & Lowder 2005) states it slightly differently and in a more complex form specifically for the Resurrection.

[2] Not to forget all manner of other ancillary claims, such as a host of dead saints rising and parading around a city, an earthquake, the sun disappearing for three hours, the Temple Veil being torn…

previous similar examples of resurrection. This makes the probability of such a new claim being true, before evidence is evaluated, to be exceptionally small indeed.

We do this kind of reasoning all of the time. When you are deciding whether to cross the road, given what you know about traffic, and the present observations at hand. This helps you conclude "it will be safe to cross the road now, given the data".

Using another example, if there is rustling in a bush in my local neighbourhood, I will conclude it is the wind as opposed to being a tiger. I take into account that tigers do not live in my country (background knowledge), it is windy, and I do not see anything orange, black and white. Alternatively, if I had heard in the news of a locally escaped circus tiger and I saw something orange, black and white, then my conclusions would adapt to this new data and I might conclude that the hypothesis "this is a tiger" is the most probable explanation of the data.

To overcome the tiny prior probability of a god-figure being resurrected after dying (and we could do a further analysis of the claim of dead saints rising and parading around a city), one must have very high consequents. In other words, the evidence must be stunningly good. Think of the examples given above in claims 5 and 6. A divine death and resurrection supposedly witnessed or attested to by many is mind-boggling as a claim. And the evidence needs to be exceptionally good to overcome the low probability of this event, to make the truth of this claim the most probable interpretation of the data. Christians are happy to dismiss other similar religious claims from rival religions, and yet they lower their evidence threshold greatly to allow a supposedly rational acceptance and belief in these resurrection claims.

Not only do we not have video evidence of the resurrection claims, but we have no independent attestation. None of the New Testament accounts were written by eyewitnesses. And the first Gospel was not written until some forty years after Jesus' death.

One would expect multiple first-hand accounts if supposedly five hundred plus people at one time (according to 1 Corinthians 15) witnessed a risen god. And yet there is absolute silence. Where one would expect to have evidence and voice, we do not have it. This absence of evidence *is* evidence of absence. Sometimes Christians claim that this does not follow – that because you don't have evidence for something happening it does not mean it did not happen. But as you will see here, this is not always the case. Where we would absolutely expect there to be evidence, and there is none, then this *is* evidence for absence.

For example, if someone claimed that there was an earthquake in my town yesterday that reached 7.5 on the Richter Scale, but I did not feel it and there was no other information about it – no news reports, no evidence provided outside of this attestation whatsoever – then I would posit that this lack of evidence certainly *is* evidence of absence, or evidence that it did not happen.

Let us examine one of the resurrection claims, from Matthew 27:51-53:

> And behold, the veil of the temple was torn in two from top to bottom; and the earth shook and the rocks were split. The tombs were opened, and many bodies of the saints who had fallen asleep were raised; and coming out of the tombs after His resurrection they entered the holy city and appeared to many.

This is a truly miraculous and improbable claim. The passage claims that at the death of Jesus, the saints rose out of their tombs – a host of resurrected bodies – and paraded around Jerusalem. What evidence do we have to judge whether this claim is veracious or not? The answer is underwhelming: An anonymously written non-eyewitness account produced at least four decades after the event by a fervent follower and evangeliser that is unverifiable and some 2000 years old. It was not recounted in any other sources we have upon which Matthew might have been based, nor in any other Gospel.[1] It is strange that these publicly resurrected saints appeared to "many" in Jerusalem and yet we have no other accounts of this event, no corroboration from any other source. And this would have been the most amazing sight in any of the witnesses' lives. In this instance, we *should* apply the criteria that extraordinary claims require extraordinary evidence. This is an event that patently demands such treatment, yet it has only very poor evidence to support it. As a result, we should discard this claim as either false or highly dubious. At the very least, I would recommend agnosticism over its verisimilitude. But, realistically, given the lack of evidential foundation, even agnosticism is seriously called into question.

The use of Bayes's Theorem to assess miracle claims has been challenged by some, including Christian minister turned atheist John Loftus, who points out[2] that assigning a prior probability to a miracle claim is problematic if such a miracle has never taken place. There is no prior data.

---

[1] Luke 23 includes the darkness and temple's veil tearing happening at a different time, but no earthquake and parading saints.

[2] Loftus points out five issues with using Bayes's Theorem to assess the probability of miracle claims in Loftus (2020).

However, on the other hand, we *do* have data concerning times when people have made miracle claims that have turned out to be false, of people *thought* to be dead coming back to life, and so on. But even if you *were* a supernaturalist who believes in miracles, that there are some examples of them, then you would surely admit that they were incredibly rare, that the prior probability of a miracle claim being true would be very low indeed. Thus, you could still employ Bayes's Theorem and still be forced to admit that extraordinary claims require extraordinary evidence.

Background Knowledge

If you ask the Christian, "Why do you know that the resurrection accounts are true?", they will likely reply, "Because I have faith (in Jesus)." Faith, in any meaningful sense, is belief absent evidence (and oftentimes merely hope). The New Testament states clearly, "Now faith (πίστις) is the assurance of things hoped for, the conviction of things not seen. For by it, the people of old received their commendation" (Hebrews 11:1–2). This becomes apparent when we ask, "Why do you have faith in Jesus", and they likely reply "Because of the Gospels and New Testament." But that is not evidential because it defers to the faith position.

The faith in Christianity comes predominantly from the New Testament, and faith that the New Testament is true comes from faith in Christianity qua Jesus. Here we have circular reasoning.

Perhaps the Christian can draw on personal revelatory experiences. But this cannot apply universally. An Amazonian tribesman will never have a revelatory vision experience that will point to Christianity if he has never heard of Christianity. Religious experiences of Christians concerning Christianity come about precisely because they already have knowledge of the Bible, specifically of the New Testament. In other words, Christian religious experiences supervene on (depend upon) knowledge of the Bible. These experiences do not truly break the problem of circularity, but actually feed into that circle.

Even given critical historical analysis such as this book that points to the claims not having veracity, the Christian can still rely on mere faith. It is an epistemic circle that is not really sound, just relying on itself. Indeed, the process ends up looking like a presuppositional stance where the Christian might as well presuppose the truth of the New Testament to shore up faith in Jesus.

This is precisely why Christian apologists like William Lane Craig try so hard to get away from mere fideism (the doctrine that knowledge depends on faith or revelation) because they know this is not convincing to a third party. Craig sets this out in his book (and resultant website) *Reasonable Faith*[1] to establish an evidential and rational basis for his belief, intending it to be ammunition to convert third parties.

Craig is absolutely intent on establishing the historicity of the Easter story and the Resurrection. I can understand this motive. He (and others, such as Christian scholar Gary Habermas with his *Minimal Facts* approach)[2] does this because he has everything to lose by not doing so. The cost of losing one's faith in terms of invested time, social networks, brand and business, so on and forth, is high. Very high. Especially in Christian America.

Let us relate this back to Bayes' Theorem, and look at the Background Knowledge part of the formula. This is where the naturalist atheist will immediately diverge from the supernaturalist theist.

The naturalist will conclude (i.e., not presuppose), based on pragmatism and inductive observation, that there is no recourse to supernaturalism in the Easter story:

- We can't assess eyewitness accounts (there are none).
- We have never experienced a god becoming a man.
- We have never experienced any living organism dying and being resurrected.
- We have no evidence of a heaven.
- And so forth.

Therefore, in order for all of these Easter story claims to be true, we have to throw out everything we know about how the world works. Which is fine if the evidence warrants this decision (it doesn't, by the way).

The theist has different axioms, but they are all circular.

The theist already believes in a world (background knowledge) where resurrections and general supernaturalism are possible – and perhaps even expected. With this background knowledge, the probabilities of the resurrection claims are massively adjusted upwards. They already believe in a world where there is a god that has been in human form, Jesus.

---

[1] Craig (2008).
[2] Habermas (n.d. & 2009).

But these are the very claims we are trying to evaluate. The existence of God as Jesus and resurrections are what we are analysing in the formula. We cannot presuppose the truth of the resurrection by already having the Resurrection or resurrections in our background knowledge.

On the other hand, the theist will accuse the naturalist of already counting out the possibility of resurrection. Craig Blomberg, in *Resurrection: Faith or Fact?* wrangles with the late skeptic Carl Stecher over the Easter story and does exactly this:[1]

> How then do we adjudicate among the remaining options? At this point the issue of preunderstanding, presuppositions, or worldviews looms large. If one is an antisupernaturalist (or, more simply, just a naturalist), then one excludes the possibility of an actual bodily resurrection at the outset. No amount of dialogue, discussion, or debate can change that. Dead men don't rise. Everyone today knows this. Therefore, however, we explain the rise of Christian faith, a literal physical resurrection is excluded *a priori*. We can debate the relative merits of the alternatives, but the historic Christian belief simply can't be the correct one.... Hume also claims that no one has sufficient reason for believing in something that has no analogy in their personal experience or an experience of anyone they know. Already in the eighteenth century, however, it was pointed out that by this logic, no person living in the tropics should ever believe in the ice.
>
> Today, the presupposition of antisupernaturalism is often phrased a little differently. Nothing may be admitted as genuinely existing, or as having occurred, unless it can be demonstrated empirically or logically. But the truth of this presupposition is merely asserted; it is never demonstrated either empirically or logically! Indeed, by its very nature it cannot be true. So the argument is solipsistic, that is, it forms a viciously circular form of reasoning and therefore has no force. Only slightly different is the claim that unless something can be proven scientifically, there are no rational grounds for believing it. But again, this affirmation itself cannot be proven

---

[1] Stecher & Blomberg (2019), p.234-5.

scientifically. We are reminded that science is not omnipotent and cannot be the final arbiter of reality.

However, the theistic approach would also support a belief in unicorns. Such a claim would obviously be nonsense and may even be an attempt to prove a negative. *Proving* that unicorns do not exist in the universe would require us to look under every rock and inspect every atomic conglomeration in the universe. Even then, we would be victim to claims of making mistakes and missing things.

We should not be able to just *assert* every divine claim (read in any ancient text) or any idea as being true without recourse to other arguments and evidence. This is a question not of proof but of probability.

The naturalist has inductive reasoning, observations over time and geography, that resurrections do not happen. A Christian usually applies this same reasoning to every other situation…outside of Christianity. However, the naturalist can also apply a *methodological* naturalism to underpin such *metaphysical* naturalism. By this, I mean that scientists always assume naturalism when doing any observational work since to posit that a ghost or God could have done something does not help any scientific experiment; these statements are untestable. This methodology has worked very well for science. Look where it has got us.

As such, the naturalist can use inductive reasoning tools to conclude metaphysically, that, in all likelihood, supernaturalism is false. But, we would really hope that this metaphysical conclusion is not merely an assertion and it is at least based on inductive evidence and probability.

My favourite quote on this topic is as follows:[1]

> The cause of lightning was once thought to be God's wrath, but turned out to be the unintelligent outcome of mindless natural forces. We once thought an intelligent being must have arranged and maintained the amazingly ordered motions of the solar system, but now we know it's all the inevitable outcome of mindless natural forces. Disease was once thought to be the mischief of supernatural demons, but now we know that tiny, unintelligent organisms are the cause, which reproduce and infect us according to mindless natural forces. In case after case, without exception, the trend has been to find that purely natural causes underlie any phenomena. Not

[1] Carrier (2006).

once has the cause of anything turned out to really be God's wrath or intelligent meddling, or demonic mischief, or anything supernatural at all. The collective weight of these observations is enormous: supernaturalism has been tested at least a million times and has always lost; naturalism has been tested at least a million times and has always won. A horse that runs a million races and never loses is about to run yet another race with a horse that has lost every single one of the million races it has run. Which horse should we bet on? The answer is obvious.

Jeffrey Jay Lowder explains further:[1]

If there is a single theme unifying the history of science, it is that naturalistic explanations work. The history of science contains numerous examples of naturalistic explanations replacing supernatural ones and no examples of supernatural explanations replacing naturalistic ones. Indeed, naturalistic explanations have been so successful that even most scientific theists concede that supernatural explanations are, in general, implausible, even on the assumption that theism is true. Such explanatory success is antecedently more likely on naturalism–which entails that all supernaturalistic explanations are false–than it is on theism. Thus the history of science is some evidence for naturalism and against theism.

The theist simply does not have this luxury because it all looks very circular:

(1) I believe in a world where resurrection is possible.
(2) Because I believe in a world in which Jesus was resurrected.
(3) Because I have analysed the accounts of Jesus' resurrection and found them a plausible account of the data.
(4) Because (1) I believe in a world where resurrection is possible.

And so the circle goes on, in perpetuity.

Read this again because this is absolutely fundamental to highlighting the foundational issues to the Christian worldview.

---

[1] Lowder (2012).

The skeptic or naturalist does not dismiss the claims of resurrection in the Easter story out of hand. To the contrary, they assess the evidence of what we know about the physical world, and the standard of evidence of the Gospel accounts. Indeed, Stecher replies to Blomberg's arguments about presuppositions in this way:[1]

> I am certainly willing to consider the evidence for the resurrection, just as I call upon Craig to consider the evidence from natural explanations and the problems with the evidence for the resurrection as a fact of history. Both of us, certainly, have presuppositions, but the hope is for both of us to make the strongest possible cases for and against resurrection as history (given the limitations of the format and the voluminous arguments on both sides), then to clarify where and why we differ, and to discover, if possible, where we are in agreement. My position is not that Jesus' resurrection did not happen, but that the evidence is scant and deeply flawed, contradictory in almost every possible way, and therefore insufficient to establish Jesus' resurrection as a fact of history. Furthermore, I argue, there are many plausible natural explanations to explain why some of Jesus's disciples might have come to believe that Jesus had been raised from the dead.

And that is pretty much my approach and conclusion in this book.

This section on epistemology should present strong enough argument for a supernaturalist who believes in resurrection, for whatever reason, to assess the historical analysis of the Easter story claims and logically conclude: "Although I believe in resurrection being possible, I do not believe that the claims of the Easter story have historical veracity because they fail on grounds of probability irrespective of supernaturalist beliefs."

Hope springs eternal, though, of course, the supernaturalist would then be invalidated in any adherence to Christianity on account of having no evidential foundation to their belief.

---

[1] Stecher & Blomberg (2019), p. 155-6.

Why Would God Create Anything at All? And a Look at God's Experiential Knowledge.

This piece will continue our current direction of travel into the territory of epistemology. I want to look very briefly at why God would create anything at all. In so doing, I will bring into play an argument addressing God's experiential knowledge.

Non-God Objects and Creating

This is taken from a chapter in a previous anthology of mine,[1] drawing on work from Justin Schieber, in what he termed "The Problem of Non-God Objects". It is crafted as follows:

> ➤ P1: If the Christian God exists, then GodWorld is the unique best possible world.
> ➤ P2: If GodWorld is the unique best possible world, then the Christian God would maintain GodWorld.
> ➤ P3: GodWorld is false because the Universe (or any non-God object) exists.
> ➤ Conclusion: Therefore, the Christian God, as so defined, does not exist.

Let me explain. An omniscient being would be aware of the fact that himself existing alone for eternity as GodWorld is the unique best possible world that could ever exist, and because (a Christian god) God is essentially morally perfect, he would not have a motivating reason to intentionally alter the overall maximal purity (and quality) of the unique best possible world. Further, any alteration in overall purity by the introduction of a universe or any Non-God object would, by necessity, be a degradation of overall purity and, therefore, overall quality. Thus, (the perfect Christian) God would not logically introduce limited entities (i.e., humans) each with their own unimpressive set of degraded great-making properties, which is what the creation myth of Genesis records. While Adam and Eve clearly do have a few great-making properties (knowledge, power), they have them to an

---

[1] Pearce (2021).

unimpressive degree. So introducing such beings would result in a degradation of overall ontological purity and overall ontological quality. To suggest God is in the degrading business is to suggest he was not maximally great or perfect in the first place.

Problem of Evil

In addition to the incoherent Christian idea of the need for God to create anything, Christians (for example) also have to address why there is suffering in the world. Such theists have to admit that suffering is necessary for some (arguably unclear) reason. Without a reason, suffering, whether stubbing a toe or 230,000 tsunami deaths, is gratuitous.

The issue here is explaining (from a Christian perspective) all of the suffering on Earth given God's supposed omni-characteristics. Not only this, but in creating at all, God admits some kind of need (as incoherent as this is with a perfect being who has no needs); or, lacking this, some kind of superfluity of love such that creation overflows out of this (as some theists claim).

Divine Foreknowledge

I believe that divine foreknowledge is the thorniest of thorns in the side of theism, especially classical theism (defined as an OmniGod who is all-powerful, all-knowing and all-loving). There are so many problems associated with divine foreknowledge, and yet to jettison the idea creates more problems for the theist.

If God truly knew everything in advance, then there would be no need to create anything at all.[1] It is not like God would be wondering, upon creation, what some outcome of it would be, perhaps providing himself some hypotheses that he would test in creation. Despite this problem, there are theistic frameworks (e.g. Open Theism) that do suggest this as the basis for God's creation. The problem with such systems, when concerning Christianity, is that they are not evidenced (at least, not without some serious theological contortions and gerrymandering) in the Bible. For Open Theists, it is almost as if creation is like some sort of almighty simulation computer

---

[1] Please see Pearce (2011, 2017 & 2021) for a host of other arguments pertaining to God's omni-skills, as well as a later chapter in this book.

game where God is hoping that by putting bricks here, humans there, and tectonic plates under there, a certain outcome will eventuate, fingers crossed.

Such an approach is not fulfilling for classical theists who see God as all-knowing. For them, God cannot be some sort of creative being who sets up the game with a wing and a prayer as to how the outcome *might* end up.

For other people, creation is some sort of test, with humans the ones being tested and God being the teacher and invigilator (who oversees exams). But if God *does* have full divine foreknowledge and knows *everything* in advance, then there would be no need to test the humans. Teachers test students in order to find out how much the students know of a given subject or what decisions they would make in a given scenario. But if the teacher knew all of these things about their students already – *indubitably* – then there would absolutely no need to test the children.

Unless, of course, the test – creation and life – is not about the outcome of each person, but about some sort of journey.

But, even then, full divine foreknowledge would surely include the experiential knowledge of each and every one of those test subjects. Let us explore this idea more.

Experiential Knowledge

If God really is perfect – as Anselm would claim: "God" is "a being than which no greater being can be conceived"[1] – then that God would have experiential knowledge of every experiencing entity in creation. God would have knowledge of all future events *experientially* without having to create those events. In theory, God should be able to feel and experience counterfactuals and future events from the beginning. (Remember, a counterfactual is an if...then scenario: if I created X, then Y.)

For example, God should be able to know the experience of a child being hit by a bus, a mother dying of malaria, or a sailor drowning in a naval battle. God should be able to experientially know the qualia (subjective experience) of a bat – what it really feels like to be one. He should also already know the experience of a believing Muslim in prayer, a Christian in religious ecstasy, and an atheist in heathen hedonism. All of this without *being* those entities, and ahead of time, ahead of the actual *creation* of said entities.

---

[1] This is the basis of what is known as the Ontological Argument.

This appears to be a viable form of knowledge, even if only conceptually (since OmniGod can do anything conceivable, within logical bounds, right)?

If God can experience "creation" without creating, then it seems he is duty-bound not to create because then God is creating suffering – real and actual suffering – needlessly (more on this later in "God Is a Consequentialist"). God could imagine the world, and get any pleasure or experiential feedback that he might need or want from creating, without actually creating. This is an important point: if creation is about entities feeling and experiencing a loving union with God, then God could know and experience such a relationship merely in the abstract. God would have no need for creation, especially if what God wants is for those experiences to be real, because they would be "real" in the vicarious experiences of God himself (herself or, as I prefer, itself).

And if this argument holds, this is another argument to disprove the existence of OmniGod.

NATURAL THEOLOGY AND THE PHILOSOPHY OF RELIGION

The term "natural religion" is sometimes taken to refer to a pantheistic doctrine according to which *nature* itself is divine. "Natural theology", by contrast, originally referred to (and still sometimes refers to) the project of arguing for the existence of God on the basis of observed *natural facts*.

In contemporary philosophy, however, both "natural religion" and "natural theology" typically refer to the project of using all of the cognitive faculties that are "natural" to human beings—reason, sense-perception, introspection—to investigate religious or theological matters. Natural religion or theology, on the present understanding, is not limited to empirical inquiry into nature, and it is not wedded to a pantheistic result. It does, however, avoid appeals to special non-natural faculties (ESP, telepathy, mystical experience) or supernatural sources of information (sacred texts, revealed theology, creedal authorities, direct supernatural communication). In general, natural religion or theology (hereafter "natural theology") aims to adhere to the same standards of rational investigation as other philosophical and scientific enterprises, and is subject to the same methods of evaluation and critique. Natural theology is typically contrasted with "revealed theology", where the latter explicitly appeals to special revelations such as miracles, scriptures, and divinely-superintended commentaries and creedal formulations....

Philosophers and religious thinkers across almost every epoch and tradition (Near Eastern, African, Asian, and European) have engaged the project of natural theology, either as proponents or critics. The question of whether natural theology is a viable project is at the root of some of the deepest religious divisions: Shi'ite thinkers are optimistic about reason's ability to prove various theological and ethical truths, for instance, while Sunnis are not; Roman Catholic theologians typically think that reason provides demonstrations of the existence of God, while many Protestant theologians do not. Unlike most of the topics discussed in an encyclopedia of philosophy, this is one over which wars have been fought and throats have been cut.

Andrew Chignell and Derk Pereboom, "Natural Theology and Natural Religion", *The Stanford Enyclopedia of Philosophy*

Why I am Not a Theist

Having set out much of the groundwork for understanding the world around us, and a framework for assessing claims, it is now time to get onto one of the most common of debated issues: God. I have long had an interest in the notion of God in classical theism and how "his" attributes intersect from various religious belief systems. Or don't. I say "his", but I mean "hers" or "its". There's another headache right there (which is compounded by "they" and "theirs"…).

"Classical theism" is the idea that God is omnipotent, omniscient and omnibenevolent. God is OmniGod™. I often give philosophical or atheistic talks to various groups, one presentation of which is a set of arguments against the existence of God that I call "God on Trial", where I present five arguments against OmniGod's existence. One point that is sometimes raised is that this is a straw man conception of what God is. They argue, "My idea of God is very different to this version you are presenting; therefore, you are wrong. I, too, admit that this idea of God is problematic!"

There are as many versions of God as there are believers, and theists of various stripes can always shift the goalposts. However, we have to start somewhere. I cannot present a case against God and take into account the several billion variations thereof. Instead, I pick the most prevalent understanding of God that has prevailed through history, revised by philosophical ruminations over time.

The ideas of OmniGod are popular and, some argue, they are necessary threads that weave their way through ideas of what God is. So, for this section, I will settle for picking my philosophical fight against this understanding of OmniGod. If you want to propose another version of God, we can have that debate another time. Which will be sometime after you have wrangled free of being labelled a "heretic" by most of your well-meaning friends. Good luck with that.

Some of the following arguments may be more relevant to certain gods than to others. You can't please everyone, I guess. At any rate, let us start with the conceptual, and narrow it down from there. Go big or go home, I always say.

Why Create at all?

I set this out earlier when discussing the experiential knowledge of God. Imagine God, causally "before" creating anything, existing in total perfection, for that is what God must be. There is, or was, nothing greater than God in human (or any other) conception. Interestingly, God could not have deliberated about creating because, after all, there was no time. God's decisions were instantaneous. Necessary, even. God "chose" to create this world. Why? What reason could God have? In order to intend to do something, there must be some kind of desire (forget, for a while, that there was no time in this process! Oh, it's all so problematic!). A desire signifies a lack of something. If you have a lack, then, we can argue that you are imperfect. A perfect being will have no needs and no desires. If God has perfect foreknowledge, then God would know all future counterfactuals (i.e., if this happens, then that would follow). God would know the future. Heck, God could *feel* or *imagine* or *experience* the future, without *even* having to create it. Essentially, God could be sitting back in his virtual armchair *really* and *actually* imagining and sensing the universe without *really* and *actually* creating it.

Alas, I am here, *really* and *actually* experiencing stubbing my toe, and wondering whether that experience was real or not. So *I* exist, whatever *I* am.

But God apparently *did* create, so God *wanted* something out of this process – something he must not have had. This renders his perfection rather problematic.

He Created Imperfectly

For the moment, let us shelve the problem that OmniGod would have had no desire or need to create anything, existing, as he did, in perfection. Let us consider actual creation. Anything created must necessarily have been a degradation of his perfect state of affairs. Unless, of course, he created absolute perfection there and then. But let's face it, although I'm pretty awesome, I'm not quite perfect. And that is even after a few billion years of trial and error…

A perfect painter is unlikely to produce a really shoddy painting and still maintain the moniker of a perfect painter. It's all about the deeds.

Likewise, a perfect creator, as God must be,[1] would surely choose to create perfectly.

But we are here. Good old humans, on good old Earth, with its good old tsunamis and malaria, in this good old universe, with its supposed heat death, and life-sucking black holes. This universe is a perfect creation. Somehow, at some point. But is it really? Is it *now*? The jury's out. Maybe we could be on a journey to perfection. Who knows…? I am just not sure that all the pain and suffering we see is necessary for the eventual perfection.

Okay, let's use an analogy (the philosopher's favourite toy). Imagine you are an extraordinarily good scientist in your lab. You have concocted a design for a new sentient creature. You know that this creature, if you were to create it, would, with one hundred percent certainty, go out and rape and pillage in the local town. These sentient beings (they have been profligate), you *know* would run amok, freely causing pain and suffering. They would also paint some lovely pictures, and be nice to people at times, too. Knowing all of this, you create anyway. And the creatures go out from your lab into the wider community and cause the expected mayhem. The police come knocking. They find you ultimately morally culpable for the crimes committed. You are deemed, rightly, to be a meddling, ne'er-do-well scientist.

To continue with the analogies, if I were a CEO (and chief designer) at a car company, and I designed a car that I knew would be faulty and would cause death when it malfunctioned, and decided to create that car anyway, releasing it to market, I would be morally and legally culpable for so doing.

These analogies show that God should not be let off the hook for the moral misdemeanours of these imperfect beings called humans. There is no way round this if God has that perfect foreknowledge, that omniscience, and was the ultimate creator of all there is and ever will be. He has chosen to create imperfect beings that he has designed, and whom he knows will cause untold havoc. And yet he is apparently perfect, and morally off the hook?

Suffering, Suffering, and More Suffering

The Problem of Evil is a well-trodden battlefield. How can there be so much (or any) suffering in light of an OmniGod who cares enough, knows enough and is powerful enough to do something about it.

The answers are generally along the lines of:

---

[1] If we listen to great Christian philosophers who thought up syllogisms like the Ontological Argument to supposedly prove this, and his existence.

1. No suffering is gratuitous – there could be/is/must be a reason for all units of suffering.
2. God moves in mysterious ways (skeptical theism) – we *don't* or even *can't* know why God allows suffering, but there is a reason (see 1.)

What this means is that every single unit of pain is explicable in terms of reasoning. There has to be a reason why God allowed (or even designed a world in which this would happen) 230,000 people to die in the 2004 tsunami.

It is actually far more wide-reaching than these rather grand and terrible instances.

I stubbed my toe yesterday. That unit of pain, let's call it nearly the smallest unit of suffering, cannot be gratuitous under an OmniGod. No unit of suffering or pain, from toe-stubbingly small to genocidally and pandemically big, can be gratuitous.

But it gets more contrived still.

Not only must there be a reason for this suffering, but the suffering must be necessary for that suffering to come about. This suffering must be the minimum amount of suffering that can be incurred for it to have the desired effect that it must have.

This causes all sorts of issues. Let us look at two separate events.

Let's consider the 2004 tsunami resulting from tectonic plates existing. and the (let's say) 227,898 people who died. This has to be the minimum amount of suffering to exist for whatever reason God had to justify those deaths. I'm not interested in whatever that particular theodicy actually was, whether it be some necessary design feature or soul-building scenario. Whatever the reason there was for that suffering to happen, that exact amount of suffering must have been the minimum required for God still to be called all-loving. God could not have allowed 227,897 people to have died. Not only were all of those 227, 897 people necessary for whatever reason God had in mind, but that extra person pushing it up to 227,898 was also necessary. There can be no single unit of suffering that is gratuitous.

And, of course, it wasn't just human death, but animal death, too (and plant death leading to further animal suffering). And it wasn't just death, but injury and emotional pain. There was not one broken arm too much, not one psychological breakdown too much.

This is the scale of the problem for the (classical) theist. They have to justify *everything*. Every unit of pain involved there, every piece of emotional and physical suffering. There was not one unit too much.

The scale, of course, goes down to stubbing my toe. That gave me 6 units of pain. I could have stubbed my toe and it be slightly less painful – 5 units. But 6 was the optimal and necessary amount for whatever reason God had in mind. Not one unit too much.

Think of every single bit of pain and suffering that happens every single minute of every single day to every single animal in one way or another. Every single unit of pain and suffering is optimally necessary for something. It's just that no one is really sure what that something is, and so all of that pain is kind of pointless.

If we can't learn from it, or learn the wrong thing, then the lesson is bad or fails in its objective. That's basic teaching.

But it gets worse.

Are you seriously telling me that *every* unit of that was necessary?

Here's the rub: the theist has to say "yes" whilst also accepting that we aren't quite certain what the theodicy or reason for that suffering was. All the theist can do with any certainty is resort to "God moves in mysterious ways".

But, given that this appears to be the answer for humans, then why can not one less broken arm, one less death still satisfy the reasoning of "God moves in mysterious ways"? Are you telling me that 227,898 deaths and untold animal deaths and untold amounts of injury, pain and psychological suffering was all *necessary* for us to think "God moves in mysterious ways"?

However, the theist sometimes retorts that there must be a stopping point *somewhere*, because otherwise there is a regression down to zero. You can keep arguing that one less death is better and so we get down to zero. Sure, but that works both ways. And you still have to accept that, somehow, 227,898 and X extra suffering was the *optimal* point, that the message could not be communicated just as effectively with one less death or broken arm or tear. And that's given that the message is not clear at any rate! Otherwise, the number looks arbitrary. It still must be the result of some calculation of God or he is metaphorically swinging his finger around in a circle and stabbing at "227,898".

And so, finally, the problem seems to go back to the source. Not only does the (classical) theist have to accept that God knew this (227,898 + X, for example) in advance and designed and created the world where this happened anyway (such that this must be the optimal blueprint in terms of his omni-characteristics), but they must accept that humans are *not even sure of why this suffering is actually happening:* they can give a host of reasons, but generally disagree, deferring to inference, and ending up at skeptical theism's "God moves in mysterious ways" anyway.

Thus, the reasoning cannot really be to teach us humans something, since we all disagree on what that reason is (unless that disagreement and necessity for blind faith, like with Abraham and Isaac, are the general point in and of themselves). The reasoning must be internal to God.

This is just bizarre and means that deaths, pain and suffering happen on Earth so that God can reconcile some design and creation deficit with himself.

God creates the world W1 in such a way that, for him, he needs Y amount of suffering in a given scenario in W1, or Z suffering in W1 overall, or some such scenario, so that the suffering isn't about teaching the sentient beings there anything (notwithstanding the pain and suffering to non-sentient beings) since they don't or can't understand the reasons for it, but it is about some internal reconciliation that results from his own design and creation criteria (none of which we have access to).

And that, there, is why I can't be a theist. (Don't worry, there's more!)

Adam and Eve

Let's put this design fault into biblical context, with the understanding that this is aimed at the Abrahamic faiths. According to Genesis, God creates Adam and Eve in this supposedly perfect scenario. They have been chosen to represent humanity in a big test: not eating a fruit from the Tree of Knowledge. This presents a conundrum from the start: Before eating from a fruit that gives them the knowledge of what is right and wrong, they have to know that it is wrong to disobey God and eat some forbidden fruit.

Damn this logic game.

Okay, let's allow that issue to slip and carry on with the story.

So, Adam and Eve represent humanity in this test. God presumably knows in advance the result of this test, but he picks Adam and Eve to do it anyway. And he knows they are going to fail. God knows he has a glaring design fault. Further, if Adam and Eve are representative of humanity, then any human taking that test would have failed, and we are all inherently faulty. This throws perfect design and creation down the proverbial drain.

If, however, Adam and Eve are *not* representative of humanity, then God has chosen non-representative people to take a test and fail. On account of this failure, all other people, given the Fall, are punished. It's bad enough to know we are being punished for the choice of Adam and Eve because we are all equally as shoddy as they are, but it's quite another to think we are being punished for the wrongdoing of this test when we could have *passed* the test ourselves!

Quite a two-horned dilemma.

God Loves Abortion

Another creative shortcoming concerns foetuses. Most religious people appear to be fervent pro-lifers: They are not fans of abortion. No one is really a fan of abortion in and of itself, but it is a useful procedure for a number of reasons, and the foetus is often merely a group of cells or something that has no personhood and feels no pain. God has designed and created human beings, and also does nothing to prevent abortion from occurring naturally and regularly in the female half of his creation. Anywhere up to three quarters of fertilized eggs are naturally aborted within the female body. They either fail to implant or are rejected by the body, or undergo other such problems. His denizens do not seem to recognise that.

This amounts to perhaps billions of individual blastocysts or embryos over time that have been naturally aborted. God doesn't appear to lift a virtual finger to stop this.

God's Not Fair

Let's reset. We have, according to the theists, a collection of human beings that God has designed and created. Or if you are a theistic evolutionist, God created the system that created the humans. Either way, with his omniscience, he knew what would come to pass.

God created a whole range of people. Men, women and others (if you don't adhere to a gender binary) is one range. People on the spectrum from neurotypical to autistic might be another range.

For the traditional Christian, since heaven and hell appear to be the consequence of what we do here in this existence, the main point for earthly humans is to enter into a loving relationship, freely, with God. We can ask what happened to people who existed before the Bible, or in the Amazon who have never heard the Gospel, who don't know the Bible. Christian theologians like William Lane Craig have an answer: God front-loaded all those souls whom he knew would freely reject him into those peoples. Dark. Fatalistic.

An alternative answer (whilst still retaining the heaven/hell concept) might be that humans have morality written on our hearts, and that we don't need the Bible, nor a relationship with the Christian/Muslim/InsertNameHere God, in order to succeed in the Test of Life and get into heaven. That's a whole problem for theists because it means we do not need God for morality, nor need the Bible for guidance. And it is a good argument for secular humanism!

Back to the point. God has created ranges of people, and science has shown that these different types of people have different probabilities in believing in God. Women, for whatever reason (it doesn't matter whether it is genetic, biological or environmental), are more likely to believe in God than men. Scientists are less likely than others. And, interestingly, certain autistic people[1] are far less likely than the neurotypical to believe in a personal deity.

One hypothesis about this last group, based on work by Norenzayan, Gervais and Trzesniewski,[2] is that certain autistic people are less able to empathize, to see life from someone else's point of view. They are less able to put themselves in someone else's shoes. Where religious believers are constantly wondering how God, as a personal agent, is viewing their life and their moral actions. Autistic people are unable to do this. That kind of intersubjectivity is much more difficult for them. And so they end up not believing in God, being almost unable to believe in a personal entity out there who is watching their every move.

What this means is that God is unfair. He is stacking the cards, loading the dice, such that certain subgroups of people are more or less likely to freely come to love him. If that is part of the endgame, then God is not fair, and not omnibenevolent.

Heaven Ain't Justification

Please do not use heaven to justify the last point on stacking the odds, or to justify how it is okay that a six-month-old baby dies of cancer. "It's alright,"

---

[1] As an utterly irrelevant sidebar here, I found the article "Identity-First Language", (reproduced later for the Autistic Self Advocacy Network [ASAN], originally titled "The Significance of Semantics: Person-First Language: Why It Matters") very interesting reading, in detailing the different ways people (autistic or otherwise) label autistic people/themselves. Language is important and so often nuanced in ways we don't realise until we step back, take a deep breath, and think. See Brown (2011).
[2] Norenzayan et al (2012).

you or your theistic friend might say, "they will live for an eternity in heaven!"

This is treating heaven as compensation; and compensation is not moral justification, especially if you are a religious believer. Theists invariably hate a moral value system called consequentialism (William Lane Craig called it a "terrible ethic") because it has no need for a benevolent god. You derive your moral value from the consequences pertaining to a given action. If I walked up to you and punched you in the face and broke your jaw for no reason, then that would not be nice. It is not morally good on almost anyone's moral value system.

But let's think about theists who believe morality is divinely commanded. We now have a conundrum. If I am made to pay you $10,000, or even if I give it to you voluntarily, it does not make the punch suddenly morally good. You may even enjoy getting that money and think it was worth it. But it is compensation; it is not *moral justification*. Theists try to fool us with this sleight of hand.

Why Don't We Photosynthesize?

Time to return to God and creation. It turns out that mere existence is predicated upon a whole raft of pain and suffering. Many organisms require the pain and death of other organisms in order to simply exist. This happens, literally, on an industrial scale, from intensive farming to the Serengeti. I once watched an online video of a water buffalo being eaten alive by a pride of lions just so I could understand this point.

It was terrible.

But that's life – or death, as may be. And it has happened for a very long time. All that pain and suffering—every unit—has been built into the design of so many organisms.

But it does not have to be that way. God could have made it any other way, surely, with his omni-skills? Carnivorousness can't be necessary, can it? We could, for example, all photosynthesize. All organisms could derive all of their energy from the sun, thus not necessitating the death of other animals. God could either create the physical constant to allow for this, or simply allow for perpetual miracles to take place in every organism.

You can take this a step further. Maybe we don't actually need energy. Conceptually, God could have created organisms, or a whole system, that didn't revolve around our understanding of energy.

Further still, God did not need to create a physical world at all. God could just have created heaven, and populated heaven directly. There's a thought.

Heaven and Hell

If the endgame is indeed heaven, then why not just create heaven and put our ethereal beings within? Let's return to his divine foreknowledge: If God knew in advance the people who would freely come to love him, then why not just create them? If he knew exactly who on earth would freely come to love him, why bother creating all those others? All those others who are condemned to an eternity in hell? That seems unnecessarily harsh: punishing people infinitely for a finite failure that God knew would happen anyway.

No, God could just create heaven. Forget earth, the universe, and everything else; just create paradise and fill it with the people you were always going to fill it with.

Job done.

Suffering eradicated. (This creating job is a cinch.)

Satan as God's Management Executive

God is supposed to be omnipotent: all powerful, almighty and all knowing. The great-making characteristics of such a god are his paragon of abilities. He could achieve anything at the metaphorical click of his fingers.

So what the hell is Satan still doing hanging around? Well, of course, Satan (or any other such evil equivalent) does not exist either. But suppose we believe that both God and Satan are real entities. Well, then, this makes no sense at all. God could make Satan disappear. Y'know, non-existent. With a metaphorical click of his fingers. Any ontological argument for God, or claim that he is perfect, such as under Perfect Being Theology, argues for God's supreme omni-abilities. To be the greatest being in conception, there can be no rival being as God could dispense with them. Therefore, Satan cannot be God's equal.

This means that if the Devil exists, he does so at the behest of God. Either God actively wants him to exist, or his disappearance would cause more grief than good, like some embodiment of the Problem of Evil and consequentialism, as previously mentioned.

Thus, it appears that Satan, if he exists, is doing a job for God; he is providing a service, if you will. God, then, must accept corporate responsibility for him. In other words, anything that is laid at the feet of Satan, in terms of blame and moral responsibility, should actually be laid at the invisible feet of God. God allows (either by design, direct causation or act of omission) everything that Satan does.

God's Omniscience Means He Has No Free Will

Of course, simply knowing everything is not so simple. If God knew his own actions in advance, and was constrained by his own omni-characteristics, then he would not have free will and could not do otherwise than he had already predicted. If God had perfect foreknowledge, and knew in advance exactly what he was going to do, he could never change his mind, or he would invalidate his perfect foreknowledge.

Second, if he is perfectly loving, then everything that he did would have to be in terms of that kind of perfection. His course of action would always *have* to be the most loving option. He would have no freedom to do otherwise. He would have no freedom or ability to act against his own nature, a nature that he had no role in creating, it was just necessarily so.

If free will is super important, as many theists claim, then the fact that God does not have it is a bit of a problem.

And We Don't Even Have Free Will!

It's free will, Jim, but not as we know it. I have steered away from talking *too much* about one of my most favourite subjects in philosophy: free will (and the fact that we don't have it). As with everything philosophical, and as you have seen from this book, it is all about definitions and making sure interlocutors have the same understanding of a term when debating its existence.

As previously mentioned, I see free will in the libertarian sense and as defined by the real and conscious ability to rationally choose and do otherwise in a given scenario. This could in principle be exemplified by making a decision at t_0, letting the universe proceed for ten minutes (t_{10}) and then rewinding to that exact moment, t_0 (let's call this "second" iteration t_0^a). Libertarian free will (LFW) believers would have it that the agent really could choose otherwise even if every aspect of the universe at both iterations (t_0

and to^a) are the same – that the universe in both scenarios is identical (for it is technically just that one universe) down to every wave function, piece of prior learning, gene, particle, and whatnot. Or, in any given scenario, an agent really could choose A and ~A, breaking the Law of Non-Contradiction.

I deny this kind of free will, the kind that theists almost always (Calvinists aside) adhere to, because they need it for their understanding of a judgemental god. Science – including psychology – also makes little sense of LFW. You wouldn't visit a psychologist to unpick a problem or understand a behaviour and allow them to wave you away with a trite claim that "It's okay, it's just your free will being enacted." No, scientists seek to understand causal relationships and why things happen, and whether we like it or not (as we can now start seeing with Big Data), humans are pretty predictable creatures.

I am in good company in my denial because it turns out that almost all philosophers (as according to the 2009 *Philpapers* survey) deny the existence of libertarian free will, and almost all of those who do rather conveniently turn out to be theists. LFW is a philosophical incoherency but it is also something of a necessity for such theists.[1]

As such, most philosophers are at least soft determinists (people who believe free will and causal determinism coexist by redefining free will), with many being hard determinists (free will, as so defined – contra-causal free will – does not exist in a causally determined reality). We can allow for indeterminism – quantum randomness, or otherwise, at a microscopic level – because such allowances do not work well with LFW. Allowing random into a decision-making process doesn't really help rational and conscious decision-making ownership.

The interesting questions come out of this: what do we do with the knowledge we do not have free will, and how do we deal with crime and punishment? These questions are where most philosophers are now concentrating their grey matter, since for many in the ivory towers, we live in a post-God world and have more pressing matters to attend.

All He Knows Is That He Doesn't Know Everything...

We cannot know that we don't know something. If we claim to be omniscient, and there is a situation where we do not know something, then this would invalidate our claim.

---

[1] A problem that I cannot spend too much time discussing, but see my chapter "Free Will" in John Loftus's *Christianity in the Light of Science* – Loftus (2016).

For example, there could conceivably be something that God does not know. Conceivably, perhaps another dimension run by another God exists that does not coincide with this dimension. If one eternal God can exist, why not another in an entirely different dimension and unbeknownst to the first God? It is unimportant whether this is actually the case or not. What is important is that God could not *know* that he did not know this by the very nature of not knowing it! Think on that for a minute.

Where does this leave God? Well, God is in a situation whereby he cannot know that he knows everything. He might *think* he knows everything. Epistemologically speaking, though, he cannot *know* it. Of course, this whole point depends on the definition of "know" and "knowledge." But if we take a Cartesian sense of indubitably to be the case, then I think we can make something of a problem for the classical concept of God.

Going back to Descartes and his Evil Daemon thought experiment (updated to *The Matrix* for modern times), there's always a chance that God is an experiment in an elaborate lab. In this scenario, he is programmed to think he is omnipotent and omniscient (yes, God could be plugged into the Matrix and he'd never know it!). There's a chance he is one of a trillion gods in a trillion different universes. Maybe he has himself been created by another, more powerful god, but that the other god made it so God god was not aware of this.

It only takes one thing you cannot know to invalidate omniscience. God cannot know that he knows everything. It might not be the case, of course, that there is a whole procession of gods leading back from God. But God cannot know that this is indubitably not the case.

Phew, being God isn't as easy as it's cracked up to be.

And the List Goes on

And so it goes for the classical notion of God. Problems beget problems, and they beget further problems. I look at many of these and more in a couple of my previous books: *The Little Book of Unholy Questions* and *The Problem with "God": Skeptical Theism under the Spotlight*.

I think what we *can* safely say is that the version of God that is omnipotent, omniscient and omnibenevolent is wholly unlikely, and thoroughly problematic. Maybe even impossible, given the above. Something has to go. One of the omnis has to be dropped. Or all of them.

Or God.

Evidence for Supernatural Gods

We have talked about epistemologies already. Now it is time to talk in a little more detail about probabilities. Divine events are incredible events that have supposedly taken place in space and time in history.

The operative word here is "incredible" – events that one cannot believe. Why are they incredible? For several reasons. First, they break the natural laws of the universe. Second, they are exceptionally low probability events anyway, irrespective of whether they broke natural laws.

We discussed the terms "naturalism" and "supernaturalism" towards the beginning of the book. And though they can be difficult to completely pin down, we can have some intuitive understanding that has pragmatic value.

Let us re-examine the example of Jesus Christ resurrecting from the dead. This breaks the laws of nature, which dictate that a supernatural event *cannot* happen. Plus, resurrection events as *claimed* in history are very uncommon. I will explain this further below.

The claims of Jesus as being a god, and his resurrection (defying and reversing death) to atone for the sins of humanity (however that might work) are undoubtedly supernatural in almost any definition of the term.

Given that, under naturalism, these claims break the Laws of Nature and contravene our Background Knowledge, they have very low prior probabilities. To overcome this very low prior probability, we would need exceptionally good evidence. But even if the divine events surrounding Jesus cohere with our Background Knowledge (as a supernaturalist), these are nonetheless incredible, low probability claims. And they *still* require exceptionally high quality evidence to overcome those odds and lead one to believe that the Christian/Bible/God hypothesis is the most plausible explanation of the data.

In the case of any New Testament claims in the Christian Bible, let us consider the four Gospels. They were written by unknown people at unknown dates in unknown places with *ex post facto*[1] agendas to evangelise, at least forty years after the death of the person they are writing about and whom they have never met, has died. Is this high-quality, reliable evidence?

Michael Martin expresses Bayes' Theorem as applied to the Resurrection as a logical syllogism as follows:[2]

---

[1] Meaning the authors already believed that Jesus was the Messiah *and then* write a "history" of his life, rendering the process and output exceptionally biased.
[2] Martin's chapter in Price & Lowder (2005), p. 46.

1. A miracle claim is initially improbable relative to our background knowledge.

2. If a claim is initially improbable relative to our background knowledge and the evidence for it is not strong, then it should be disbelieved.

3. The Resurrection of Jesus is a miracle claim.

4. The evidence for the Resurrection is not strong.

5. Therefore, the Resurrection of Jesus should be disbelieved.

There really is nothing about this with which I disagree. As Martin rightly alludes to in his chapter, even the Catholic Church starts with the inductive conclusion that any new claim for a miracle at Lourdes is likely to be false. They then apply very charitable metrics and evidential value to conclude that a minority of the claimed miracles are true. This reality suggests that the initial probability of a miracle claim is still very low indeed, even if we are the very charitable Catholic Church.

As Stephen T. Davies, Christian philosopher and apologist (and miracles believer), concludes: "naturalistic explanations of phenomena ought to be preferred by rational people in the vast majority of cases".[1] Irrespective of whether you are a naturalist or supernaturalist (however you define those slippery terms), miracle claims have a very low probability of being true and require a high level of evidence to support them.

And it is not just Christianity. I could pick any religious claim from any religion in the world and we would get to the same problem: does the level and quality of evidence overcome the low prior probability of the claim being true? And in every single case, the answer is no. Every religious adherent dismisses the claims of every other religion and religious adherent. Atheists take it one religion further.

Simply put, the evidence required – offered by the Bible, the Qu'ran, individual revelatory claims, etc. – is not good enough to convince any properly rational person of believing in any given religion.

I have set this out in the context of Christianity in much more detail in my books The Nativity: A Critical Examination and The Resurrection: A Critical Examination of the Easter Story.

---

[1] Davies (1993), p. 13.

And with this two-pronged approach of philosophy of religion (in the abstract) and evidentialism (using rational arguments to deal with the concrete), we can see that atheism is a more rationally secure belief than belief in God...any god.

TELEOLOGY

Design arguments are empirical arguments for the existence of God. These arguments typically, though not always, proceed by attempting to identify various empirical features of the world that constitute evidence of intelligent design and inferring God's existence as the best explanation for these features. Since the concepts of design and purpose are closely related, design arguments are also known as teleological arguments, which incorporates "telos," the Greek word for "goal" or "purpose."

Design arguments typically consist of (1) a premise that asserts that the material universe exhibits some empirical property F; (2) a premise (or sub-argument) that asserts (or concludes) that F is persuasive evidence of intelligent design or purpose; and (3) a premise (or sub-argument) that asserts (or concludes) that the best or most probable explanation for the fact that the material universe exhibits F is that there exists an intelligent designer who intentionally brought it about that the material universe exists and exhibits F.

Kenneth Einar Himma, "Design Arguments for the Existence of God", *The Internet Encylopedia of Philosophy*

The Meaning of Life.

"I very rarely think either of my past or my future, but the moment that one contemplates writing an autobiography – and I am sitting down with that intention today - one is forced to regard oneself as an entity carried along for a brief period in the stream of time, emerging suddenly at a particular moment from darkness and nothingness and shortly to disappear at a particular moment into nothingness and darkness. The moment at which officially I emerged from non-existence was the early morning of November 25th, 1880, though in fact I did not personally become aware of my existence until some two or three years later. In the interval between 1880 and today I have lived my life on the assumption that sooner or later I shall pass by annihilation into the same state of non-existence from which I suddenly emerged that winter morning in West Cromwell Road, Kensington, so many years ago. This passage from non-existence to non-existence seems to me a strange and, on the whole, an enjoyable experience. Since the age of sixteen, when for a short time, like all intelligent adolescents, I took the universe too seriously, I have rarely worried myself about its meaning or meaninglessness. But I resent the fact that, as seems to be practically certain, I shall be as non-existent after my death as I was before my birth. Nothing can be done about it and I cannot truthfully say that my future extinction causes me much fear or pain, but I should like to record my protest against it and against the universe which enacts it.

"The adulation of the deity as creator of the universe in Jewish and Christian psalms and hymns, and indeed by most religions, seems to me ridiculous. No doubt in the course of millions of millions of years, he has contrived to create some good things. I agree that 'my heart leaps up when I behold a rainbow in the sky', or 'the golden daffodils, beside the lake, beneath the trees, fluttering and dancing in the breeze', or 'the stars that shine and twinkle on the Milky Way'. I admit that every now and again I am amazed and profoundly moved by the beauty and affection of my cat and my dog. But at what a cost of senseless pain and misery, of wasteful and prodigal

145

cruelty, does he manage to produce a daffodil, a Siamese cat, a sheepdog, a housefly, or a sardine. I resent the wasteful stupidity of a system which tolerates the spawning herring or the seeding groundsel or the statistics of infantile mortality wherever God has not been civilized by man. And I resent the stupid wastefulness of a system which requires that human beings with great labour and pain should spend years in acquiring knowledge, experience, and skill, and then just when at last they might use all this in the service of mankind and for their own happiness, they lose their teeth and their hair and their wits, and are hurriedly bundled, together with all that they have learnt, into the grave and nothingness.

"It is clear that, if there is a purpose in the universe and a creator, both are unintelligible to us. But that does not provide them with an excuse or a defence."

Leonard Woolf (1960)[1]

Let us begin. Are the views expressed in this passage reasonable?

What have we achieved so far in this set of essays? First, I have sketched for you my understanding of the ontology of the world and how concepts merely exist in our mind as conceptual representations of the world outside our minds. From the sense data that our minds take in, we build up an epistemology that itself constructs knowledge. As a group of humans, we build that knowledge through being able to store information, using tools (writing, computers) and through extensive communication (language and technology). We use our faculties to observe the world around us and the scientific method to continue the journey towards an ever more accurate appraisal of the universe around us. In my opinion, this includes the conclusion that no gods exist.

Our conceptual map allows us to navigate the world around us, but we must remember not to confuse the map for the terrain. The map is a conceptual overlay of the universe, and serves as an interpretative framework that we can use to navigate and understand that universe. But that conceptual overlay is not the world itself. Maps are useful to navigate the mountains and oceans of reality – but it is not the fundamental fabric itself.

Part of the map-making process concerns meaning and purpose (teleology) and it is to this topic that we now turn.

---

[1] Woolf (1960).

Back to the quotation.

There is much we can analyse and debate in this long quote by Leonard Woolf (the husband of the author Virginia Woolf) from his autobiography *Sowing: An Autobiography of the Years, 1880–1904*. In this essay, I will illustrate the main ideas in this quote before debating them at greater length. There are too many salient points (as seen below) to cover in this essay – some of them have caused more ink to be spilt than would result from a riot at the Parker pen factory. For ease of review and economy of space I have set out the ten main points as follows:

1. We are nothing before birth and shortly become nothing at death.
2. Our lives and existence are sadly short.
3. We do not have immortal souls.
4. We should not worry about finding the meaning of existence. ("I have rarely worried myself about its meaning.")
5. He resents the fact that he will be nothing at death as before life. Therefore, there is a lingering inference of the futility of existence. ("And I resent the stupid wastefulness of a system…they…are hurriedly bundled, together with all that they have learnt, into the grave and nothingness.")
6. Death is not to be feared.
7. The worship of a god is ridiculous as illustrated by the problem of evil.
8. There is pointlessness (or wastefulness) in undergoing a lengthy process of acquiring knowledge only to lose it, shortly after gaining it, in death before using it to give service to mankind.
9. With age there comes pain and shame.
10. God is unintelligible to us, as is a purpose in the universe, even if they do exist. (A purpose suggests a universal objective purpose for humans in the universe.)

The main areas that I will discuss are Point 8 and Point 10, which I will look at in reverse order. Also, Woolf uses the terms "meaning" and "purpose" interchangeably throughout. I will discuss whether that makes a difference to our understanding … or not.

Point 10: God is unintelligible to us. Woolf says that if there is an objective purpose to life, it is unintelligible to us. I will agree with the idea that if meaning and purpose exist objectively, then they are effectively unintelligible. This points towards the need for a subjective purpose. I take this a step further by claiming that objective purposes are themselves effectively and philosophically incoherent or impotent.

Point 8: Learning is important and yet wasted. Woolf claims that (like philosophers from John Stuart Mill to A.C. Grayling) learning is integral to happiness and the service of mankind. But unfortunately, our learning is short-lived and wastefully left behind at the annihilation of our death. I will partially agree that happiness is certainly a worthy goal (as a subjective purpose). But I disagree with Woolf by arguing that happiness, like knowledge, is not necessarily wasted.

Meaning of Life

Let us look at whether there is meaning to life as hinted by Woolf in the following words: "It is clear that, if there is a purpose in the universe and a creator, both are unintelligible to us." Let us debate the term "meaning"; as in, the question "What is the meaning of life?" And is that the same question as "What is the purpose of life?" mean? But before venturing too far, first, we have to define "life" and "meaning" to decipher the question.

Life is a process, and a collection of experiences and actions taken by an individual until the individual dies. Life, in its early form, is without self-awareness, and so is described in even more basic and biological terms, including living cells and functions.

Meaning gets even more complicated. What does "meaning" mean (a little meta-humour for you there…)? There are many interpretations of the word "meaning":

> *Pain* means bread in French.
> Did you mean to hurt him?
> The smell of cut grass means a lot to me.
> What is the meaning of this whole debacle?
> The colour red means danger.
> I mean business.
> Running into her in the café was meant to happen.

The list is very long. There are multiple basic linguistic issues to muddle through. But the meaning of life is different from the meaning of *pain* in the sense that we are trying to decipher the meaning of a phenomenon and not just a simple word. It makes no sense to say "What is the meaning of a tree (or a pebble, or a puddle)?" As philosopher Oswald Hanfling said, "The difficulty that faces us here is as if we were asked about the meaning of grass, or of the Atlantic Ocean."[1] Intrinsically they have no meaning outside of the definition of the word and what it signifies. Life is potentially no different in this respect, and the question is possibly meaningless. But life is different. It has *significance* in that it has, as British intellectual Terry Eagleton states, "point, substance, purpose, quality, value and direction".[2]

A postmodernist might point out that "meaning" calls for something to stand in for something else, to represent something else. In this way, though not without its critics (such as linguistic philosopher Ludwig Wittgenstein). Terry Eagleton opines:[3]

> Meaning and interpretation imply hidden messages and mechanisms, depths stacked beneath surfaces ... it still needs to be dug out, since the world does not spontaneously disclose it. One name for this excavatory enterprise is science, which on a certain view of it seeks to reveal the invisible laws and mechanisms by which things operate.

It may be true to say that science determines the mechanisms and establishes data, but finding meaning and purpose is out of its remit. The knowledge and understanding of data and mechanisms are not synonymous with understanding the meaning that may or may not lie behind them. Understanding that evolution is the mechanism that defines life as we know it does not infer that evolution is the meaning of life (although it still may be). The conflation of method and meaning is all too common.

Purpose of Life

Returning to Eagleton's quote, about life having significance because it has "point, substance, purpose, quality, value and direction". It is the words *point* and *purpose* that are really more poignant than the term "meaning". What is the point to life? Why are we here? What is our purpose? This is arguably a

---

[1] Hanfling (1987), p. x.
[2] Eagleton (2007), p. 37.
[3] Ibid., p. 16-17.

more sensible approach than seeking the meaning of life. But these questions are potentially fraught with issues themselves.

"What is the purpose of life?" is problematic too, because it implies the existence of a purposer, or it demands subjective purposing (thus meaning there is no objective "purpose of life"). In order for an object to have a purpose, there would have to be some entity that is giving the object that purpose. A puddle does not intrinsically have a purpose. Nor does an ant, unless we mistakenly conflate method with purpose. In other words, the method or mechanism of evolution does not necessarily imply that the purpose of an ant is to do ant things that lead towards the survival of the colony and thus the species.

Contrary to the previous statement, we *can* argue that evolution gives purpose to living things. This actually implies that the underlying principles of evolution that provide the purpose (the mechanisms of survival and reproduction). And the end result of evolution (existence of the species) represents the purpose.

Can we really say that the purpose of life is to survive? This is possibly the only purpose that we can provide for life without much doubt, since in order to think about existence, we need to exist. And none of us can exist as a living entity without having been produced via reproduction and surviving up until reading this essay. This sounds obvious, but it is hugely important. The foundational purpose of life, before working out any overarching or highly philosophical ideas, is to survive as an individual, and as a species. Evolution provides a good framework for that purpose. That being said, could these intermediary aspects (survival and reproduction) simply be the methods that entities use in order to achieve their ultimate purpose?

But surely existence is just the corollary of those methods. Perhaps this form of purpose doesn't quite entail the meaning that we want it to. Animals don't adapt to an environment *so that* a particular gene survives; it just so happens that a particular gene survives when the animal is best adapted to that environment. The gene isn't a mind and has no intention, nor is the environment. The animal may have intention to survive, and this is hard-baked into it as survival intuition (or not in lesser animals and plants) because it just so happens that this characteristic lends itself to survival and reproduction better than some kind of suicidal tendency.

Following the above argument, we could be back at square one – still needing to interpret what our purpose is. It could be that evolution, and all the baggage that comes with the process, provides the mechanistic purpose and method for existing, but that there is a greater purpose that humans aspire towards that exists alongside, or overshadows, evolution. This touches on the unintelligible nature of purpose as hinted at by Woolf in the opening quote ("It is clear that, if there is a purpose in the universe and a creator, both are unintelligible to us"). Whatever our purpose is, given a creator or not, it is not exactly explicit. Not only is it not explicit, but it *may* not exist at all. The mere fact that I, after many thousands of thinkers, am still trying to tease out potential meanings and purposes to life shows that these things are clearly *not* explicit.

Objective Purpose – Can It Exist?

An objective purpose is a purpose that exists for a human irrespective of time or place, and outside of their mind. If there is an objective purpose[1] (one that exists in all possible worlds), we must undergo a highly subjective process of trying to decipher exactly what it is! This is very important to note, and is analogous to objective morality. If we do not know what our objective purpose is, then we all make up our own subjective purpose to replace it. This subjective/objective interplay provides ample reason to cast doubt on the existence (or usefulness) of objective purposes.

Let us return, though, to the idea that to have a purpose requires a purposer (someone to import purpose onto something else). If we ask, "What is the purpose of a spade?", we assume that the spade has a purpose outside of itself to another entity, for a specific end (i.e., for a gardener to dig). Thus, the same question with regard to (human) life purpose would imply there is another entity outside of humanity that can use humanity to achieve a certain end. In this case, humans *serve* a purpose rather than *have* a purpose. This obviously raises the question as to whether there is an entity outside of humanity that can give human life a purpose. Is there a creator who gives us purpose?

If we assume that there is a god, and that we do indeed have an objective purpose, where does that leave us? If we say that our objective purpose is provided by a god, it simply becomes a subjective purpose to that god.

Let's use that spade analogy again. If the spade was sentient, and decided that it didn't fancy being used to dig holes in my garden at my behest (I am the purposer here, the god), but wanted to take on a nobler cause of digging gardens in the community, and helping criminals rehabilitate their ways in a gardening program, then the spade is entitled to feel that its own purpose was superior (even if it was something *less* morally upstanding). As a god, I could chastise and cajole the spade, through punishment and reward,

---

[1] Woolf possibly implies this in his last sentence with "*a* purpose".

towards aligning its purpose with mine. But then objectiveness simply gets transformed into a consequentialist purpose, with the spade only adopting a purpose to avoid punishment (banishment to the tool shed) or gain the reward from me as the god. There is an intuitive lack of objective purpose in the happiness of the spade, since pleasing me gives the spade less punishment and more reward. Thus objective purpose is replaced by the subjective gaining of happiness.

Similarly, if we believe that a god might have an "objective" purpose for us, it does not make it superior (which is indeed a completely unmeasurable and subjective notion) to a subjective purpose set by ourselves. Furthermore, the idea of an objective purpose is rendered pointless or meaningless by this. If there is an objective purpose, the only "duty" to follow it would be in terms of a consequence of punishment for not adhering to it, or reward for doing so. A sort of "so what" to an objective purpose. *Duties* and *oughts* are, in my opinion, conditional notions (ideas of if … then). There is only a *duty* to do something if there is a *consequence* to not doing it, or a *reward* for doing it (either abstract or concrete). The duty of a schoolteacher to take the register at the beginning of the day may be for the following reasons:

- To avoid being disciplined by the school management.
- To ensure that all the children are present, which in turn ensures that the school has accurate records.
- To allow the teacher to know who is present so that he/she may alter their planning accordingly.
- To ensure a thorough process is in place to facilitate child protection etc.

However, the register being taken is not an *objective* duty in and of itself. In other words, there is no objective duty; the teacher is not bound by having to take the register on its own merit. As long as there is a "because" after the "ought", then it is a conditional, consequentialist notion. I ought not punch a passer-by in the face because:

- I will get in trouble for it;
- he might retaliate to my disadvantage;
- a sound society relies on decent and reliable behaviour;
- a sound society is beneficial for all concerned;
- and so on.

As soon as there is no "because", then a behaviour or action is committed on its own merit – there is true objective duty. However, I can see no situation whereby this causal circumstance exists. Even if there is a god, as mentioned, we may have moral duties, but these duties exist within a framework of consequences and repercussions, positive and negative. I will lay this out in more detail in the short piece on "oughts" to open the morality section in this book.

Obviously, this is in direct opposition to the beliefs of moral absolutists or deontologists – objective morality – and Divine Command Theorists – religiously defined objective morality. Things can get very tricky when trying to argue as to whether or not objective morality exists (where philosophers will wrangle over the term "objective"). Deontology (whether an action is intrinsically or objectively right or wrong) seems to be under threat from itself, as expressed by the issues within the trolley problem.[1] These thought experiments continue to cause headaches, and arguments rage on much as they have for hundreds or even thousands of years. This is not a settled debate. Just as we struggle to define what our purpose or meaning might objectively be (remember Kant and not being able to know the thing-in-itself?), so we struggle to know what is objectively right or wrong.

As philosopher Jeremy Bentham stated, deontology looks rather similar to popular morality. Especially since, as John Stuart Mill added, when the rights conflict, no one can *absolutely* say which ones take priority. Deontology simply cannot provide an absolute moral guide. (Remember, I am sketching things out here with a lot of over-simplification – please read elsewhere for analyses of deontology and its strengths and weaknesses. I will also be discussing this in the Morality section of the book.) Certainly, for many "consequentialists", the consequence that a moral action brings about defines its goodness or badness. Things – people or actions – are a means to an end, an instrument used towards a goal.

From this train of thought, we can extrapolate that life might not be an end in itself, but possibly a means to an end (a theist might posit heaven), and it is that end that we often seek to fathom out. The ought in life, like the student register, is a means towards a goal.

But this does not answer the question of whether there is actually an objective purpose to life and what that might be. From a religious point of view, that purpose would be down to the followers of each religion to interpret (for example, leading a morally decent life whilst maintaining a loving relationship with a personal god). There are too many religions vying

---

[1] The thought experiment where someone has maliciously sent a trolley hurtling towards five innocent and immobile people at the end of a track. The only way to stop the trolley and save the five is to throw one innocent bystander in front of the trolley.

for my attention to give a quality assessment of the different purposes. So I will sweep this massive subject aside in a huge atheistic gesture. Essentially, the purpose for the religious person is not in the hands of the human believer, but in the hands of a god. And without explicit and indubitable revelation, then the purpose is unintelligible and subjective.

Because of the plethora of choices offered up by the myriad different religions, I do not want to focus primarily on Christianity simply because I was born (through a natural lottery) into the geographical area in which Christianity was prevalent. Instead, I will assume a position of atheism with life's purpose not emanating directly from any god. This is similar to the existentialist approach of thinkers such as Sartre, who believed that meaning is not given but is achieved through the actions and interactions of people. For example, the case of the spade assumes that the spade is given a purpose by the creator (the gardener/designer/manufacturer). But without an overarching creator for the universe, we are devoid of the purposer. As such, we have two "choices":

(1) There is no objective purpose, and so we have to create subjective purposes ourselves; or

(2) Objective purposes can exist naturally to which we are not obliged to adhere, and thus create subjective purposes anyway.

Let us look at whether objective purposes can exist naturally. Essentially, the short answer, given the opening chapter to this book and given that both meaning and purpose are abstract ideas, is "no". But let us still look into this problem.

As far as I can see, the only way that we can naturally derive an objective purpose or meaning to life would be if it depended upon unarguable objective foundations upon which the purpose can be built. And the only framework that seems to be fit for purpose would be logic. Logic, and the rationality that derives from it, has an "objectivity" to it. This is why it is in some manner universally accepted in the discipline of philosophy.[1]

Logic even applies if we return to considering a god (who is omnipotent); defying logic is outside of even his[2] bounds. For example, he cannot make a rock that is too heavy for him to lift, or a square circle. These examples are seen as logical and semantic paradoxes and propositions that do not apply to God's omnipotence. Such propositions defy the objective nature of logic (though many theists would argue that this is still contingent upon, or a necessary reflection of, their god in such a framework).

---

[1] There are many different logical systems and much argument to be made of logic and its ontology. I am simplifying here.

[2] Assuming, of course, that god is a 'he'.

Rather like discussions concerning morality, does logic exist separate from God, so that God is somehow bound by it, or is it a reflection of God's very nature, or some such ruse?

Could it be, then, that if we could rationally develop (based on sound logical premises) an argument that defined a purpose to (human) life that was universally accepted, we could have an objective purpose? I have seen similar arguments be used to arrive at theories of objective morality, such as by Francois Tremblay.[1] He states that a unit of ethics (such as a unit of energy might be a Joule) is value. Therefore:

> By evaluating what values are being effected by a given action in its context, we can express a sound moral judgment on that action (this was a good thing to do, this was a bad thing to do). This is true regardless of your actual moral system – we all have values, implicitly or explicitly. The real argument is about those scientific and social facts and what values they entail.[2]

In order to establish his theory, Tremblay attempts to marginally redefine objectivity to be "based on reality" (rather than having an ontic foundational existence in and of itself). This is arguably similar to Sam Harris's approach in his book *The Moral Landscape*.[3] Determining an objective purpose is not a case of evaluating a single action against a scale of good to bad using logic and rationality. Life is wholly more complicated and multifaceted; there is a phenomenally rich complexity to human life (let alone any other life form). To find a *single, all-encompassing* purpose does not lend itself easily to natural objectivity. More importantly, if there is one, then it is effectively unintelligible, since (as mentioned before) it is a subjective process of interpreting and arguing what that may be.

To conclude this section, abstract ideas are conceptual and dependent upon the conceiver. Thus, assuming no god exists, objective purposes do not exist. And if a god does exist, then we cannot know the thing-in-itself – the purpose – anyway, and so the whole enterprise becomes subjective.

Other than that, we all know the answer is 42.

---

[1] Tremblay (2005).
[2] Ibid.
[3] Harris (2012).

Purpose Is Unintelligible

Woolf implies that an objective purpose, if it exists, is unintelligible to us. And I have argued in this essay that (divinely derived) objective purposes are either philosophically incoherent or subjective to the creator. Let me set out the logical arguments for all of the options.

Although Woolf is not emphatically concerned with whether God exists or not, it is a useful place to start in order to tease out exactly what the ramifications of his arguments are. Talking about the purpose of life requires at least a cursory walk through the landscape of theism with regard to its impact upon the nature of purpose. Here are three simplified arguments that set out to show that all purposes for humanity are subjective.

Syllogism A
If there is no god, or if there is a god but he has no purpose for us:
1) There is no god (or godly purpose).
2) There is no objective purpose.
C) Therefore, humans make up their own subjective purpose.

Syllogism B
If there is a god and an objective purpose exists:
1) God has an objective purpose for humanity.
2) Humans do not know this purpose.
3) God's "objective" purpose is unclear (since it is not, for some reason, adequately communicated).
C) Therefore, humans make up their own subjective purpose, or interpret the divine purpose subjectively.

Syllogism C
If there is a god and the purpose for humanity is subjective to that god:
1) God has a purpose for humanity.
2) This purpose is subjective to that god.
3) Humans either do not know this or can reject the purpose.
C) Therefore, humans make up their own subjective purpose.

With regard to Syllogism B, an agent may hit the jackpot and align their purpose with that intended by the god. However, it seems that the agent wouldn't or couldn't *know* that they had done this.

These logical arguments together conclude that whether or not a god exists, and whether or not an objective purpose does actually exist, purpose for humans is effectively subjective. It is because of this subjectivity that objective purpose is in effect "unintelligible". Purposes are not explicit (objectively) and therefore are up to us to define. People have been arguing over them for thousands of years, and philosophers have written innumerable essays trying to decipher a conclusive answer as to what universal purposes humanity should adopt. This leads me to believe that they are either non-existent or unintelligible. In this, therefore, Woolf and I are in agreement.

Happiness as a Goal

Woolf's quote never states that the purpose of humanity is to learn to achieve happiness. But there is certainly an implicit acknowledgement that this is (at least one of) our purpose(s). Happiness is an end – a goal. Woolf seems to believe that happiness and service to society are long-term goals (purposes) that can be achieved by learning, experience and the accumulation of skill. Now let us look at whether one of those, happiness, is a worthy purpose, and if it can be achieved by learning.

If we accepting that humanity's purpose is subjective in nature, does happiness offer itself as one of the most promising purposes to a human? On an obvious note, if this is our one and only life, then it would be pretty senseless and masochistic if we were not trying to make it as enjoyable as possible.

But a religious person might point out the potential for reward in the afterlife as a purpose for this life. This warrants a mention again. We will call upon Ockham's Razor[1] here. The theory of an afterlife assumes a lot of extra phenomena that have not been adequately evidenced. It requires another dimension, usually a god, and a soul or immortal vessel carrying the self onwards and upwards, so to speak. Without evidence for these things,[2] then

---

[1] The idea that postulates that the simplest theory (the one with the least unnecessary entities) is more often the correct one. In other words, if there are competing hypotheses to explain something, and assuming they all satisfactorily explain the phenomenon, then the one with the least extra assumptions should be deemed the most likely.

[2] As I have set out in Pearce (2010), p.54-58, and earlier in this collection, there are many good arguments against the existence of the soul. For such a belief, evidence is very important, and there simply is none for the soul, unless it is conflated with

the theory that there is no afterlife offers a simpler and more effective explanation for what happens after our death. Given the assumption (along with Woolf) that we have no afterlife, it seems fairly self-evident that we need to make the most of the life that we have.

Is it easy to promote happiness as our raison d'être? Epicurus[1] certainly felt that happiness was the prime goal of life. This is philosophically known as *hedonism*. Epicurus realised that we apparently returned to atoms at death, and that there was no afterlife. So this seemed eminently sensible. Aristotle[2] made the point that happiness is the only thing that humans strive for, for its intrinsic value. For example, we might want to be healthy, but this is only relevant in the context that it leads to happiness. Aristotle's term for happiness, *eudaimonia*, was defined in light of activity as opposed to an emotional state per se (the "pleasure" definition of happiness used by Epicurus). But it certainly holds true (for me at least) that most of what we do leads towards the intended end goal of happiness. Playing sport at the weekend, working (for the wage and what the wage can bring), buying clothes, going to the cinema are all activities undertaken to promote happiness.

It gets controversial when we think about charitable actions, and whether we do them to make ourselves feel better (psychologically and subconsciously) or whether we are being truly altruistic (but even this is often seen in terms of improving the happiness of others). Aristotle overlaid his own theories of happiness with virtuous ethics, which is a step away from the last point. He had Platonic ideals that actions could be abstractly and objectively good. As I have previously pointed out in this book, this sort of realism does not sit coherently for me. I prefer a conceptualist, or even nominalist approach. That means I do not believe that abstracts or universals (such as strength, redness, this table here, or Barack Obama) exist as objective entities in abstract form. Plato suggested that there was another dimension where abstract ideas existed (in a sort of spatial sense). This notion seems problematic,[3] because it certainly appears that ideas only exist subjectively in the mind of the beholder.

---

consciousness. The eternal existence of either begs many questions, and seems, as I argue, exceptionally improbable.

[1] Living at around the end of the fourth century BCE, Epicurus was well known for the paradox that is now expressed as the Problem of Evil.

[2] In his landmark *Nicomachean Ethics*, see Arostotle (trans. Crisp 2000).

[3] Though I explain the incoherence in the next sentence, it is worth also exemplifying that by my mind inventing the object or abstract 'ftyangyang', realists arguably have to assert that the 'ftyangyang' would pop into metaphysical existence in some domain somewhere. This would be the case for every idea that any human (or non-human)

For example, if you or I saw the same table, we would have marginally different ideas about what the abstract idea of that table would be. Furthermore, we could argue about the idea of a table itself, and hopefully ultimately reach some kind of mutual agreement over the properties. However, I might argue that a sawn tree stump that I use for my picnic is a table, whereas you might disagree entirely. Thus, even seemingly obvious abstract ideas are open to subjective gainsaying. In this way, I dispute that actions can be objectively virtuous (in the sense of Aristotle's idea of happiness). And even morality is just another example of an abstract idea that exists conceptually in our collective minds.

Utilitarianism

Utilitarians such as John Stuart Mill decreed that people should behave in a way that brings the maximum amount of happiness to the maximum number of people.[1] It becomes much more difficult, though, to define objectively (or by accurate consensus) exactly what such behaviour should be. We might take a course of action thinking it is for the benefit of many, but end up causing less happiness. For example, we could instinctively save a person from being run over by a trolley, only to find out the person later became a mass murderer. Furthermore, choosing between the pain caused to an individual versus the resulting happiness to a larger majority is inherently problematic. I could poison the water system in the world's most overcrowded city of Manila, killing off a third of its inhabitants. One could argue it to be of huge benefit to the surviving population that would allow them far more resources and a greater standard of life. My actions would hardly be considered "good" in any ordinary sense, but this is what can be argued when proposing certain forms of moral consequentialism.

There are many similar issues with utilitarian or consequentialist ethics, and, as a result, many philosophers have refined and adapted the idea so that it is fit for purpose in a more universal manner. This has led to a plethora of different consequentialist ethical value systems.[2]

Having said this, utilitarianism is seemingly the common-sense moral approach adopted by most people, whether they know it or not. Some

---

might ever had. Thus, though the represented matter exists empirically, such abstract labels, or any abstract idea, only exist in the mind of the communicator.
[1] He developed the work of predecessors such as Jeremy Bentham.
[2] There are several developed versions of consequentialism such as act, rule, aggregate and preference consequentialism, to name but a few.

research has suggested that some 89% of people would pull the lever in the aforementioned trolley experiment.[1]

However, let us focus on happiness at an individual level. We know much about how happiness manifests itself.[2] And we know that our happiness depends in no small measure upon our daily actions (further research shows that social networks, for example, are one of the foremost contributors to happiness), goal-setting and achieving those goals. Thus, long-term goals and aims, and working to achieve them, can bring a sense of purpose and can contribute to achieving consistent biological happiness.

In Pursuit of Knowledge

So how does learning fit into this goal of happiness? Interestingly, it is not explicitly seen as one of the primary contributors to happiness, such as are notions of social interaction, employment, health, optimism, and so forth. That is not to say, though, that learning and education cannot be important variables in achieving these ends, which in turn achieve happiness. Woolf sees knowledge, experience and skill as part of a matrix of things important in life, though not necessarily the main goal. To support the importance of such intentions, Aristotle is quoted as saying of a predecessor:

> They say that Anaxagoras, when someone raised just these puzzles and asked him what it was for which a person would choose to be born rather than not,

---

[1] However, research has also found that the percentage switches when people have to push "a fat man" off the bridge rather than merely pull a lever, showing the psychological influence on our supposedly rational decision-making. See Khazan (2014).

[2] Such as in neurobiological terms, about the effects of hormone levels and so on. This more instantaneous gratification is a very important aspect to happiness, but it is not everything, or at least needs to be sustained on a lower level with consistency if "happiness" is to be holistically achieved. We have an idea through various research that happiness is about 50% genetically dependent (Lyubomirsky et al (2005)), about 10-15% (Blanchflower and Oswald (2004)) determined by variables concerned with life circumstances (health, socioeconomic status, sex etc.) and the remaining 40% or so dependent on an unknown set of variables and the actions an individual may do to purposefully engage in becoming happier.

answered that it would be "in order to apprehend the heavens and the order in the whole universe."[1]

Humans have a predisposition towards searching for knowledge. It seems that we search out answers and seek knowledge about anything and everything.[2] Personally, it has been my primary pursuit for the last goodness knows how many years of my life! Knowledge does have practical applications, obviously, and is useful both for ourselves to acquire and for our children. Consequently, education is seen as hugely important in society. However, it does not follow that it is valuable in and of itself. The advantages and consequences to knowledge acquisition are obvious. But does it have intrinsic value and does it makes us "better" than a mere dog with no hope of such knowledge? Yet, to confuse matters, a dog may possess all sorts of different forms of knowledge that we may have no hope of ever gaining.

Knowledge is incredibly valuable for the ends it produces. Without *any* knowledge[3] we would not be able to achieve anything, living in gross ignorance (or even not being able to survive). Thus, knowledge is a crucial *consequentialist* ideal. It is a key necessary ingredient in being able to achieve anything, whether as an individual, or as a collective society.

What seems to follow from here, though, is that knowledge (and related skills) is not valuable intrinsically, but has great value in being able to facilitate almost everything else. Remember our talk of non-derivative value currency? Well, knowledge can be derived back to further values: Why do I want knowledge? Because it gives me X or Y. I cannot achieve the happiness of a secure job, of being married, of reading a good book, or playing sport, without any knowledge of how to do these things. And related to the ideas of goal-setting, goal-achieving, and goal-resetting as discussed earlier, it is natural that when we achieve a certain level of knowledge we have the urge to push ourselves to setting a goal of achieving the next level of knowledge.

So knowledge and skills (that are learnt) are almost elementary particles in the physics of achievement. It is fundamental, then, to decide how to employ such knowledge. Knowledge cannot be an end in itself, since it does not appear to be the last link in the chain. There is no intrinsic value in knowledge. As the old adage goes, knowledge is power. It is what you do with knowledge – the end – that matters. Knowledge is a means to that end,

---

[1] As in Hanfling (1987), p.139 who quotes Aristotle (1982 edn).
[2] The success of the internet, and of sites such as Wikipedia, are evidence of this.
[3] And I mean no knowledge whatsoever, such that mere survival would be almost impossible. If I was living as a hunter gatherer and did not know how to hunt or gather, then I would be unable even to fill the basic physiological needs of Maslow's Hierarchy, let alone approach ideas of self-actualisation.

whatever end that may be. Again, it is difficult to get away from happiness (pleasure, pain avoidance) as being a non-derivative currency here. Does knowledge merely and inexorably derive back to happiness (or lack of pain)? Is happiness that golden goal?

Now, we have arrived back at setting ourselves an overarching goal, a purpose to life. But our goal or purpose cannot be to gain knowledge for knowledge's sake – that arguably has no value in and of itself. It has to be done for a further goal (e.g., the gratification of being the most intelligent mind in the physics faculty – but then why would you want that status?). No, what we do is set ourselves goals that may well necessitate the gaining of knowledge.[1]

There is something to be said for setting goals. Happiness comes, in many cases, not from reaching some objective, from achieving some goal, but from the *journey* and the sense that one has some *purpose*, some destination. This is why, when we achieve a goal, we almost always immediately set another one. We need that sense of being on a journey to *somewhere*. The challenge for humans and for humanity is to work out where that destination might be in order to embark on that journey.

Perhaps, in this way, we don't have a single, overarching goal, but many. Perhaps our purpose is to *have a purpose*, or to have goals! Meaning and intentionality (the ability of minds to be *about* something, to deal in representation) might be our purpose in a sense that this is what separates us from most of the rest of the animal kingdom.

However, I still do not think we can have an objective, universal purpose without a purposer (i.e., a god), so I think that humanity and humans do *not* have a purpose, but that we *do* find meaning to life. This is the purpose of our next section.[2]

Ultimate Meaning

Humans do not, however, have ultimate meaning. There is no meaning that transcends our existences. If all humans died, then there would be no meaning to our previous lives still existing in some realm, at least to us (other

---

[1] Unfortunately, there is the chicken and egg paradox here. We need to gain sufficient knowledge in order to work out the machinations of the world and ourselves, in order to work out what goals we should strive for, which will necessitate the gaining of knowledge[1] to achieve. What comes first, the goal setting for knowledge, or the knowledge to set goals?

[2] Do you see what I did there?

sentient creatures may derive meaning from humanity's existence…or extinction). Meaning, in terms of the conceptualism we have been talking about in this book, is in the mind of the conceiver. And this, is very much an individual affair. We might dress up our meaning with talk of larger, humanity-wide goals and ideas, but this is essentially a subjective, individual thing. We might sign up, collectively, to ideas and meanings that align with other people, or align with (or derive from) collective, organisation ideals. But these meaningful ideas are still individualistic at heart.

This may be hard news for certain people who feel like they need meaning to be more transcendental, more objective, more ultimate and absolute than that. But we must not commit the fallacy of wishful thinking.

We are living short lives on a pale blue dot in a galaxy far, far away. We will not only soon meet our own deaths but (at some point) the universe will experience a heat death (or similar). And our lives will eventually come to nought…no matter what.

We live on in those around us, in society, for as long as we are remembered in some way – through our legacy. But that memory, that legacy (on a naturalistic worldview), is not transcendent or eternal.

This is also why I have expressed the problems involved with the afterlife and the soul. The soul (if it existed) would be the vehicle for transcendence for humans, but in the absence of this, we are left with our Earthly lives.

Therefore, we need to (or simply just do) make our own meaning whilst we are here, but we should also understand that there is nothing ultimate about it.

Woolf's point – that it all seems tremendously wasteful and thus largely futile that we spend our lives acquiring these skills only to die and be annihilated – is powerful. I concur with the realisation that spending your entire life learning and acquiring skills only to die and not be able to use them is seemingly futile. But that is only true if futility is derived from eternal transcendence. However, the process of living and learning, loving and giving, is something that can be thoroughly enjoyable, even addictive. It is a purpose in and of itself, arguably. (Conversely, though, it is often posited that the more knowledge you have, the more prone you are to depression, though this is often not a causal relationship, but a correlation.[1] Ignorance is bliss, they say.)

---

[1] As King Solomon said, "For in much wisdom is much grief; and he that increases knowledge increases sorrow" (Ecclesiastes 1:18). Woolf himself suffered from depression, as if to prove this point, and elements of such can be gleaned from nuances in the initial quote.

To focus on knowledge, Woolf claims that the gaining of knowledge is wasteful. But it is difficult to know whether these views should be taken at face value or be seen to have an air of irony.[1] Perhaps it is that people do not use their knowledge beneficently before they die, and, therefore, do not achieve happiness before they die. As I have said, there is happiness to be gained in the *pursuit* of knowledge, of the goal-setting, achieving, and further goal-setting, and often involving knowledge acquisition. Look at how different society is today to society 100,000, 10,000, 5,000 and 500 years ago. To imply that there has been no service to mankind and no gaining of happiness is obviously untrue. Humans all over the world exist (not consistently admittedly) in moments of great pleasure and happiness. We might, however, ask whether humans are happier now (using some comparable metric) than we were 10,000 years ago, and how any differences might be explained. But with knowledge comes security, health and general wellbeing. And there is little doubt that, on average, these are in greater abundance now than they were in times long past.

There is regret that we don't live for longer than we do – we would all like to live longer (but not too long for fear of philosophical boredom). Our knowledge could be put to a more sustained good use, and the longer we lived, the more knowledge we could gain, and the greater amount of good we could do. This is the basis of Woolf's regret, but we can still recognise the service to mankind and happiness that is achieved, even if it has no eternal longevity.

Having argued that meaning is individual and conceptual, there is also some use in looking at universalising meaning, purpose and goal-setting. Once we have a goal in mind, we can go about sorting out how best to get there.

Let us look at the idea that our individual knowledge and goals might not be wasted in view of the larger picture of humanity (even if they are "ultimately wasted" when we die). If we could argue that there is value for the individual in safeguarding the human species and even the world, so that an individual's actions in their one finite life can have a lasting beneficial effect for the whole species, then the playing field could look very different. The key here is that we would need to come to consensus as to a mission statement for humanity. This would then cohere with the acquisition of knowledge and skills, since we would have a framework to build our knowledge up in order to achieve the ends set out in the mission statement, with happiness/wellbeing ensuing from the pursuit, and the achievement, of goals. This mission statement would be beyond the scope of our immediate

---

[1] Surely, he cannot think that our knowledge is "bundled into the grave" at our death?

and individual lives, but would benefit humanity as a whole and would lessen the wastefulness of our individual learning. It also depends upon whether it is possible to argue that there is objective value, or at least universal subjective value, in setting goals for the whole of humanity that go beyond the scope and duration of a human life.

"Why bother?" about leaving a legacy, or about trying to improve the lot for humans, or the world. We could look from an evolutionary perspective and see things in terms of genes. It is baked into our very biological existence that behaviours and traits are in place for the benefit of continuing our genetic lineage. Our purpose (of sorts) is to survive and pass on those genes to the next generation…and so on.

None of this seems fulfilling enough, or of high enough philosophical value (for want of a better term). Although I am cognisant of my life being very finite, and the existence of life in the universe being finite (short of some pretty staggering future technology or some kind of far-fetched sci-fi scenario), I also feel that my life has more meaning if I can envisage a kind of legacy that exists after my life is over. Is this a self-indulgent egocentrism, in that I want to be remembered, that I want to feel like I have made an impact?

Perhaps.

But feeling like my life has some positive impact that stretches out beyond its mortal coil is something that has intuitive attractiveness.

What Do You Want the World to Look Like?

What we would need to do is to set out the goal of what we want the world to look like. Unfortunately, people do not seem to be interested in properly setting out this goal in any kind of explicit manner. We spend a phenomenal amount of time arguing over politics – which is *how you get to the destination* – and yet no time arguing about *what the destination actually is*. If we are to give meaning to our collective lives, as humanity on a journey to some worthy destination, then knowing that destination is very important (even if, from a happiness point of view, it helps just to be on a journey, as we discussed above).

The scope of this essay does address the topic of what I would want the world to look like. That is enough to fill a book in its own right and would take into account populations, cultures, the environment, sustainability, education, kindness, crime and all sorts of different areas. It is self-evident that there is value in happiness (it makes us happy!) and it is an emotion that can be seen as an end in itself. Therefore, whatever objective we set for ourselves, it should involve happiness or wellbeing (there is no point living our one and only life in perpetual sadness if it can be avoided). We acknowledge that our wellbeing could be linked to the wellbeing of the planet, or other living organisms that share our living space. Again, this is a discussion to be had elsewhere.

Returning to the universal mission statement, let us look to see what objectives get somewhat close to a decent, universal ideal. The United Nations (UN),[1] with its humanity-wide global perspective, looks to create a set of objectives[2] for achieving the maximum amount of happiness for humanity (through equality, the minimising of suffering and so on). Their charters serve as mission statements and mechanisms towards these ends.

Philosophically speaking, the UN arguably provides a tangible embodiment of the utilitarian ethics of John Stuart Mill. The gaining of knowledge and skills that feed into the achievement of these universal goals will eventually feed back into the happiness of the individual. The individual in a safe and secure society is arguably happier, on average, than an individual in an anarchistic, warring society. Therefore, if you were a betting person, you might wager that the happiness of the individual would be inexorably linked to the happiness of the whole species, which would more likely be in a peaceful society.

In this way, we can argue that the goal of the individual should be aligned to the goal of the whole society as defined by organisations such as the UN. This idea runs contrary to Woolf's claim of wasted knowledge as we move collectively towards what many will agree to be a better world (socially, in terms of health, welfare and justice) than the world of 500 years ago.

Consequently, it can be argued that we should individually set our goals to obtaining the knowledge and skills to achieve the objectives of (say) the UN in order to achieve the maximal happiness for humanity as this would ensure the most average happiness for an individual.[3]

By applying this worldview, our experience, skills and knowledge are not wasted and can be utilised towards achieving a happier world. And happiness is an emotion that has intrinsic value – an end in itself.

I say we "should" do this in the full knowledge of the prediction that life in the universe will eventually come to an end, and with it will end all the accrued benefits of the goals we and happiness achieved.

---

[1] Which can broadly be seen as a "service to mankind"!

[2] See Appendix 1 for the objectives of the UN.

[3] And yet I used the term "can be argued", because to do this, it is essential to argue that a universal subjective goal for the society is also good for the individual, even though the benefits of said goals would most likely be arrived at after the individual dies.

Carpe diem, and all that.

APPENDIX 1

Below are the objectives for the United Nations, taken from https://www.un.org/en/about-us/un-charter/full-text (retrieved on 01/02/2021).

CHAPTER I: PURPOSES AND PRINCIPLES

Article 1

The Purposes of the United Nations are:
1. To maintain international peace and security, and to that end: to take effective collective measures for the prevention and removal of threats to the peace, and for the suppression of acts of aggression or other breaches of the peace, and to bring about by peaceful means, and in conformity with the principles of justice and international law, adjustment or settlement of international disputes or situations which might lead to a breach of the peace;
2. To develop friendly relations among nations based on respect for the principle of equal rights and self-determination of peoples, and to take other appropriate measures to strengthen universal peace;
3. To achieve international co-operation in solving international problems of an economic, social, cultural, or humanitarian character, and in promoting and encouraging respect for human rights and for fundamental freedoms for all without distinction as to race, sex, language, or religion; and
4. To be a centre for harmonizing the actions of nations in the attainment of these common ends.

Article 2

The Organization and its Members, in pursuit of the Purposes stated in Article 1, shall act in accordance with the following Principles.

1. The Organization is based on the principle of the sovereign equality of all its Members.
2. All Members, in order to ensure to all of them the rights and benefits resulting from membership, shall fulfill in good faith the obligations assumed by them in accordance with the present Charter.
3. All Members shall settle their international disputes by peaceful means in such a manner that international peace and security, and justice, are not endangered.

Jonathan MS Pearce

4. All Members shall refrain in their international relations from the threat or use of force against the territorial integrity or political independence of any state, or in any other manner inconsistent with the Purposes of the United Nations.
5. All Members shall give the United Nations every assistance in any action it takes in accordance with the present Charter, and shall refrain from giving assistance to any state against which the United Nations is taking preventive or enforcement action.
6. The Organization shall ensure that states which are not Members of the United Nations act in accordance with these Principles so far as may be necessary for the maintenance of international peace and security.
7. Nothing contained in the present Charter shall authorize the United Nations to intervene in matters which are essentially within the domestic jurisdiction of any state or shall require the Members to submit such matters to settlement under the present Charter; but this principle shall not prejudice the application of enforcement measures under Chapter VII

MORALITY

Moral theories are large and complex things; definitions are not. The question of the definition of morality is the question of identifying the target of moral theorizing. Identifying this target enables us to see different moral theories as attempting to capture the very same thing. And it enables psychologists, anthropologists, evolutionary biologists, and other more empirically-oriented theorists to design their experiments or formulate their hypotheses without prejudicing matters too much in terms of the specific content a code, judgment, or norm must have in order to count as distinctively moral.

There does not seem to be much reason to think that a single definition of morality will be applicable to all moral discussions. One reason for this is that "morality" seems to be used in two distinct broad senses: a descriptive sense and a normative sense. More particularly, the term "morality" can be used either descriptively to refer to certain codes of conduct put forward by a society or a group (such as a religion), or accepted by an individual for her own behavior, or normatively to refer to a code of conduct that, given specified conditions, would be put forward by all rational people.

Which of these two senses of "morality" a moral philosopher is using plays a crucial, although sometimes unacknowledged, role in the development of an ethical theory. If one uses "morality" in its descriptive sense, and therefore uses it to refer to codes of conduct actually put forward by distinct groups or societies, one will almost certainly deny that there is a universal morality that applies to all human beings. The descriptive use of "morality" is the one used by anthropologists when they report on the morality of the societies that they study....

In the normative sense, "morality" refers to a code of conduct that would be accepted by anyone who meets certain intellectual and volitional conditions, almost always including the condition of being rational. That a person meets these conditions is typically expressed by saying that the person counts as a moral agent. However, merely showing that a certain code would be accepted by any moral agent is not enough to show that the code is the moral code. It might well be that all moral agents would also accept a code of prudence or rationality, but this would not by itself show that prudence was part of morality. So something else must be added; for example, that the code can be understood to involve a certain kind of impartiality, or that it can be understood as having the function of making it possible for people to live together in groups.

Bernard Gert, "The Definition of Morality", *The Stanford Encyclopedia of Philosophy*

Checking in: Where Have We Got to?

Let us take a little breather here to see where we have got to in this meandering wander through ~~philosophy~~ my mind. I started off by looking at definitions of atheism and of Christianity in order to clarify what I meant by some pretty important terms. After this, I looked at abstract ideas and what they are, in an ontological sense. This is because I wanted to build my worldview from the bottom up. In discussing those terms "atheism" and "Christianity" at the beginning, we could see that (by comparison) "atheism" was considerably easier to pin down than "Christianity". "Christianity", as a collection of properties and ideas, is a lot more nebulous.

This introduced the idea of conceptualism, a form of nominalism that sees abstract ideas as existing as concepts in the minds of human conceivers. This then provides a lens through which to see the everything else (in the universe and/or in this book).

With this in mind, we looked at epistemology: knowledge and truth. We finished this section with using the epistemology to conclude that Christianity is most probably false.

After this, and with using the same lens, we argued that there is no overarching purpose to life, and any meaning we garner is subjectively derived. But to provide a positive spin, we mentioned a few ideas to play with so you can start trying to work out any goals or meaning to life you might see as fit for your purpose.

And now, finally, we come to the section on morality. In this section I want to introduce the idea of morality being goal oriented (fitting in with the previous piece on the meaning of life and the need for goals). This will help demonstrate that, despite what Christians think, their own moral value system is very secular indeed.

We will conclude matters after that last section.

A Short Foray in to the World of Oughts

Let me lay out the idea of *oughts* mentioned in the last essay in somewhat more philosophical terms, and we might also see how it is connected to teleology (do we have a purpose?) as previously discussed.

I need to set out some basics here first. What is morality? Generally, the study of morality is split into three components: *descriptive morality*, *meta-ethics* and *normative morality*. Normally philosophers interchange the term "morality" and "ethics". We will do likewise. Descriptive ethics is concerned with what people empirically believe, morally speaking. Normative ethics (which can be called *prescriptive ethics*) investigates questions of what people *should* believe about morality. Meta-ethics is more philosophical still in attempting to define what moral theories and ethical terms actually refer to. Or:

- What do different cultures actually think is right? (descriptive)
- How should people act, morally speaking? (normative)
- What do *right* and *ought* actually mean? (meta-ethics)

Morality, as the term will be used here, will generally be understood as: "normatively to refer to a code of conduct that, given specified conditions, would be put forward by all rational persons."[1]

So, what is an *ought* and why should we care? Well, oughts should be seen in their larger context. In normal situations, we use language in a way that we take linguistic shortcuts. For example, if I say "I ought to change the oil in my car engine" then most people understand what I mean by implication and inference. This is actually an *apodosis*, the part of a conditional sentence that usually starts with *then*. The problem is, we are missing the *protasis*, which is the first part of the conditional sentence that usually starts with an *if*. This is because we are clever enough to make the correct inference and work out what the speaker means.

However, if we were being specific and accurate, we would include the protasis. In this case, the protasis would be "*If* I want my car engine to work well, *then* I ought to change the oil in my car engine." Without the protasis, the sentence "I ought to change the oil in my car engine" is literally

---

[1] Gert (2002).

meaningless. This is because you can place anything as the protasis and completely change the overall meaning of the sentence or, indeed, render the apodosis incorrect. In this case, if I said "If, as a scientist, I am testing how well engines work without oil in them" then adding the apodosis, "then I ought to change the oil in the car engine" might not make sense, and the whole sentence is problematic.

Thus, the point to make here is that, although we often eliminate it for general conversations, if we are to be precise, then we should always include the protasis in a conditional statement.[1]

Religionists claim that atheists are not able to ground moral oughts in a sentence. But I argue that oughts are goal-oriented and the goal is contained in a viable protasis. Let's now turn the tables and see how this works with the theist. The theist states, "You ought to be good." The theist then claims that they have more philosophical right to say this than the atheist. But if I were to ask "Why?" to the theist, then we start to see how problems can arise. Remember our talk about grounding claims and deriving value. The theist is in danger, without a viable protasis, of merely asserting oughts in a vacuum – you must be good…in order to be good. This is circular or tautologous and tells us nothing. It is the same as "You ought to change the oil in the engine in order to change the oil in the engine." So, as it stands, the theist has no coherent grounding for their own moral obligations.

How else can the theist ground their claim? On further inspection, there are two other choices:

a) In order to get into heaven and avoid hell.

b) Because God told you so.

The first one looks rather consequentialist in nature and is very self-serving, though I suspect this is the reasoning that underpins a lot of religious thinking. On the other hand, *because God told you so* faces all the many problems that Divine Command Theories face. Essentially, the only reason to do what God says is to be good, without any recourse to moral reasoning. This means that morality is at best arbitrary, a-rational, and is simply the behaviour, essence or nature of God (as claimed).[2]

When we ask the *why* question to the atheist, the answer continually derives down until we reach an axiom or self-evident truth. This, in many moral value systems, ends up being happiness or pleasure (or lack of pain). These are self-evidently good: pleasure/happiness is self-evidently positive

---

[1] I received much joy from re-reading this sentence to find a protasis and an apodosis being used to explain protases and apodoses! I need to get out more.
[2] See Pearce (2016b) for sixteen arguments against divine command theory, summarised in the last essay in this book.

(with certain caveats). An axiom is a preferable starting point, especially if it is a properly self-evident truth, than a circular argument or an infinite regress.[1]

If the atheist uses a consequentialist moral value system (and this is not the only option for the atheist), then they might want to establish the greatest amount of pleasure for the greatest number of people. The idea is that they are really and truly trying to make the world a better place. That's a pretty noble objective. This can hardly be said of the Christian, who appears to be trying to make *their* world a better place, but not *the* world as a whole. This means that atheists arguably have a better and nobler ground for moral oughts. If I want the world to be a better place, then I should be kind in this particular way.

What, then, is the viable protasis for the Christian? What is the *if* statement? Here are some options:

- If I want to go to heaven/avoid hell, …
- If I want to please God/be in union with God, …
- If I want to be good, …
- If I want to make the world a better place, …

The first three are either self-serving or tautologous. The fourth is at most equivalent to the atheist. However, if you are merely following what you think are God's rules, then you are making the world a better place devoid of moral reasoning. Otherwise, the reasoning is what underpins the moral action as it does for the atheist. But if the Christian is merely putting blind faith in the idea that by merely following God's orders, he will make the world a better place, then he does not have to make a rough calculation that it *actually* will. Obedience to God appears to be the only moral reasoning, here. Doing what God asks, irrespective of what it is, is good, and we should be good. This seems to be devoid of meaningful moral content.

Moral oughts are goal-oriented and require viable protases. It is not good enough for the theist to simply assert that atheists have no grounds for moral oughts. There are all sorts of oughts in every society on Earth, and many have little or nothing to do with religious diktats. The UN Charter of Human Rights does a damned sight better job than the Bible at grounding moral oughts. Laws are passed by humans using moral and political reasoning all of the time without recourse to a divine lawgiver, and often, in different countries, with recourse to the *wrong* divine lawgiver!

---

[1] These three ways of grounding are known as the Münchhausen Trilemma, already laid out earlier in the book.

The Christian might ask something like this: On the brute fact of naturalism why *ought* anyone do anything if in the end it all ends up the same? But don't let some kind of fallacy of wishful thinking get in the way of accuracy. This is the power of the promissory note of heaven or the threat of hell: it can add force to moral diktats. This, though, is still a case of using ultimate transcendence to infiltrate a moral proclamation. "You should do X" is really "If you want to get into heaven and avoid hell, then you should do X."

We must first establish the protasis. On what basis the *if* statements are grounded is the job of the moral value system.

And, as we know from over three thousand years of moral philosophy, there is no decent moral value system that universally works. Every moral value system has its shortcomings. In this way, and taking into account the main opening chapter on conceptualism, I am a moral skeptic. Morality does not exist objectively, "out there" in the aether. It does exist "in here", in our minds. And it is our job to collectively agree, by consensus, what it is and where it will take us. I will lay this out a little more in the final essay in this collection.

For now, and to simplify, I would suggest using the moral value system that makes the world the most pleasant place to live for us and our children, and for the natural world around that supports us.

You may argue that this is eventually self-serving; perhaps it is. But not more than the theist. And that's *the best case argument* for the theist. The theist may get to match the atheist in the domain of moral oughts, but they cannot beat us.

God is a consequentialist.

Morality is one of the cornerstones of any philosophy. This is because almost every action one can conceive of has a moral dimension. When we eat, is what we eat morally or ethically sourced? When we buy a car, are we making a morally good decision or could we make a better choice in our method of transport, or model of car? Is our money better spent on a charity organisation or donated directly to the end-user? Should I fly to a poorer country on the other side of the world for my holiday to help boost their tourist industry but contribute to climate change? Every person in the world faces these and infinite other choices every moment of every day. Thus, any and every religion that purports to have a prescriptive or descriptive interest in the actions of its adherents is inherently entangled with notions of morality.

This crossover from religion to morality is something I aim to investigate in this essay. In particular, I look at claims of morality from proponents of Christianity, most notably philosophers such as William Lane Craig, who claim that God is the grounding entity of objective morality. I will also show that God is, through the evidence shown in his actions (permissive or direct) of recent times and from the Bible itself, a moral consequentialist. I will then contrast these actions with the Christian claim that God is the arbiter of objective morality, without whom objective morality could not exist. Christians use this line of thinking both as an argument for God or for objective morality, depending on which direction they need to go. Finally, I will conclude that God is either (a) not an adherent to objective morality, or (b) he values moral actions on their consequences over and above any intrinsic value they may or may not imbue. In effect, this conclusion will seek to undermine both the claims that God exists, and/or that he is the arbiter of objective morality.

Furthermore, this essay fits into the overall claims concerning morality within this section. So whilst I may not give an account of other moral positions here, this will come.

However, let us first look at defining terms within the discipline of moral philosophy, from morality itself through to objective morality and consequentialism.

With regard to the definition of key term itself, as *The Stanford Encyclopedia of Philosophy* claims, morality is one of two things[1]:

---

[1] Definition of Morality, *The Stanford Encyclopedia of Philosophy*, http://plato.stanford.edu/entries/morality-definition/ (retrieved 03/02/2021)

(1) descriptively to refer to certain codes of conduct put forward by a society or a group (such as a religion), or accepted by an individual for her own behavior, or

(2) normatively to refer to a code of conduct that, given specified conditions, would be put forward by all rational people.

Though there are two definitions here, I will be using the second definition, the one of normative morality, for two reasons. Firstly, normative ethics (and though there are some nuanced differences, I will use ethics and morality interchangeably here) means a code of ethics that, as British moral philosopher R.M. Hare claimed, is "universalisable".[1] This is crucial because it implies that the moral code can and should be understood by all rational persons. This is unlike moral relativism or moral nihilism (the beliefs that facts can differ from society to society or morality as a whole does not exist at all)[2].

I am assuming moral realism for this discussion – the belief that an action can be right or wrong, and that these constitute moral facts. This is necessary because I am seeking to tackle views of theists who themselves believe in moral facts. Thus, I am looking to meet the theists on their own grounds. In a sense, it is almost irrelevant as to whether this position is tenable or not. After all, as I have expounded upon earlier in this book, knowledge and abstract ideas – such things exist in our minds and not objectively in the aether. I am playing theists at their own game.

Secondly, I will use a normative definition of morality, as opposed to a descriptive one, because a normative definition attempts to rationally prescribe how one *should* act, which a descriptive definition cannot do. This again fits into the mode of arguing that theists themselves adopt – claiming that humans should act in a particular way, and this duty is grounded in God. Normatively speaking, actions can be moral or immoral, good or bad, because there is some kind of framework with which we can evaluate such actions. In simple terms, an action that is moral (as opposed to immoral) can be seen as good, and one that is immoral can be seen as bad. We should strive to do that which is good. As mentioned, there is much that can be said about this, but for the sake of this essay, I shall leave it at that.

---

[1] Hare (1955).
[2] This is oversimplifying matters, necessarily, as I could also introduce ideas of moral and / or reasons internalism and externalism here. For further reading, I would advisw seeing Williams (1981) p. 101-13.

Next, let us look at objective morality, what is meant by the term, who argues for and adheres to it, and why.

The Moral Argument

William Lane Craig is a prominent American philosopher, theologian and Christian apologist, presently working as research professor at the Talbot School of Theology, Biola University, California. He has written many papers, journals, and books. But he is just as well known on the debate circuit, where he has a formidable reputation as a debater for the existence of God and has debated many prominent philosophers and academics of various disciplines. Heralded by many Christians as being a thinker who epitomises a faith defended by reason, evidence, and academia (one of his most famous books is called *A Reasonable Faith*), he often uses what he calls The Moral Argument to propose a proof for the existence of God. The argument is formulated as follows:[1]

> (1) If God does not exist, objective moral values and duties do not exist.

> (2) Objective moral values and duties do exist.

> (3) Therefore, God exists.

As we can see, this argument proves that God exists if we first allow for the truth of premises (1) and (2), that objective moral values rely on the existence of God for their own ontology.

Regarding premise (1), (especially naturalist) moral deontologists, who believe in objective moral oughts on their own merit (e.g., the Categorical Imperatives of Immanuel Kant), would object to this claim. They argue that such imperatives are absolute moral laws (like "you must not lie") and they exist, somehow, whether or not there is a god.

The second premise claims that objective moral values *do* exist. Let us investigate what this claim entails.

---

[1] Craig (2008) p. 172.

Objective Morality

As mentioned previously, "objective" can be a very slippery and difficult term since it can be applied in so many contexts. Objective, in this case, is defined by Craig himself:[1]

> To say that something is objective is to say that it is independent of what people think or perceive...
>
> ... To say that there are objective moral values is to say that something is good or evil independently of whether any human being believes it to be so. Similarly to say that we have objective moral duties is to say that certain actions are right or wrong for us independently of whether any human being believes them to be so.

Craig claims that this "objective morality" has its ontology existing as God; but Craig merely asserts that it comes from (finds its locus in) God. He claims that theism is the only pathway towards an objective morality without establishing a value code for said morality. There seems to be no explanation as to *how* we can value separate actions and compare them to each other. And yet there is an implicit understanding that acts can be more or less good/bad than other acts (actions carried out intentionally by people). For example, is raping a small child more morally reprehensible than stealing a loaf of bread, or not giving a beggar some money, or kicking the beggar? All of these actions, for one who adheres to objective morality, must surely have different moral worth, different moral value. Craig provides no method of comparing these acts, no formula with which to calculate moral worth or value of any given action. It is merely how much it reflects God – something that, for us, is somewhat unknowable. Unless there is explicit revelation on any given matter (where revelation is not providing moral *reasoning*, but producing an assertion of God's commands).

So, where is this objective morality? In *A Reasonable Faith*, Craig refers to the thinking of moral philosopher William Sorley to try to clarify matters:[2]

> Where, then, does objective moral value reside? Sorley answers: in persons. The only beings that are bearers of intrinsic moral value are persons; non-personal things have merely instrumental value in relation to persons.

---

[1] Craig (2008) p. 173.
[2] Craig (2008), p. 105.

> Only persons have intrinsic value, because meaningful
> moral behavior requires purpose and will.

In "The Indispensability of Theological Meta-Ethical Foundations for Morality", Craig also asserts:[1]

> On the theistic view, objective moral values are rooted in
> God. God's own holy and perfectly good nature supplies
> the absolute standard against which all actions and
> decisions are measured. God's moral nature is what Plato
> called the "Good." He is the locus and source of moral
> value. He is by nature loving, generous, just, faithful, kind,
> and so forth.
>
> Moreover, God's moral nature is expressed in relation to
> us in the form of divine commands which constitute our
> moral duties or obligations. Far from being arbitrary,
> these commands flow necessarily from His moral nature.
> In the Judaeo-Christian tradition, the whole moral duty of
> man can be summed up in the two great commandments:
> First, you shall love the Lord your God with all your
> strength and with all your soul and with all your heart and
> with all your mind, and, second, you shall love your
> neighbor as yourself. On this foundation we can affirm
> the objective goodness and rightness of love, generosity,
> self-sacrifice, and equality, and condemn as objectively
> evil and wrong selfishness, hatred, abuse, discrimination,
> and oppression.

God just *has* these qualities. God is a being in a non-spatio-temporal existence (though maybe not after the creation of the universe), and the location of this morality is within God. God somehow grounds these in his nature, although Craig goes on to say elsewhere that God has no moral obligations or duties. So does this mean God isn't a moral character. Because we owe our duties or obligations to God, we are moral, but since God has no obligations to any other entity, the same does not apply to God. Morality appears to be more about accountability:[2]

> I think of God as the embodiment of the moral good. He
> is the paradigm of goodness. He defines what goodness

---

[1] Craig (1997).
[2] Craig (2008c).

is. Think by way of analogy of judging music in terms of being hi-fidelity. We used to hear the term that a recording was hi-fidelity, which meant that it approximated to the sound of a live orchestra. But a live orchestra wouldn't itself be hi-fidelity because it doesn't have anything to approximate to – it is the standard. In the same way, moral values are defined by God. He *is* the standard of goodness. His character is the paradigm of goodness. Whether or not our actions are good or bad will be based upon how faithful they are to the standard. Whether they are morally hi-fidelity or not or whether they fall away from the standard and are therefore evil.

For Craig, actions are moral if and only if God is in the equation, thus rendering the morality objectively grounded. Craig denies any subjective form of morality as being, well, moral (no longer counting as good or evil):[1]

Today I want to argue that if God exists, then the objectivity of moral values, moral duties, and moral accountability is secured, but that in the absence of God, that is, if God does not exist, then morality is just a human convention, that is to say, morality is wholly subjective and non-binding. We might act in precisely the same ways that we do in fact act, but in the absence of God, such actions would no longer count as good (or evil), since if God does not exist, objective moral values do not exist. Thus, we cannot truly be good without God. On the other hand, if we do believe that moral values and duties are objective, that provides moral grounds for believing in God.

Craig is defining his way to his conclusion by exclude the idea that good and bad can possibly be anything other than objective, and that objectivity can only be grounded in God.

It seems that humans have moral obligations and accountability and so our actions, as intentional extensions of the agent, have moral value (or the intentions do). Yet, things are never simple: we might question as to whether a moral intention A with outcome A_1 has different moral value than moral intention A with outcome A_2 where A_2 is intuitively a much "worse" outcome, but where the intentions were identical. Which action or person better reflects God, ceteris paribus?

---

[1] Craig (1997).

For example, in "Moral Values and Abstract Objects", Craig says:[1]

> It follows, then, that the Good cannot be an abstract object, since there are no uncreated abstract objects. So on my view neither numbers nor moral values are abstract objects. Rather I take the Good to be a concrete object, namely, God Himself. God Himself is the paradigm of Goodness.

God is, at least before creation, a non-spatio-temporal being who embodies, who *is*, good, and yet is not abstract? What does concrete mean here, absent spacetime? This is mere pie-in-the-sky thinking and mere assertion to me. I imagine if Craig was challenged on this, on the ontology of God, he would defer to mysterianism – it's just a mystery.

Craig, elsewhere,[2] admits that "human beings do possess intrinsic moral value" such that there is intrinsic moral value within humanity. This goodness is seen in relation to God himself. As Paul Copan states in his book with Craig:[3]

> We would not know goodness without God's endowing us with a moral constitution. We have rights, dignity, freedom, and responsibility because God has designed us this way. In this, we reflect God's moral goodness as His image-bearers.

Such intrinsic moral value in people and their actions (as opposed to their moral sense and understanding of moral actions) is echoed in the *Blackwell Companion to Natural Theology*, where Mark D. Linville states:[4]

> Moral agency is thus what we might call a *dignity-conferring* property.
>
> If such an argument is to succeed at all, one requirement is that morality itself must be of intrinsic rather than instrumental value.

---

[1] Craig (2011).
[2] Craig (2008b).
[3] Copan (2007), p. 91.
[4] Linville in Craig & Moreland (2009), p. 431-446.

This still does not really allow us to compare actions against other actions to decipher a comparative moral worth. Instead, we have a claim that moral worth lies in the actor, the human agent. This is predominantly because Craig denies the Platonic existence, the abstract existence, of "good". He argues[1] that goodness must reside in God or the person doing the action (as opposed to the action itself). Either way, then, there is intrinsic moral value whether it be in the action itself or in the agent. This intrinsic moral value is nonrelational or non-derivative. It could be either in the form of the action holding an intrinsic, non-instrumental value,[2] or in the form of the agent and their intention, which is based on a reflection of God himself.

For the purposes of this essay, I am not going to argue further on whether this, as a moral meta-ethical theory, holds in light of any criticism (other than any I may duly give). I will remind the reader of the opening section of this book dealing with abstract ideas, of which, to me, morality is clearly one. But Craig's viewpoint is held by many Christian philosophers and apologists. It is also worth saying that Craig is not representative of all Christians; there are many different schools of thought. I have chosen Craig for his prominence and volume of his writing.

Consequentialism

Now let us turn to an alternate view of morality known as consequentialism. This theory, as one might guess, implies that moral worth is conferred by the consequences to an action, as opposed to the action itself. These normative properties are themselves universalizable – they are moral facts. This is a moral realist theory, despite how it may intuitively appear. There are many different kinds of consequentialism, but we will look here at how moral rightness can be in some way derived from the consequences of an action, or indeed the intentions behind said action. In this way, consequentialism will enable us to compare moral actions. If the consequences are measurable, then we can determine whether the rape of a child is worse than stealing a loaf of bread.

The most common version of consequentialism is utilitarianism. Classic utilitarianism, which was championed by the likes of Jeremy Bentham and John Stuart Mill in the 18th and 19th centuries, claims that an act is good if

---

[1] Craig (2011).

[2] An example of instrumental value would be money, which is not valuable in and of itself, but construed by the person(s) doing the valuing such as society or the individual.

the total amount of good minus the total amount of bad resulting from the act creates a net good. My opinion is that the intrinsic value that is necessitated from any comparable moral system is pleasure[1] (with the antithesis being pain). And the value/utility (e.g. pleasure) is intrinsic because it cannot be broken down any further – it is non-derivative (as previously mentioned in this book). This means you cannot see it in terms of anything else.

> The concept of intrinsic value has been characterized … in terms of the value that something has "in itself," or "for its own sake," or "as such," or "in its own right."… [L]et us … focus on what it means to say that something is valuable *for its own sake* as opposed to being valuable *for the sake of something else* to which it is related in some way.[2]

For example, one might buy Fair Trade tea instead of normal tea. This is because the Fair Trade tea commands a higher price, which is fed back to the original farmers and workers, paying for schools and education for their children, which in turn gives pleasure to the families. The money and services provided for the workers are further derived into pleasure. Pleasure, often seen as happiness, is seen as intrinsic because you can no further derive it.

When someone talks of reasons for doing something, we can always continue asking the why question (such as "why is that good?"), as we might do in the above example. We don't stop asking "why" at the point where it is stated that the tea commands a higher price (that would not make the act 'good'). However, when we are greeted by the answer "because it makes him happy" and then follows this with a "why", the answer becomes tautologous such that "it makes him happy because it makes him happy". This tautology is not fallacious since the feeling of pleasure or happiness is pleasurable. This pleasure is an axiom that cannot be further reduced. Rational and sane (neurotypical) people would rather feel happy than sad because happy is a positive feeling – *it feels good to be happy*. This is the basis of utility and utilitarianism, at least as far as original utilitarian Jeremy Bentham was concerned.[3]

---

[1] You may disagree, and there are pluralistic theories of intrinsic value, but I argue that they are always further derivative.

[2] As ever, all of these claims can be challenged. A good place to start is Zimmerman & Bradley (2019).

[3] As Jeremy Bentham (1789) p.1 said, "Nature has placed mankind under the governance of two sovereign masters, pain and pleasure. It is for them alone to point

The idea of consequentialism can clearly be seen in the famous Trolley Problem (discussed previously).[1] Utilitarians would invariably flip the switch[2] so that the trolley would go along the track that would kill only the single person as opposed to the five people, since less pain would result. The theist, believing in objective morality as previously mentioned, would not do so since this would be using a human as a means to an end, using them instrumentally. However, I wonder how many Christians in the US defended the use of atomic weapons at Hiroshima and Nagasaki…

The theist usually believes that human is imbued with moral dignity and cannot be morally instrumental. Craig says that no human being has the authority to take an innocent human life. Such an action is tantamount to "playing God".[3] This is a clear distinction between the two moral systems. Theists would assume that not pulling the lever is more reflective of God than pulling the lever (perhaps this is why God let's earthquakes happen!).

This simplified look at the two separate (albeit objective) moral codes will suffice for the purposes needed here. The next aspect of morality to visit is the action of God himself. Throughout the Bible, there are countless examples of deaths, injuries and actions that can be seen in a moral light, from the destruction of Sodom and Gomorrah to the sacrifice of Jesus himself. I am going to take one event from the Bible and one event from more recent times and investigate them further.

---

out what we ought to do, as well as to determine what we shall do. On the one hand the standard of right and wrong, on the other the chain of causes and effects, are fastened to their throne. They govern us in all we do, in all we say, in all we think …"

[1] "The original problem runs like this: Suppose that a judge or magistrate is faced with rioters demanding that a culprit be found for a certain crime and threatening otherwise to take their own bloody revenge on a particular section of the community. The real culprit being unknown, the judge sees himself as able to prevent the bloodshed only by framing some innocent person and having him executed. Beside this example is placed another in which a pilot whose aeroplane is about to crash is deciding whether to steer from a more to a less inhabited area. To make the parallel as close as possible it may rather be supposed that he is the driver of a runaway tram that he can only steer from one narrow track on to another; five men are working on one track and one man on the other; anyone on the track he enters is bound to be killed. In the case of the riots the mob have five hostages, so that in both the exchange is supposed to be one man's life for the lives of five." Foot (1978); originally appeared in the Oxford Review, Number 5, 1967.

[2] It is interesting to note that, according to the *philpapers* results,[2] a large majority of 68.2% of philosophers would flip the switch as a utilitarian would.

[3] Craig (2007).

God's Actions

First, let us look at the global flood involving Noah. I will assume a literal understanding of the Genesis passage that narrates the event, though I am cognisant of symbolic and other interpretations of the passage. In Genesis 6-9, God is revolted by all the sin committed by humanity and sends down a flood to kill all of humanity bar eight (Noah and family), and all animals bar two of each kind (Genesis 6:7):

> So YHWH said, "I will blot out man whom I have created from the face of the ground, man and beast and creeping things and birds of the air, for I am sorry that I have made them."

But wait. The classical interpretation of God is that he is at the same time omniscient, omnipotent and omnibenevolent. His omnibenevolent characteristic is the one with which we find most interest in this context. Let us look at the act of destroying all the world's population (bar eight) and all the world's animals (bar two of each kind). Is this an act that could be said, in and of itself, to be benevolent? Surely not. Surely such destruction of people apparently endowed with moral dignity, and of animals with no moral value per se, must not have intrinsic moral goodness. So how can such an act be seen as being morally good, if not seen in its intrinsic value?

From what we have previously heard from Craig, can we really accept that this is the outpouring of God's moral character? It just *is* good? We can't employ moral reasoning since it is *just* God's *nature*? This carries no rational weight for me.

Context is everything here. There are two ways of looking at this. The first is retribution. Humans could have been so sinful as to deserve almost entire eradication. Indeed, this is actually what most Christians seem to claim. Aside from this being an incredibly unlikely scenario (but let us assume that this might be the case), this retributive punishment is incoherent with the death of a myriad of morally unaccountable, yet sentient, animals (and not to mention children, foetuses, newborns etc.). Furthermore, retribution actually offers little in the way of constructive usefulness past a sort of deterrence that could be achieved in other ways without so much death, I wager.

Maybe retribution has some moral value itself, but only insofar as it pertains to gaining pleasure for the agent (in this case, God). It would be easier to argue that putting humanity through a successful rehabilitation programme would be a morally greater course of action than the retributive one described in Genesis. I am fairly sure that rehabilitation is prima facie more moral than genocide and mass animal death. Is God's nature death before rehabilitation? Whatever happened to forgiveness? Or had this not been invented yet?

The second way of looking at this is that God was trying to achieve a greater good in this seeming "evil". Perhaps God needed to do this harsh act in order to achieve a particular (all-loving) end. If this is the case, then God (whose acts can only be seen as morally perfect, according to the theist) is *using* this event and the lives of all those who perished *to achieve an end*. This is clearly a form of consequentialism. The moral value of the event was not in the event itself, but derived from the consequences, even though we might not know what these were (or are). As is often cited as an answer for difficult moral dilemmas involving God, who knows the mind of God? God moves in mysterious ways!

Let us look, then, at a more recent event. The tsunami of 2004 has some poignant parallels with the global flood event. The world was shaken by the sheer force and fallout of such a massive natural phenomenon. Some 230,000 people died, as well as entire ecosystems and probably billions of organisms perishing. God, with his classic characteristics, would have known this was going to happen and would have had the power to stop it. Being all-loving, all we can possibly conclude from his permissive will is that the tsunami must have served some greater good in order for it to be permitted by an omnibenevolent Creator deity.

It is difficult to second guess such reasons for allowing destruction of this magnitude. It could be a combination of reasons, seen by theologians as *theodicies*, or theories that seek to answer the Problem of Evil.[1] Maybe this event is character-building or soul-building (the Irenaean Theodicy) for the survivors (or even those who perished). The generally accepted maxim by

---

[1] There are many formulations of this and I have selected this one:
1. God exists.
2. God is omnipotent, omniscient, and perfectly good.
3. A perfectly good being would want to prevent all evils.
4. An omniscient being knows every way in which evils can come into existence.
5. An omnipotent being, who knows every way in which an evil can come into existence, has the power to prevent that evil from coming into existence.
6. A being who knows every way in which an evil can come into existence, who is able to prevent that evil from coming into existence, and who wants to do so, would prevent the existence of that evil.
7. If there exists an omnipotent, omniscient, and perfectly good being, then no evil exists.
8. Evil exists (logical contradiction).
Trakkakis (n.d.)

Christian philosophers is that we cannot know the mind of God and that he has his reasons. Or perhaps we do not have the capabilities to understand but that *there must be a reason* or a greater good to come from such suffering. This is known as "skeptical theism". In a debate with skeptic Jeffrey Jay Lowder, Phil Fernandes (a theologian and philosopher of religion) stated:[1]

> "A theist... would have to argue that this is the greatest possible way to achieve the greatest possible world... God often uses evil and human suffering to draw people to himself. Now God's ways and thoughts are far above our understanding and even the Scriptures state that. At best atheistic arguments show that limited minds can't fully understand why God allows so much evil..."

This sort of rationalisation is commonplace, and William Craig has also reached similar conclusions when talking and writing of the Problem of Evil:[2]

> Again, such an assumption is not necessarily true [that an omnibenevolent God would prefer a world without evil]. The fact is that in many cases we allow pain and suffering to occur in a person's life in order to bring about some greater good or because we have some sufficient reason for allowing it. Every parent knows this fact. There comes a point at which a parent can no longer protect his child from every mishap; and there are other times when discipline must be inflicted on the child in order to teach him to become a mature, responsible, adult. Similarly, God may permit suffering in our lives in order to build us or to test us, or to build and test others, or to achieve some other overriding end. Thus, even though God is omnibenevolent, He might well have morally sufficient reasons for permitting pain and suffering in the world.

This is a clear exposition of the value of God's decisions as evaluated by an analysis of the consequences. This is acceptance, as clear as day, that God can use people instrumentally as a means to an end to achieve some greater good.

---

[1] On September 26, 1999 at the University of North Carolina at Chapel Hill, Jeffery Jay Lowder, then President of Internet Infidels, Inc., and Phil Fernandes, President of the Institute of Biblical Defense, debated Naturalism vs Theism.
[2] Craig (n.d.).

Therefore, we have a situation whereby theists claim an objective, intrinsically-based moral system. And yet we have clear evidence and acceptance by those same theists that God employs a consequentialist moral system himself with a great deal of actions. We must remember that by accepting that there are successful theodicies, such as the free will theodicy (whereby suffering is a corollary of humans being able to have free will), then one accepts that the consequences justify the action. In other words, (by their definition) *theodicies are consequentialist.* Where does this leave us? Well, there are two options.

First, moral consequentialism could be mutually exclusive with regard to any other moral code. Given the evidence for divine consequentialism, there may be no objective morality such as is suggested by the likes of William Lane Craig. This would entail that theists "had their ideas of morality all wrong". This would require some serious rethinking from said philosophers since they often criticise atheism from a moral standpoint, denigrating philosophies such as consequentialism and utilitarianism as being inferior to a morality grounded in God. For example, Australian philosopher David S. Oderberg states:[1]

> I have given a number of fairly abstract reasons why consequentialism is on the face of it unintuitive and unmotivated. But I also think it is straight out false, and not only false but an evil and dangerous theory – a view I am not alone in holding.

Alternatively, such moralities night not be mutually exclusive but could be used in conjunction with each other. Thus an act might be intrinsically morally good as well as being consequentially good. However, a major problem presents itself here. What happens when one morality delivers a "good" verdict whilst the other a "bad" verdict? Is the consequentialism evidenced in God's "reasoning" more meaningful, more valuable, than any intrinsic moral value? In other words, the moral value of the consequences of these acts of God outweighs any potential intrinsic value that may be claimed of the acts. This implies that intrinsic moral value, if it does exist, is effectively meaningless or valueless since it is consistently, throughout the Bible and history, trumped by value of the consequences.

Let us look at the events of both floods – one directed by God and one permitted by God (such an "act" or *not acting* to intervene is often seen as a *moral omission*). It may not only have been permitted, but the theist must declare that it was even designed into the system. God allowed or directed

---

[1] Oderberg (2007), p. 5.

these similar events causing widespread pain, suffering and death, involving both humans and animals. Moreover, he (or theists) seemingly rationalises these acts by valuing the other consequences (greater good) of the acts over the suffering resultant from those acts.

In fact, by God allowing every single bit of suffering, every single death, that has ever happened to any human being or animal since the Big Bang (or Genesis Creation), on every single occasion, God has been a consequentialist. The consequences of every single piece of suffering must outweigh the intrinsic "badness" of the suffering (if God is all-loving, powerful enough to have it otherwise and knowledgeable enough to know how to have it otherwise). Thus, even if intrinsic moral values exist as well as consequentialism, it seems that consequentialism trumps intrinsic moral value every time God allows suffering to happen.

There are many guises to such moral consequentialism because every "choice" God made in designing the world had a moral dimension. As I wrote in *The Little Book of Unholy Questions* as a direct question to God:[1]

> 297. Couldn't we all have been photosynthetic organisms, using sunlight and inanimate molecules to make our energy thereby avoiding the need to kill other animals for survival?...

> There is no reason why, from an all-loving point of view, animals should exist by necessarily killing other animals and plants.

Of course, for the purposes of this essay, we don't need to know *what* the greater goods are, just *that they exist*. Plus, if we are a theist, we know that God acts as a morally perfect being, and the acts are morally valued by their consequences, by their greater goods. Having pitted these two moralities against each other and seen that consequentialism appears to come out as the winner, let us look at some possible objections, which I present as an essay in itself.

Remember, such consequentialism is seen by theists as "a terrible ethic" because it does not necessitate God existing for there to be moral facts. Showing that God is consequentialist is, therefore, a problem for theists and their whole moral system.

---

[1] Pearce (2011), p. 124-7.

Dealing with Objections to "God Is a Consequentialist".

William Lane Craig, our previously heavily quoted Christian theologian and philosopher, was involved some time back in a series of discussions in Australia with theoretical physicist Laurence Krauss regarding philosophy and science.[1] Unfortunately, Krauss is no great philosopher, which is what most of their discussion revolved around. Rather crucially for our purposes here, both Craig and the (very annoying) moderator claimed that "consequentialism is a terrible ethic" and that utilitarianism and consequentialism had been "renounced" by the Abrahamic faiths. This seems to be a contradiction to my claim that God is, indeed, a consequentialist.

I am in no need of proving that moral consequentialism holds and that it has no problems, only that theists use it to justify God's actions, and that their defence that God's actions are not consequentialist do not hold.

This is something of a marginally more technical nature than some other chapters here, but I feel it important to include in order to defend my thesis that the morality of (Christian) theism is, indeed, highly problematic (in this case, from their own perspective).

The Authority Defence

Some theists claim that God has the right, through his maximal authority, to intervene consequentially, using humans as a means to an end (in a way that humans ought not do). This argument sidesteps the consequentialist form of morality. In philosopher David McNaughton's paper "Is God (almost) a consequentialist? Swinburne's moral theory", McNaughton looks at noted Christian philosopher Richard Swinburne's approach to God's moral dimensions. Bringing back the trolley track example, many theists argue that we humans do not have the right to interfere in another's life, either for their own good or the good of another. This is based on the notion that we do not have the "*authority*" to do so. And so we should not switch the track for the trolley no matter how many lives it might save. McNaughton argues against this logic. He states, instead, that *carers* do have this right, whether in the guise

---

[1] Found variously online, such as here:
https://www.youtube.com/watch?v=mj4nbL53I-E (retrieved 24/03/2021).

of parents, a care home or even the state. But does this right get God out of a moral corner?

> If it is wrong for us to harm others for good ends, how could God make it permissible and even obligatory by his commands? The answer is that for Swinburne the only reason why we may not do these things for good ends is that we lack the authority. Since God has that authority, he can authorise us. So the underlying structure of Swinburne's moral theory is much less deontological than might at first appear. This is made clear in his proposed amendment to Kant's famous second formulation of the Categorical Imperative: 'It is ... permissible to use someone for the good of others if on balance you are their benefactor, and if they were in no position to make the choice for themselves' (1998, 233).[1]

McNaughton seems to conclude that God is *almost* a consequentialist based on a distinction of rights. But, to me this is a red herring. Whether one has the right to use a consequentialist morality or not is not under consideration when the evidence clearly points to the fact that such a code is regularly being employed. Both Swinburne and (to a lesser extent) McNaughton are trying to derive deontological[2] duties from the rights of humans and apply these to humanity and God. However, it seems they fall into a trap of the slippery slope fallacy of being unable to define when an act remains a deontological act, and when it slips into consequentialism. As McNaughton also says:[3]

> Sometimes harming someone is morally acceptable. For example, to save them from worse harm, or when inflicting a justified punishment, or when the person harmed is a willing volunteer seeking to achieve some considerable good. But it is generally accepted that it is wrong seriously to harm innocent people, without their consent, even when it is done for the general good.

There is no discernible way to separate consequentialism from a greater deontological duty other than to appeal to intuition. Thus our claims of divine consequentialism hold in light of a failure to properly establish that

---

[1] McNaughton (2003), p. 27.
[2] The belief that moral obligations or rules drive reasoning for moral actions.
[3] McNaughton (2003), p. 9.

God really does have the *moral* authority to cause a great deal of harm for a supposed moral duty, and how this is not, in fact, consequentialism.

There is something prima facie wrong with claiming that God has the right to just extinguish life at will because he's God, and he created us. It feels like a dodge of sorts, inoculating God from moral evaluation, and thereby permitting God to do anything at all in human conception.

This is how skeptical theism also works (God moves in mysterious ways – there *could* be a good reason why he allows such suffering). With both skeptical theism, and God being morally excepted due to having the right and authority to do anything, the following can be justified:

God could destroy the entirety of human and animal life in a one thousand-year project of torture. In fact, your whole family were the last to go, tortured in front of your eyes in the most disgraceful way. You are the last life form in the universe and have now had your life extended to allow for one hundred years of personal torture.

Even given all that, you can either say that God has the right to do this, that he is not morally obligated not to, but also that there could be a greater good that could come about.

This is the theist's eventual answer to every philosophical thorn in their side.

God Has No Moral Duties

Perhaps a more robust defence of accusations of divine consequentialism comes from William Lane Craig himself. The intrinsic moral value of people is a reflection of God's nature and moral actions are appropriated through divine commands. Divine Command Theories are moral theories that derive moral *obligation*:[1]

> According to the version of divine command ethics which I've defended, our moral duties are constituted by the commands of a holy and loving God.
>
> … On divine command theory, then, God has the right to command an act, which, in the absence of a divine command, would have been sin, but which is now morally obligatory in virtue of that command.

---

[1] Craig (2007).

However, there certainly seems to be a circularity to this approach – morality is defined by the command, and yet we have no independent benchmark against which to judge the goodness of such commands. In this way, we cannot decipher whether something is good or not on its own merits, or whether it is good merely because it was commanded by an entity deemed good.

Craig's approach is to establish our morality in a reflection of God's commands (such as "Love thy neighbour"), but to deny God the same moral obligation:[1]

> Since God doesn't issue commands to Himself, He has no moral duties to fulfil. He is certainly not subject to the same moral obligations and prohibitions that we are. For example, I have no right to take an innocent life. For me to do so would be murder. But God has no such prohibition. He can give and take life as He chooses. We all recognize this when we accuse some authority who presumes to take life as "playing God." Human authorities arrogate to themselves rights which belong only to God. God is under no obligation whatsoever to extend my life for another second. If He wanted to strike me dead right now, that's His prerogative.

However, I would contest this sort of approach for several reasons. Initially, it is problematic in a pragmatic sense, as atheist P. Wesley Edwards states:[2]

> As we've seen, when confronted with what would normally be considered crimes against humanity, the theist will respond in various ways, none of them satisfactory: "We are His creations, and He can do as He pleases," or "God is good regardless of His actions, just in ways that are beyond us." Stripped of our own ability to know an evil deed when we see it, we now have to first ask: "Who did it?" One is reduced to saying, "I don't know if it was evil until you first tell me whether or not God did it. I'll even do the deed myself, no matter how bloody or genocidal, if you first convince me that God ordered it." Uncritical obedience to orders ultimately becomes the only criterion of moral behavior, even when the rule is

---

[1] Craig (2007).
[2] Wesley Edwards (2018).

infanticide, such as illustrated in Gen 22:2 where Abraham is told to slaughter his own son. Indeed, Abraham's willingness to blindly follow orders – even with the tortured, frightened screams of his own child in his ears – is held up as the supreme example of moral "goodness" we should all follow.

If it is true, as some theists claim, that "God communicates to us our sense of judgment for determining right and wrong," then shouldn't we naturally sense moral *beauty* in these O.T. [Old Testament] atrocities, since they were sanctioned by God? Fortunately, few do. But even if our moral instinct is one of revulsion, we are told to remember that good is *defined* by God. Anything He does is good by definition, no matter what: healing sick children or having them ripped apart by wild animals. Curiously, many Christians have often complained at this point that "things were different in the Old Testament." In other words, their "absolute" morals were different in the past. Such a view ironically turns their absolutism into a rather extreme form of moral *relativism*.

I think Edwards points out the flaws to Craig's approach with clarity and force. Divine Command Theories (DCTs) are circular in nature. Moreover, they are not particularly good pragmatic guides of how to act morally since we are unable to fathom exactly what would be morally commanded by God. They do not help us to comparatively rate different actions morally. There is an epistemological issue with how we would know if God had communicated a command to us. I heavily critique DCTs and their circularity in my following chapter.

Divine Command Theories imply that morality only comes from (God's) power, status and relation in giving particular commands. As you will see, this is fraught with problems.

Craig tries to drive a wedge between moral *obligation* and moral *good* such that God is exempted from moral obligations or moral duties/oughts. However, this does not exempt his actions from being morally valued. Craig would say that the value is necessarily good, since it comes from God's nature but this is begging the question. Moreover, the moral value (which may well also be good) seems to still be derived from the consequences of the actions. Religious thinkers like Craig admit to this in other contexts (such as theodicies with the problem of evil). From every design facet to every death in the Bible, to every unit of pain and suffering experienced in the

197

world, God must be valuing his own actions and omissions on the basis of their consequences. I can see no way around this conundrum.

I am particularly perturbed by Craig's claim that "God doesn't issue commands to Himself". What does this really mean? I may live on a desert island with no other human being. I might decide, after some time, to become vegetarian, so as not to cause any pain or suffering to other sentient creatures. I do this because I am trying to make my behaviour as morally good as possible, irrespective as to whether any other human being (i.e., moral creature) exists on Earth. The obligation I have is to my desire to be as moral as possible. I am obligated to my own desires and nature.

Craig seems to be saying that God has no obligation to anyone else, so he therefore has no obligations. He is at the top of the pecking order, and created all contingent beings below him on that order; he is not obligated to them. But I do not see morality as exclusively being an obligation to other people. Indeed, in its purest form, it is an obligation to oneself and to one's standards and desires. The theist could say that God has no desires,[1] but he has a nature to which his actions must be benchmarked. If, as many theists will claim, God has free will, then God surely has the ability to act in any number of ways (though he will necessarily choose the action that most reflects his OmniGod nature – a prickly problem).

I posit that moral obligations will derive from any kind of relationship between any sentient beings. That includes between God and humans. I see no reason why God is not morally obligated to humans in the same way. And I do not understand why Craig sees this as a one-way street, other than from motivated reasoning to get God off the hook.

It seems, from all of this reasoning, that God has moral character and will. It seems perfectly clear to me that any sentient entity that interacts with other living creatures is moral – their actions have moral dimensions. Therefore, God has a moral dimension. God is love, after all, right?

Perhaps we can see this from a different direction: one of love rather than suffering. God is love and God loves humans. Love, I argue, is an action imbued with positive moral properties. Christians appear to allow this intention of love and action to come from God to his subjects. Therefore, Christians see God as a moral, loving entity.

---

[1] After extricating God from the problem of desiring creation, as previously discussed.

Unpicking Moral Obligation

Catholic philosopher Joseph Lombardi sets out in *American Catholic Philosophical Quarterly*, in his essay "Against God's Moral Goodness":[1]

> Questions about the moral goodness of God usually arise in discussions of the problem of evil. But matters other than the quantity and types of evil in the world might also call divine moral perfection into question. Consider the following argument. God is not perfectly good in the moral sense unless God always fulfils his moral obligations. This, in turn, presupposes that God has moral obligations. But there are features of the divine nature which make it impossible for God to have such obligations. Therefore, God is not perfectly good in the moral sense.

Christian philosopher William Alston, in his 1989 paper "Some Suggestions for Divine Command Theorists"[2] discusses the term obligation at length, saying the "*S* has a moral obligation to do A" essentially means "*S* (morally) ought to do A", and:

> It leaves us without any adequate way of construing the goodness of God. No doubt, it leaves us free to take God to be metaphysically good; but it forecloses any conception of God as morally good, as exemplifying the sort of goodness that is cashed out in being loving, just, and merciful. For since the standards of moral goodness are set by divine commands, to say that God is morally good is just to say that He obeys His own commands. And even if it makes sense to think of God as overbearing commands that He has given Himself, that is not at all what we have in mind when thinking of God as morally good. We aren't just thinking that God practices what He preaches, whatever that may be....
>
> For if God is good in the right way, there will be nothing arbitrary about His commands. On the contrary His goodness will ensure that He issues those commands for the best.

---

[1] Lombardi (2005).
[2] Alston (1989), p. 305.

Alston continues by discussing how incoherent moral obligation is when attempting to apply it to humans and in the same way to God. "For if it is the same, how could it be constituted so differently in the two cases? And if what it is for God to have an obligation is something quite different from what it is for a human being to have an obligation, how is divine obligation to be construed? I have no idea."[1]

Alston sees there being a problem with moral obligation existing within the context of God, but rather than dropping the God hypothesis (as an atheist does), he attempts to distort the moral obligation concept to fit with God and the God hypothesis.

To return to William Lane Craig, it appears that he claims that God "can give and take life as He chooses".[2] God certainly can do this (he has the ability if he exists) – but taking life gratuitously and causing pain gratuitously falls into the trap of the problem of evil.

What Craig is saying here is essentially that God can do whatever he likes: murder and rape an entire species of sentient creatures, and be let off the hook because he is not moral. He has no moral obligations. It is all grounded in God's perfect nature... How can these same people say God is love and God is good, and yet believe he biblically sanctioned genocide, and designed Covid-19? How can they say that God is perfect? Again, this is a case of a solution to one theistic conundrum not cohering with other theistic conundrums and solutions.

Let's see if Craig's claims that God is not moral chime with the Bible:

Nahum 1:7

"The LORD is good, A stronghold in the day of trouble, And He knows those who take refuge in Him."

Mark 10:18

"And Jesus said to him, "Why do you call Me good? No one is good except God alone."

James 1:17

"Every good thing given and every perfect gift is from above, coming down from the Father of lights, with whom there is no variation or shifting shadow."

---

[1] Ibid., p. 306.
[2] Craig (2007).

Romans 2:4

"Or do you despise the riches of His goodness, forbearance, and long suffering, not knowing that the goodness of God leads you to repentance?"

Romans 8:28

"And we know that God causes all things to work together for good to those who love God, to those who are called according to His purpose."

Romans 12:2

"And do not be conformed to this world, but be transformed by the renewing of your mind, so that you may prove what the will of God is, that which is good and acceptable and perfect."

There are many more, but you get the point. The Bible explicitly claims God is (morally) good.

The key to what Alston proposes in the following solution is to maintain that God is good but has no obligations in the sense of DCTs: "If this move is to work, we will have to develop an account of divine moral goodness that does not involve the satisfaction of moral obligations."[1]

God Must Be Good Without Having Obligations to Be Good

Christian philosopher William Alston sets out that some say God is "*essentially perfectly good*"[2] and it would be impossible for him to fail to be good when speaking of God's duties or oughts. The scenario might defer to the issue that God's nature determines his actions so that he cannot act freely; he cannot have free will. Nonetheless, Alston maintains that, even though there is no way that God can fail to, say, love his rational creations, he still *ought* to do so. Even if there is an overwhelming obviousness to a statement, it does not invalidate the truth of a statement. This, Alston calls "the inappropriateness argument". (I have to admit, I get somewhat confused in Alston's paper as he presents arguments, then adds Devil's Advocate

---

[1] Alston (1989), p. 307.
[2] Ibid.

arguments, and counter-arguments. Often, I am not sure which of these he *actually* adheres to.)

Alston continues by separating some conception of moral goodness from moral obligation:[1]

> The fact that it would be, morally, a good thing for me to do A must not be confused with the fact that I morally ought to do A, that it is morally *required* of me, that I am morally blameworthy in case I fail to do it.

There is this idea of *supererogation*: It might be morally *good* that I teach children in a Siberian village to play the piano, but I'm not morally *obliged* to do so. We aren't obliged to do all things that are good. Alternatively, what Craig's defence seems to do is to say that God is *not* morally obliged to love his creations, but also that in loving them, this is somehow *not* morally good (i.e., it has no moral value because God is not moral). It is as if there is some kind of moral vacuum when considering God. On the other hand, Alston appears to end up saying that God *cannot* have moral obligations qua divine commands, as he is not obligated to anyone else, but he *can* still have moral goodness in his actions, diverging from Craig.

Of course, the problem for theists is when a critical analysis of the Bible shows that God is in contravention of those perfect moral standards. He breaks promises, and his followers have to end up justifying rape or genocide. Does this invalidate God's perfect moral goodness, his omnibenevolence? And we return to the problem of evil.

Eleanore Stump, Catholic philosopher, has pointed out[2] that God has entered into covenants and promises with people in the Bible and this constitutes an *obligation*. Breaking these, should God do so, would be less than morally perfect and show that God is under some kind of moral obligation. Alston's defence of Stump's example is that it is an anthropomorphism (such as God "stretching out his arm"). I don't buy this. If God promises to do something, then he promises to do something (it reminds me of the Jewish concentration camp prisoners of war taking God to court for breaking the covenant).

Alston concludes: "In particular, we can think of God as perfectly good, morally as well as otherwise, even if that moral goodness does not consist in the perfect satisfaction of obligations."[3] Or, there is more to moral

---

[1] Ibid., p. 312.
[2] Stump (1992).
[3] Alston (1989), p. 316.

goodness than moral obligation. Terms like justice, mercy and love all have moral dimensions, and all supposedly apply to God.

This conversation, and discussion of Divine Command Theories, is all in context of Plato's Euthyphro Dilemma,[1] which can be set out like this: Whatever God wills is good and just. But is it good and just because God wills it, or does God will it because it is good and just. This dilemma looks at whether justice and goodness are arbitrary, whether they can exist outside of God (so that we don't need God for goodness), whether it is a case of "might is right", or whether they belong to the necessary and eternal truths of God.

Is it that:

We ought to, e.g., love one another because God commands us to do so.

Or:

God commands us to love one another because that is what is good.

Alston explains the problem:[2]

> The two classic objections to divine command ethics (to the acceptance of the first horn of the dilemma) that I shall be considering are the following.

> A. This makes divine commands, and hence, morality, arbitrary. Anything that God should decide to command would thereby be obligatory. If God should command us to inflict pain on each other gratuitously we would thereby be obliged to do so. More specifically, the theory renders divine commands arbitrary because it blocks off any moral reason for them. God can't command us to do A because that is what is morally right; for it doesn't become morally right until He commands it.

> B. It leaves us without any adequate way of construing the goodness of God. No doubt, it leaves us free to take God to be metaphysically good, realizing the fullness of being and all that; but it forecloses any conception of God as morally good, as exemplifying the sort of goodness that is cashed out in being loving, just, and merciful. For since the standards of moral goodness are set by divine commands, to say that God is morally good is just to say

---

[1] See variously, for example Hare (2006).
[2] Alston (1989), p. 305.

that He obeys His own commands. And even if it makes sense to think of God as obeying commands that He has given Himself, that is not at all what we have in mind in thinking of God as morally good. We aren't just thinking that God practices what He preaches, whatever that may be.

Alston later explains the issues with not having morality grounded in God:[1]

We are nor confronted with that horn in the original form, "God commands us to love our neighbors because that is what we ought to do," but with a closely analogous form, "God commands us to love our neighbor because it is morally good that we should do so." And that possesses the sort of feature deemed repellent to theism just as much as the first form, viz., that it makes the goodness of states of affairs independent of the divine will, thereby subjecting God to valuational facts that are what they are independent of Him. It thereby contradicts the absolute sovereignty of God; it implies that there are realities other than Himself that do not owe their being to His creative activity. If it is true, independently of God's will, that loving communion is a supreme good, and that forgiveness is better than resentment, then God is subject to these truths. He must conform Himself to them and so is not absolutely sovereign.

In showing that consequentialism might be a viable moral value system, or more accurately that it is a system employed by theists themselves, I am showing that this second horn is a real problem for theists. God can tell us to do something good because it is good, and not because it is grounded in God.

When Alston uses these arguments of moral obligation to evade the issues of the first horn of the Euthyphro Dilemma, he says: "We evaded the first horn by taking God's moral goodness, including the moral goodness of divine actions, not to be constituted by conformity to moral obligations, and hence not to be constituted by conformity to divine commands, even on this ethical theory."[2] He is saying that *there is* moral goodness in divine actions, though he is not obligated to carry them out.

---

[1] Alston (1989), p. 318.
[2] Ibid., p. 318.

Craig differs, as mentioned. The issues with Craig's approach, as I see them, and even taking into account his fellow Christian philosopher William, Alston, are then:

- You *can* have obligations to yourself.

- You *can* have obligations even if you are constrained to act to a single outcome.

- You *can* be moral outside of obligations (as Alston sets out).

- God *is* moral (if he exists).

- Theists incoherently argue for moral consequentialism (theodicies, biblical defences) whilst simultaneously calling it a "terrible ethic" and denying God is moral because he has no obligations.

- And, therefore, the claim that God is a moral consequentialist maintains.

To conclude, despite various potential objections, it seems apparent that the moral value derived from the actions of God have their basis in the consequences of those actions, and not in their intrinsic morality (if this exists at all). Either the objective morality claimed by theists does not exist, or it is consistently trumped by the consequences of the actions. Whether the consequences are defined with a classical utility, or something else – such as justice or love – is not important to this discussion, and this can be investigated elsewhere. If this is the case, then theists might do well to adjust their own moral philosophy, or to explain why the moral code of God is different to our own, if God is supposed to be the moral benchmark against which we all act, and whose moral nature is reflected in our own personal moral dignity.

My Atheistic Morality

This piece is hopefully a succinct synopsis (as much as can be reasonably be possible) of *my* moral philosophy, as an atheist. In setting it out, I will also counter positions adopted and claimed by theistic thinkers and apologists (am I implying apologists aren't thinkers?).

Abstract Ideas

First, morality is an abstract idea. So surely we would need to know what an abstract idea is and what its ontology (principles of existence) is? Luckily, you have read my position on this already. That of a conceptual nominalist. Before moving on, let me flesh out some of the terminology of abstract ideas. Here are the three main positions and their nomenclature, with the definitions pertaining to how they deal with universals (known as the Problem of Universals, such as how we explain "catness", "redness" and "chairness"):

Realist: The realist believes that all red things are red in virtue of the existence of a universal "Red", a single abstract thing that exists as a component part of all the red things. In this way, concerning the "redness" of a red apple, molten lava, and a red car: one of their parts is identical. In some meaningful sense the three parts are literally one. Redness is repeatable because there is one abstract, ontic, objective thing that manifests itself wherever there are red things.

Nominalist: The nominalist denies the existence of universals. One initial problem is determining where such universals could exist. Particulars (particular physical objects) instantiate the universal – that is, they exemplify them in individual scenarios. Nominalists believe that one major problem for the realist is this: where is this universal realm? Is it outside of space and time? For naturalists like myself, claiming something is outside of space and time by mere assertion is something of a problem. Some Neoplatonists, such as the philosopher Augustine, have implied that universals are contained within the mind of God (this led to the development of conceptualism). But if God doesn't exist…

Conceptualist (or **conceptual nominalist**): The conceptualist holds a position between nominalism and realism, saying that universals do exist but only within the mind and have no external or substantial (ontic) reality.

Moderate (immanent) realist – one amongst several other position. Adherents hold that universals don't exist in a realm, per se, but that they are located in space and time wherever they are *instantiated*. The problem being that for realists redness is supposed to exist in multiple places at the same time. The realist maintains that all the instances of redness are mind-independent and *particularised*, held together by the exemplification relation, but this relation cannot be explained.

Further reading will be necessary for the reader to understand all of the positions in much more detail.

The end result? Realism is, in my opinion, untenable. On the other hand, conceptual nominalism is not only a more coherent argument (consistent with other philosophical positions and systems), it is also borne out by actual data and the world around us. The fact that no moral philosophy works perfectly, the fact that we all believe slightly different things of morality, shows that there is, descriptively, some form of subjectivity concerning moral philosophy.

As a point of history that may (or may not!) be of interest to the reader, conceptualism has wound its way to us though many of the philosophers mentioned in this book: from medieval scholastics such as William of Ockham, through Descartes, Spinoza, Locke, Leibniz, Berkeley and Hume, to Hegel and Husserl (arguably with Kant thrown in), landing us in the modern era.

Objective Morality

We apply the abstract labels of moral evaluation to actions and intentions of humans. Actions are events with real, physical properties. Intentions are different from actions in that they are states of minds. But if we take the position that the mental supervenes on the physical (as I claim and as I briefly set out earlier in this collection), then there is a sense that such mental states of intentions are themselves reducible to physical properties.

When we talk about "morality" as a whole, we talk about the moral laws and prescriptions, and the truth values of a moral proposition. For me, there is no aether or locus for morality outside of our brains where such ideas can exist in an ontic sense. In this way, **morality is a conceptual enterprise that is constructed by our brains to create a moral map of the world that we can use to navigate the social landscape.** I have emphasised this because I think it is a pretty key conclusion.

We can use science to help us to arrive at the best course of action,[1] given a particular goal. But I think setting out that goal is a philosophical project and that requires some abstract thought, perhaps setting out axioms in one's framework. We can argue that there is an objectively better course of action given two options, A and B. For example, if you are looking for wellbeing or happiness as your endgame for morality, then perhaps option B empirically gets us more of those things. However, setting that as the endgame is not an objective ideal. It is a subjective, conceptual ideal. Most people might agree on it because we have similar brains and social environments, but it would still be subjective and conceptual. With a different goal, we get different journeys, and this might include the same goal but seen in different ways. For example, looking to maximise wellbeing for a certain population measured over an average of ten years as opposed to over fifty years might produce different moral actions.

As I have stated a number of times, I would add that for morality to make any coherent sense it needs to be goal-oriented, and setting those goals is a subjective project.

I struggle to be able to make sense of "objective" abstracta (e.g., "redness", "hero-ness") as mind-independent "things", since all conceptual entities must be mind-dependent; they are things *of* the mind.

Simply put, if there were no minds to conceive of morality, there would be no morality.

What do the Experts Believe?

Love it or hate it, if we are going to discuss ideas of morality and moral philosophy, then we might do well to consult with some of the experts. Not, of course, in a fallacious manner of *appealing to authority* or, indeed, an *argumentum ad populum*. But it is sheer folly to ignore the views of the people who spend their lives investigating moral ideas. I would not build a nuclear power station without having a few chats with well-qualified particle and nuclear physicists, whilst at the same time bending the ears of some proven structural engineers.

So what *do* philosophers think? Luckily, in 2009, the biggest ever survey of professional and graduate philosophers took place—the *philpapers survey*. In this survey we learned some important things. 27.7% of philosophers are moral anti-realists. This means that roughly a quarter of philosophers deny the objective truth value of moral statements. Further to this, some 25.9% of philosophers

---

[1] As Sam Harris does in his book *The Moral Landscape*.

accept or lean toward moral deontology (objective morality such as categorical imperatives), 23.6% to moral consequentialism, and 18.2% to virtue ethics. Now we are getting into the pertinent detail. These are the three main contenders for moral theory, split roughly equally.

What we can learn from this is that there are a variety of different moral theories that one can adopt, including the denial of moral theories. Moreover, one can actually hold to virtue ethics *and* consequentialism at the same time.

But the important result is as follows: 72.8% of philosophers are atheists, with 14.6% being theists. A huge majority of philosophers deny the existence of a god of any kind. And yet we have just learned that some 67.7% believe in deontology, consequentialism, or virtue ethics. So, clearly, many philosophers believe that you do not need to believe in a god to coherently hold a moral philosophical worldview.

I have already discussed what a moral ought is, so now let us look in a bit more detail at these main three moral positions of consequentialism, deontology and virtue ethics. At the end of the day, whilst I deny the objective existence of morality, I still see morality as crucial for the success of humanity and the rest of our world. That we have to construct it ourselves is all the more reason to understand better the rules of moral structural engineering.

All Moral Value Systems Are the Same

Richard Carrier wrote an essay that concluded that all moral value systems are the same. It was entitled (obviously) "Open Letter to Academic Philosophy: All Your Moral Theories Are the Same", in which he shows how deontology reduces down to consequentialism:[1]

> Kant argued that the only reason to obey his categorical imperatives is that doing so will bring us a greater sense of self-worth, that in fact we should "hold ourselves bound by certain laws in order to find solely in our own person a worth" that compensates us for every loss incurred by obeying, for "there is no one, not even the most hardened scoundrel who does not **wish** that he too might be a man of like spirit," yet only through the moral life can he gain that "greater inner worth of his own person." Thus Kant claimed a strong sense of self-worth is not possible for the immoral person, but a matter of course for the moral one, and

---

[1] Carrier (2015).

yet **everyone wants such a thing** (more even than anything else), therefore everyone has sufficient reason to be moral. He never noticed that he had thereby reduced his entire system of categorical imperatives to a single hypothetical imperative.

He then claims that consequentialism reduces to deontology:

> Besides these, there are many other respects in which a full-fledged consequentialism actually ends up entailing every preferable conclusion of any deontological ethical system. Duties are morally compelling because of the wide social consequences of not obeying them. Consequentialism thus collapses to deontology, in respect to anything deontology ever had to offer. Philosophers ought therefore to be analyzing every deontological conclusion they think is sound so as to expose what *consequences* actually make it morally preferable to what any *incomplete* consequentialism seems to entail. Notably, some philosophers have been doing this without even knowing it: it's called **rule utilitarianism.** But overall, instead of just saying some deontology entails you do *x*, do the hard work of asking yourself why you really think doing *x* is consequentially better. Because really, you do. And it is doing philosophy no service to ignore the consequences you are preferring and why.

Before finally claiming they both reduce to virtue ethics, anyway, where virtue ethics is defined as:

> In this theory, morality consists of those behaviors that are entailed by *the best virtues of character.* It is distinguished both in emphasizing the need to cultivate habits of character (and thus not just following rules, consequentialist or deontological) and in its casuistic situationalism: moral truth derives not from rules but from the combination of the particular situation one faces and the best virtues guiding action in all situations.

Such that:

> If a certain set of behaviors is morally right (as both deontological and consequentialist theories assert), then it is by the same reasoning morally necessary to cultivate those

habits of character that will make those behaviors common, consistent, and easy to perform. Any categorical imperative will in turn entail this, as will any consequentialist imperative.

Deontologically, if you will something to be universally performed, you are *de facto* also willing that people cultivate those virtues that will produce this universal behavior. Because "I would will that everyone behave thus" entails "I would will that everyone cultivate those moral virtues that will cause them to reliably behave thus." It would be self-contradictory not to. And the categorical imperative rules out self-contradiction. The same reasoning will follow for any coherent deontological system that has any claim to being true. The fact that Kant and later deontologists didn't think this through so as to notice it is just another example of the same blindness that caused consequentialists to fail to see the kinds of consequences deontologists didn't realize they were arguing as more important.

Consequentially, if you want the greatest good, you need to accept those behaviors that produce it, and that therefore must include behaviors that produce the character that produces those behaviors (more commonly, consistently, and easily). Thus, virtue ethics is entailed by consequentialism as well. It is only the more pertinent that science has established the needs of this: moral behavior only reliably issues from persons who have fully habituated moral virtues (such as compassion for others, a passion for honesty and reasonableness, etc.). Systems of rules are simply ineffectual, unless moral agents feel naturally inclined to follow them. And that requires cultivated virtues.

Which is to say that, in any pragmatic sense, a moral consequentialist or deontologist will be a virtue ethicist. This is perhaps to step away from morality seen in its most abstract form and understand it more as an applied philosophy. Which is what virtue ethics is, and why one can be a virtue ethicist *and* an adherent to another moral value system. They are not mutually exclusive. He continues:

And the reduction goes both ways. Deontological and consequentialist ethics reduce to virtue ethics, as just demonstrated. And virtue ethics reduces to deontology and consequentialism. The justification for virtue ethics (that which motivates anyone to obey it) has always been explicitly consequentialist: the production of personal happiness, or more precisely that state of contentment with oneself and one's life Aristotle described as eudaimonia (which is egoist, but Aristotle also implied a non-egoist consequentialism: society will function better for everyone if the members of that society live by moral virtues). Deontologically, a justification for virtue ethics arises from the same fact that reduces deontology to virtue ethics: you would will to be a universal law that everyone live by moral virtues. Deontological ethics has long been about what sort of person you become in the act (as opposed to ignoring that and focusing solely on the external consequences of the act), so it is surprising no one realized that "who you become as a person" is quite simply virtue ethics.

Philosophers therefore should abandon an exclusive focus on moral rules and recognize that moral virtues must also be fully integrated into any true moral theory. Virtue ethics can no longer be treated as a side option. It is fully a component of any valid consequentialist or deontological ethics. Not surprisingly both, as they reduce to each other.

Welcome to the quagmire of moral philosophy.

God, Divine Command Theory and Objective Morality

Let us return to the subject of God to show how the idea of divine morality is broken, and why I reject it in favour of building up my own moral edifice. As Kant would say, we cannot know things in themselves. We use our subjective minds to access *everything*. If God did embody moral law in some meaningful way, then we have a whole series of issues. God embodies, in his nature and commands, moral prescriptive law, and then we must interpret what has supposedly been revealed to do what he says in order to be moral ourselves.

Let us look at this scenario in critiquing divine moral philosophy. The most common version of this is divine command theory (DCT) whereby God's commands are what determine what is good. I shall list sixteen arguments against such a position in order to put it to bed. The Christian/DCTer would need to successfully refute all 16 points for their position to be coherent:

1. **Arbitrariness** – There is no third-party benchmark and so the idea of goodness becomes arbitrary if it is a non-rational assumption made of

God. We cannot use some other moral reasoning or scale to morally rationalise God's nature, as this would then become the moral grounding itself, and this would not necessitate God. But if God is that grounding, what makes his commands good are merely arbitrary assertions lacking any such rationalisations. Good becomes merely a synonym of God and lacks any useful meaning.

2. **Direction of causality** – The direction of causality works like this: God has lovingness, mercy, kindness etc., but these are not good characteristics, because goodness is rooted in God. These are good *because* God has them. They do not make God good. So if we ask why human lovingness is good, it is because it reflects God, not for any other reason. Justice and lovingness are only good on account of God having them, not because they obtain any good consequences within or for society, or have intrinsic moral value, or for any other moral reasoning.

3. **We are good only because we reflect God** – Think about the previous point on a practical, everyday basis. If we use DCT, then when you are being good, you cannot use moral reasoning to define that goodness, only that it reflects God. Moral reasoning cannot ground morality, because then the grounding would not be in God. This leaves us with a weird scenario such that we cannot provide any reasoning for moral actions. "Why is this behaviour good?" cannot be answered in any way other than "because it reflects God's nature". You can't use moral reasoning to teach a child why they are being good other than to appeal, each and every time, to reflecting God. Thus moral reasoning becomes impotent. It also means that God cannot have reasons for doing as he does, because then it would ground the moral value of the action in moral reasoning outside of God!

4. **Defies everyday moral reasoning and intuition (i.e., consequences)** – An action such as rape is wrong, for us, because of the harm it causes. For the DCTer, it is because God commanded us not to rape. Although, he kind of endorsed it in the Old Testament! We say, "Look how horrible rape is! Look at the harm it does." But this in itself does not make it wrong for the DCTer! It carries no intrinsic or extrinsic moral value, since the moral value appears to be in following a command of God or reflecting him as much as possible. Of course, this seems patently ridiculous. None of this plays well with our sense of moral intuition; moral intuition is wrong. We feel we are being good by doing A for X and Y reason, and yet A is actually good because it is reflective

of God. Yet most everybody being good on a daily basis believes X and Y rather than thinking of reflecting God in each and every instance of being good.

5. **Which God? Which Commands?** – We are also unclear as to which god we are talking about, and what his/her/its commands are. The commands in the Old Testament appear to have been replaced overnight with the commands of the New Testament. Incidentally, this looks like moral relativism (something I call Inter-Testamental Moral Relativism) because the historical and geographic context of the Jews defined the morality of their actions. So there is a gross lack of clarity in what actions *do* reflect God's nature – we might call this the Argument From Divine Miscommunication. Is stoning adulterers good? Is it bad? Is it only good before 33 CE? Did God's nature change then? Is all the Bible literally true? If so, then Jesus is literally a door. If not, then Jesus and the Bible talk at times in metaphor. What is metaphor and what is literal? We do not have commands for a good-many things in the Bible, what of these? Such divine commands are indeed muddled and unclear at best. Slavery (for example) appears to be morally bad, and yet God countenanced it in the Bible.

6. **Genocide and ordinary morality** – The idea that God commanded genocide in the Old Testament is also problematic and does not fit well with ordinary morality. But given DCT, it must be morally good. This potentially gets you to an uncomfortable reality: DCT depends on who tells you stuff. Genocide from God = good. Genocide from Hitler = bad! It all starts looking like the context (moral relativism, again) and the consequences are all important. Hitler gets a lot of bad press for his terrible genocide. God less so. The scales are skewed, methinks.

7. **Is God a better stopping point?** – Theists have done nothing to show that God is a more appropriate stopping point than the moral properties of kindness, generosity and justice themselves. Why is it, in any rational sense, that grounding morality in God is actually any *better* than grounding it in real and observable features of the world, such as the consequences of moral actions? There seems to be this assumption that a framework set outside of our minds and our reality, dictated to by some being that we cannot access or remotely understand, is somehow better.

8. **Why follow the commands?** – Why should we follow such commands? Only to get into heaven and avoid hell? If so, that is not really a reason to be good. If it is because they are good things to do based on moral reasoning, then again, the DCT framework fails because God does not have to provide a moral reason. In this way, there is no *reason* to accept DCT, even if it is true![1]

9. **Things not commanded are okay?** – Anything *not* commanded by God is potentially allowable. Since we cannot access the source directly (God), then we end up having to guess what is good or bad. This is a guess because it cannot be based on moral reasoning (because it's a DCT)! So anything not covered by divine commands in the Bible is potentially morally acceptable. Those actions lacking moral clarity leave us with either having to do moral reasoning, or simply not having a moral clue about what actions we should do in order to be reflective of God. This is even harder when it appears some things are both good and bad, depending on the context!

10. **But God would never command rape! Apart from he did.** – DCTers argue that God would never command bad things like murder and rape (i.e., that it is not in his nature) but this is falsified by the very fact that he *did* command them in the Bible! Including the death of all men, women, children and animals in different contexts. Some examples: Murder, rape, and pillage at Jabesh-gilead (Judges 21:10-24); Murder, rape and pillage of the Midianites (Numbers 31:7-18); More Murder Rape and Pillage (Deuteronomy 20:10-14); Laws of Rape (Deuteronomy 22:28-29); Death to the Rape Victim (Deuteronomy 22:23-24); David's Punishment – Polygamy, Rape, Baby Killing, and God's "Forgiveness" (2 Samuel 12:11-14); Rape of Female Captives (Deuteronomy 21:10-14); Rape and the Spoils of War (Judges 5:30); Sex Slaves (Exodus 21:7-11); God Assists Rape and Plunder (Zechariah 14:1-2). Nice.

11. **But God would never command rape! Er, how can you know?** – Again, the defence is common: *But God would never command rape!* Yet, in order to say that God would never command rape, we would have to know that rape is *already wrong*, independent of God! We cannot say he would never command it because he has never not commanded it (though see above), and to say that he wouldn't would involve moral

---

[1] See Pearce (2016b).

reasoning, which is contrary to what the DCTers believe about God! We have this problem with causality, because the Christian can't say "We know he wouldn't command rape because we know it is bad because of X and Y reasons". Christian apologists get seriously hamstrung when they cannot appeal to moral reasoning!

12. **God cannot know he is all-good…** – God cannot even know that he himself is all-good because to do so, he would need to judge himself on an objective standard! This is quite a difficult concept to think about, but how would God be able to have the self-reflective knowledge to be able to claim that he was all-good? All God could say was that he was Godlike. Good, being tautologous with God, means that God would work himself into a circle in trying to define himself. It is quite similar to God being unable to know that he is not a God-in-a-vat, and that there isn't a chain of gods, Matrix-style, above him.

13. **Moral development of children** – In *Morality Without God*, Walter Sinnott-Armstrong states:[1]

> …anyone who helps and refrains from harming others just because God commanded her to do so might not be hard-hearted, but her motivations are far from ideal. It would be better for them to help and refrain from harming other people out of concern for those other people. That is what we ought to teach our children. Studies of development and education show that children develop better moral attitudes as adults if they are raised to empathize rather than to obey commands without any reasons rather than to avoid punishment. To raise children to obey God's commands just because God commanded them will undermine true caring and true morality.

14. **Non-Christians who have no access to Christianity** – People who have not read the Bible or experienced the Christian God would have no idea how to be moral (unless there is an acceptable recourse to moral reasoning, which has no need of God). Think of horrible people existing before biblical times, or in different countries without access to those divine commands. Is murder acceptable because they have not had divine commands?

---

[1] Sinnott-Armstrong (2011), p. 110.

Apologists like William Lane Craig have even posited ideas saying that God knew that these people would not freely come to love him, or would simply be bad people, so he front-loaded their souls into these pre-biblical times as cannon fodder.

15. **Stephen Maitzen: Ordinary Morality Presupposes Atheism** – Here is an argument from Stephen Maitzen (W. G. Clark Professor of Philosophy Chair, Research Ethics Board, Acadia University). This is an analogy used by Christians themselves. Imagine that you are a five-year-old being taken to the doctors for an injection against a deadly disease. You do not understand how immunisation works. Your parents cannot adequately explain it to you. You just have to know that a greater good will come about from your immunisation. It is a piece of necessary pain and suffering, the needle going in, that will bring about a greater good. An onlooker would never, upon seeing the doctor about to inject this poor boy, run over and rugby tackle the doctor so as to stop the pain. That would stop the greater good from taking place. However, as illogical as this is, that *is* what every god-fearing Christian *should* do. Let me explain.

Imagine an old lady being set upon by some youths across the road. Using our ordinary morality, if we saw this, we would like to think we would step in and stop this from happening. But there can be no such thing as gratuitous evil in this world with an all-loving God. This old woman getting beaten up, as horrible as it is, is necessary for a greater good to come about. By stepping in and helping this woman, we are stopping the greater good from coming about. We would be rugby tackling the doctor to stop the pain, thus denying the greater good, if we were to stop those youths! In other words, as Maitzen states, ordinary morality simply does not make sense under theism. Ordinary morality presupposes atheism. Moreover, this whole scenario of the problem of evil and greater goods coming from suffering is consequentialist in nature. God is *using* people as a means to an end. This is the sort of utilitarianism that theists decry, and attack atheists for holding to.

16. **God is a consequentialist** – And finally… A fundamental problem for Christians is that theologians claim that things like DCT are correct, but actually, most of the population tend to be consequentialists. As William Lane Craig has declared: "consequentialism is a terrible ethic", which we have already discussed. However, it turns out that about 90% of people are intuitively consequentialist. The most famous experiment to look

into this is the trolley problem. 89% of people would pull the lever to save multiple people by killing one man. This goes dramatically down if they have to *push* a fat man off the bridge (same calculation, put pushing a person directly rather than disconnectedly pulling a lever), which shows that morality is a function of psychology. It turns out that (as psychologist Jonathan Haidt would say in "The Emotional Dog and the Rational Tail"[1]) we intuitively moralise and then scrabble around for reasons as to why we did something. But Christians supposedly decry such consequentialism. This is rather interesting because (as we have seen) it turns out that God is the biggest consequentialist of them all. Theists argue that God moves in mysterious ways, that there is a reason for everything. Extending that logic, the Problem of Evil dictates that there can be no gratuitous evil, that every bit of suffering must be necessary towards eventuating a greater good. So the moral value of the action that brings about suffering is in the consequence of the eventual greater good. It cannot be good in itself that all of the world, except the eight in Noah's family, and all of the animals bar a small number died in a great flood. No. So the goodness comes from the greater good that this brought about. Everything happens for a reason and God moves in mysterious ways. Jesus was sacrificed for the sins of the world. This was pure consequentialism. In fact, every atrocity in both the Bible and the real world is explained in this way. But, according to Christians, this ethic is terrible. The ethical system employed by theologians to use in *every single theodicy* is consequentialist, and apparently terrible!

That should really close the case on God being the objective basis of morality. Let us dwell for a short while on deontology.

Deontology is a moral framework championed best by Immanuel Kant. Deontologists believe that there are things that we categorically should do, things that ought to be done irrespective of the context. In reverse order, no matter how good the effects of an action might appear, the action might still be bad. Kant, as the deontological flag-bearer, argued there were moral laws and prohibitions that ought to be adhered to, regardless of the consequences. He argued that people should not be used as a means to an end. Imagine again a scenario where someone needs to be saved. A deontologist would act according to a rule such as Kant's Categorical Imperative: "Act only according to that maxim whereby you can, at the same time, will that it should become a universal

---

[1] Haidt (2001).

law."[1] Saving others could be willed as a universal law and we should do it, unconditionally, as an end in itself.

Let's apply deontology, then, to the Bible and Christianity:

(1) It is wrong to commit genocide. (But God and Yahwists did it, e.g., 1 Samuel 15, Exodus 17.)

(2) It is wrong to lie. (But God did, certainly by proxy, e.g., 1 Kings 22:23, Jeremiah 4:10, 2 Thessalonians 2:11 and others.)

(3) It is wrong to rape. (But God sanctioned it, e.g., Judges 21, Numbers 31, Deuteronomy 20, 21, 22 etc.)

(4) It is wrong to own slaves. (But God allowed for it, e.g., Leviticus 25, Exodus 21 etc.)

And so on. You get the point.

Christian apologists claim to adhere to some form of deontology and yet this causes moral mayhem for them when looking at the Bible. That said, I am not a fan of deontology – and this larger idea of moral realism – and I *do* think it is a harder system to defend for a naturalist (well, for anyone). Specifically, arguments like the Inquiring Murderer offer problems for establishing any such system that doesn't seem to actually derive back to a form of consequentialism:[2]

> The situation in a nutshell is this: you are cornered outside of your house by a bloodthirsty madman who is looking for your friend. You know that this friend is inside of your house. The madman tells you in no uncertain terms that he will kill this person as soon as he finds him, and demands to know his whereabouts. For some reason or other, you do not have the ability to remain silent but must answer this villain with truth or falsehood. Is a lie in this case morally permissible?...

> Kant's answer, of course, is that not even this horrific circumstance would validate a deliberate falsehood; lying is a priori wrong because it is not an action that can be universally enacted according to the moral law, representing a contradiction in nature.

---

[1] Kant (1993), p. 30.
[2] "Extract 3: Kant's enquiring murderer", *Philosophical Investigations*, 26th June, 2010, https://peped.org/philosophicalinvestigations/extract-3-kants-enquiring-murderer/ (retrieved 02/02/2021).

This is at odds with our sense of ordinary morality and with our intuitive empathy, I argue. More on this in the next section.

It seems clear to me from the above arguments that morality does not necessitate God, and that the notion of God grossly corrupts and problematises the idea of morality. Conversely, atheists have several very good cases for morality, which can take on many guises depending on what properties our reality has. It appears that morality and God are not good bedfellows; indeed, morality requires atheism to make sense.

So what do I believe?

At an ontological level, I am a moral skeptic. Morality has no ontic existence. Since abstracts do not exist outside of our minds, morality, being abstract, does not exist outside of our minds.

Well, that was quick.

The reality is, the hard work now starts.

Morality *does* exist, it's just that this existence is in our minds, conceptually. We pragmatically use our interpretations of morality in order to operate successfully as a social species.

My view, but I am open to change, is that morality is largely psychological. As someone on my blog once stated:[1]

> ...the foundation and core of our intuitive, emotional empathic responses, and I would guess, also of all our basis for cognitive moral reasoning, is the seemingly simplistic understanding that there are things we wouldn't want others to do to us, and, just maybe, it seems like a reasonable guess that others also wouldn't like it if we were to do those things to them either.
>
> The funny thing is, although religious people often float the silly idea that a god is somehow involved in morality, the law of reciprocity is an entirely secular and humanistic statement, and depends solely upon the existence, not of gods, nor of religious texts, but just two or more human beings. Nor does it depend upon some unfathomable feat of wisdom such that

---

[1] The commenter "ephemerol" stated this in a comment section to one of my articles and re-presented in "My Atheistic Moral Philosophy; Objective, Subjective and Theistic Morality" – Pearce (2018).

it could only have come down from on high; it just requires someone to be neurotypical enough to possess the capacity for empathy. In fact, there's even a fly in this ointment, such as it comes down to us, that indicates that "the golden rule" isn't quite as wise or as golden as it might at first appear, ruling out some sort of perfectly wise divine source.

Of course, the golden rule – "Do unto others as you would have them do unto you" – predated Jesus by a long way and has turned up in pretty much every society and every religion. It is a fundamental psychological and functional mechanism – indeed, we see it in other animals, too.

The Golden Rule implies the basic assumption that people would like to be treated the way that you would like to be treated. The alternative to the Golden Rule is the upgraded Platinum Rule: "Treat others the way they want to be treated."

We use our psychological metrics and systems of morality as a good guide – good, because they allow us to operate with social success. We interpret this as "goodness" (amongst possibly other characteristics).

We teach people not to lie because it feels intuitively bad when people do it to us, and if everybody did it (universalising the act), the world would be a worse place.

The reason why consequentialism, as a system, is so intuitively powerful, is that a) it seems to be psychologically ingrained (89% of people would pull the lever in the trolley experiment, and the percentage is reversed if we have to actually push someone to do it), and b) it is non-derivative (meaning it is the most basic logical axiom).

Let me remind you yet again: To ground any claim, from morality to anything else, we have to face the Münchhausen Trilemma: a circle, an infinite regress, or an axiom. Given the weaknesses of the first two, we are left with the last. Axioms, as self-evident truths, ground the "why" answer with a sort of "just because". In morality, happiness (pleasure, lack of pain) is a really useful moral currency because it is self-evidently good: Why did you do that? To give optimal happiness? Why? Because happiness is good. Why? It just self-evidently is. It makes me happy. And this is as good an axiom as I think you will find.

Compare consequentialism with God as a moral command-giver and not being allowed to use moral reasoning. In the latter case, all you get is do good either "because heaven/hell", or do good "because God is good, and that is good because God". It is all rather circular and devoid of actual moral reasoning.

Now, consequentialism is not perfect. No moral value system is. After thousands of years of discourse, we all still disagree, so we can be assured that there simply is no right answer, and this is because it is a conceptual, subjective construction without an objectively "right" manner of being.

Consequentialism is also strong because it seeks to perpetually make the world a better place. As a general principle, this is pretty noble. It can also be a weakness because it is never-ending and we end up sweeping the streets of micro-organisms in front of us so as to minimise moral impact – we become like the Jains[1].

It is worth saying that consequentialism has many different flavours and add-ons. And I haven't even talked about the difference between desire and intentions, and end results (e.g. I could give someone in need some money with good intentions, but they go and spend it on drugs, etc.). As a rule of thumb, though, I think it is intuitively attractive and pragmatically useful. Indeed, we use it politically all of the time. For example, NICE (The National Institute for Health and Care Excellence), the non-departmental body of the UK's Department of Health responsible for procuring drugs and treatments (amongst other things), uses outcome-based formulae to evaluate drugs and treatments in order to calculate the best use of finite money and resources to choose between different drugs and treatments. In terms of politics in general, you can see consequentialism at play in each and every area of governmental policy, both domestic and international.

I strongly believe that morality is heavily entwined with empathy, although the term "empathy" can be a catch-all one that needs closer defining. So, for me, morality is not some simple-to-box-up neat and succinct theory. It is problematic and messy, and it depends whether you are talking about ontology, normative values, logical constructions, truth, or axioms.

In light of Richard Carrier's conclusion on the interrelatedness of the main moral value systems, I adhere to all of these systems, in some way, in order that the world becomes a better place, which is involved in making me and others have a greater wellbeing.

Rather than arguing about whether I am a consequentialist or a virtue ethicist, it is probably safer to say: "I am a humanist". Which is to say I am someone who:[2]

---

[1] A religious sect whose first pillar of belief is intentional non-violence or noninjury", whereby adherents vow to cause no harm to other human beings, as well as all living beings (particularly animals). This is their highest ethical duty, applying to actions, speech and thought. Ascetics in this tradition often use a *Dandasan*: a long stick with woolen threads used to gently remove ants and insects that might come across their path

[2] The first three bullet points are taken from "Humanism", *Humanists UK*, https://humanists.uk/humanism/ (retrieved 04/02/2021)

- trusts to the scientific method when it comes to understanding how the universe works and rejects the idea of the supernatural (and is therefore an atheist or agnostic).

- makes their ethical decisions based on reason, empathy, and a concern for human beings and other sentient animals.

- believes that, in the absence of an afterlife and any discernible purpose to the universe, human beings can act to give their own lives meaning by seeking happiness in this life and helping others to do the same.

- desires to live in greater harmony with the rest of the world, and to work towards maintaining the biodiversity of the world, and to live more sustainably within it, as a collective. I don't do this because some god has tasked me with stewarding the world, but for its own moral rationale. I see other animals around me, all over the world, and there is still an element of empathy and of the Golden or Platinum Rule. We could try and unpick whether this is true altruism or whether this is in the best interest of myself qua humanity at some deeper level. Perhaps I'll never know the answer. But it certainly *feels* right, and I am pretty confident that I can justify that feeling.

Indeed, the journey of this book, through its various essays and chapters, has been one of justifying the above list, in terms of both the how and the why.

Conclusion

Objective, divinely-based moral value systems don't work at all.

Indeed, no moral value system works perfectly - they are all flawed in some way(s). This, aside from my ontological approach, is another reason why I am a moral skeptic.

However, I think we *can* make the world a better place by implementing the aforementioned Platinum Rule. It is useful to use consequentialist rules of thumb. We reasonably want to try to make the world a better place for generations to come. It is inherent within us, for genetic reasons, and due to empathy and psychology. And these immediate actions can have effects well into the future. It feels good to do so; it feels right; and it benefits us and the world universally (if done well).

Admittedly, there is ample opportunity for an awful lot of argument here. Do we calculate goodness over a 5, 10, 50, or 100-year basis? Is biodiversity morally better than human flourishing? How do we calculate an equilibrium?

What *is* a better world? Can we justify our goals and axioms (when, by definition, axioms cannot be justified as they are supposedly self-evident)?

The whole crux to morality is setting out the goal, the protasis (because, within a fully fleshed out protasis, you can embed the methodology of getting there)[1]. Once we agree on that, all else follows fairly well. The world is a complex place full of untold numbers of variables. This means predicting the future is extremely tough, which means being moral is equally tough (as in, tough to calculate). Hence the rules of thumb that we develop (e.g. don't lie[2]). We need to teach empathy well and to understand the world better, and the consequences that come about from different actions. This will underwrite good, evidence-based (moral) policy-making.

The problem for many is that this is a rough sketch, and we often desire certainty; certainty makes us feel good and secure. On the other hand, making things up that give the appearance of certainty (because you like the sound or feel of them) can end up being dangerous.

Look at religion over the years.

---

[1] To exemplify this, somewhat arbitrarily, if I said "I want the world to be a place where everyone has equal opportunity" then this would not just be the outcome, but the way by which we would get there.

[2] A good example, since, as a rule, this is worth following. Universalise lying – imagine the world if everyone lied – would that be the sort of world we would want? On the other hand, this works as a rule of thumb, but sometimes, by the consequences, it can be right to lie (e.g. to the Inquiring Murderer).

What Can We Learn from This?

It has been a long and winding path to get here. Let me briefly recap: I am an atheist – someone who actively disbelieves in gods. I am a naturalist – someone who disbelieves that supernatural minds interact with the physical world and overcome Laws of Nature in unfalsifiable ways. These definitions are *for me* because specific labels are subjective and conceptual, although we can write dictionaries and encyclopaedias when we agree. For example, there is no True Christianity™. We make the best of these things that we can.

Here is an interpretation of my interpretation of how we interpret reality:

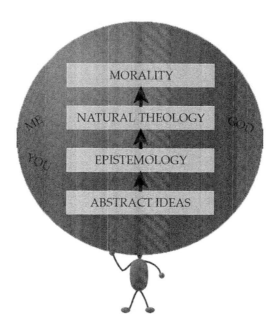

So whether I am arguing against someone who believes in God and that all morality and moral rules somehow reside in God's nature, or whether against someone who believes the US Constitution somehow accurately reflects inalienable natural rights that exist mind-independently, this is the framework I return to.

In fact, and let me really emphasise this point, my arguments here can be used in all sorts of really rather important contexts. For example, I have used my worldview (and advise you do the same, hence this book) to argue from an ontological (think abstracts) position against the following position and people:

- Racism, racists and "race realists" (this phrase is an attempt to couch racists in a more agreeable manner, but it gives the game away – it depends on a form of realism to work). Races are mental constructions – concepts we use to categorise the world. They don't exist out there, and, for many people, in here.

- Second Amendment advocates and deregulation of guns and gun ownership. People who argue for inalienable natural rights to bear arms require an objective realist existence of those rights (including the Constitution) for their position and arguments to hold. Those rights are mental constructions codified onto a piece of paper. You can amend that paper and you can change laws. See the following paragraphs.

- Anti-choice activists who argue human *beings* and personhood start at conception. Both terms are mental concepts.

- God (the Ultimate Abstract?) and the belief that she underwrites all morality. See the following paragraphs.

- In fact, my worldview means that I can and have pretty much argued with everyone about everything…

Remember, The Constitution and the Bill of Rights are just old bits of paper. You can amend them, get rid of them, supersede them – whatever.[1] They only become meaningful in a pragmatic sense when codified, enacted and enforced. This is, of course, trivially true. The Constitution *literally is* an old piece of paper (written by a bunch of long-dead old [white] guys[2]). It *literally includes* amendments and changes. It *literally is* encoded into law, enacted and enforced, thus giving it practical importance and implication. To add to this, the Supreme Court routinely tests and modifies interpretations of the statements in both documents.

It's the ideas that are important.

But, as stated, ideas are only practically meaningful when they have ramifications or influence: in other words, when they are codified and acted upon.

---

[1] See both documents and their amendments in the *National Archives* at https://www.archives.gov/founding-docs/constitution and https://www.archives.gov/founding-docs/bill-of-rights (retrieved 20/09/2021).

[2] I mention this because it shows how ideas are contextualised and adapt to the needs of the conceivers. In terms of the Constitution, many of the Founding Fathers were slave owners, and it wasn't until the 13th Amendment – the 13th change, if you will, that the moral proclamations were adapted to new needs and contexts. See the *National Archives* here: https://www.archives.gov/founding-docs/amendments-11-27 (retrieved 20/09/2021).

We don't dig into the sands of an ethereal dimension like abstract explorers to *discover* already-existent individual ideas or frameworks of abstract ideas. We are builders, not discoverers.

This whole debate is *where* these ideas exist, as already set out at length. So we have these alternative options. If not in the individual's mind (or in addition to), abstracts exist in…

(1) some Platonic realm where there is the right to bear arms (that in this realm, there is some absolute moral law or diktat that sits there, as an abstract idea, naturally),

(2) or in the mind or existence of God.

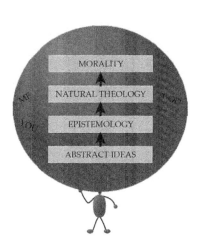
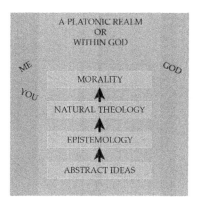

The broad point for me is that unless you set out your ontology of abstract ideas, you simply cannot do epistemology (how you know stuff, or go about seeking truth and what this means, since "truth" is an abstract concept), you cannot then do natural theology (whether gods exist, and how to make them coherent) and you cannot do morality (the ultimate of abstract objects).

All 2nd Amendment advocates, anti-choicers, religious zealots, and other such people do is argue from God outwards, or morality downwards, but they make a hash of abstracts, and their whole framework falls apart.

Not just those people. I once wrote an online piece on moral skepticism and plenty of humanists and atheists didn't like it. They're wrong, too (in my humblest of opinions, sorry!). They are arguing from a realist ontology of morality – an assertion that there are indubitable moral facts that exist irrespective of human/sentient minds, or some such thing. This may be the case, but they often, outside of the ivory towers of academia, present no cogent argument for how this is so. Thus it is merely wishful thinking.

I will admit, if I am wrong at the bottom, everything else falls apart and I will have to rebuild my foundations to see where it leads me (don't start with the conclusion and work back!). The only thing that has come close – though it might be a paradigm shift rather than a complete deconstruction – is idealism, as I discussed earlier in the book.

For the theist, or the ontological realist, we then have the following epistemological headache, *even if we were to accept the existence of God or a Platonic realm!*

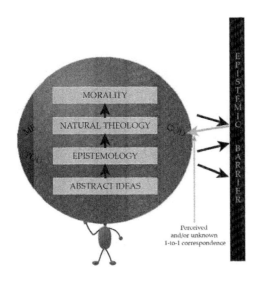

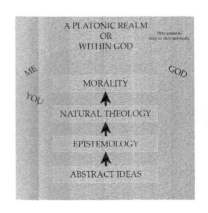

Even if they do happen to hit the jackpot by "getting their god right" or mapping a moral rule accurately, *they cannot know this!* As a result, they still have to map everything out using their own conceptual mechanisms and frameworks!

This is one of the famous areas of issue with Divine Command Theory – the epistemic criticisms. To remind you, here follows a typical conversation.

Christian: Goodness comes from God's nature. What he commands is by definition good.

Skeptic: God commanded rape in the OT.

C: No he didn't. At worst, that's a human mistake in the Bible.

S: But how do you know God wouldn't countenance rape?

C: Because God is good and rape is bad.

S: But in order to tell me that God wouldn't command rape, you are using secular moral reasoning to tell me rape is bad such that it wouldn't be part of God's nature since it seems he did command it in the Bible!

This and many other connected issues show that we do morality and apply it *to* gods, we don't derive morality *from* gods. Our divine revelations throughout the world have been so wildly at odds with each other over time and place. There is simply no way of knowing you are accessing God's moral dimension of a PR.

But this doesn't have to be about God, it is also about, say, the Second Amendment – the right to bear arms. Where does that "inalienable right" exist? How does it compete with my asserted right to not be surrounded by people with guns? How do the rights of a blastocyst trump the rights of a fully-grown, perhaps voting and civically engaged (or not) woman? Who gets to be the arbiter of the accuracy of any correspondence?

This is an epistemological problem because we cannot access either God or the Platonic realm (PR). As such, there is an epistemic barrier, first formulated by Descartes: all we can know indubitably is *cogito ergo sum* – "I", as a thinking or experiencing entity, exist. Past that, anything could be happening. *The Matrix*, Descartes' Evil Daemon, a simulation, idealism, and so on. So we build up our epistemologies, but these are often measured on their success in pragmatic terms. We don't know that our thoughts and beliefs entail 1-to-1 correspondence to an ultimate, foundational reality.

We all live in our worlds of our minds and hope that other minds think like ours. Often, we change our minds, and often we seek to change others in the endless journey towards the ideal of cognitive alignment.

If God exists, or a PR, we simply can't know that our idea of morality is correct; 42,000 denominations of Christianity will show you this. In reality, we mirror our own moral views, abstracts and ideas onto God or some kind of objective PR.

We are not made in God's image; God is made in *our* image.

Can that epistemic barrier be breached? Revelations depend on epistemologies, and epistemologies depend on abstracts and how we see the fundamental and ontological nature of reality. A theist (Let's call him Mark) could ask the following:

> If there is an epistemic barrier between my abstract ideas and God's, is there also an epistemic barrier between my abstract ideas and yours? If not, how do they interact?

It's *all* about epistemology, and this book has been largely about setting out my methods and standards.

When my idea of morality is different to that of Mark, I can know this almost definitely because we communicate, and our communication is validated and verified by others, and by our own data and analyses. I say X, Mark says Y. We disagree. There is effectively no barrier (past the Descartes' Evil Daemon or *The Matrix* scenario) because I can simply reply to him or email him. Or, heck, even go and see or Zoom call him if we so desired. I can get first-hand confirmation, and also confirmation of everyone else on Earth if they have access to the internet.

Essentially, we interact.

So what are the differences between this scenario and interacting with God?

Well, all the usual ones. If God is revealed in a 2000-year-old book, then we don't have epistemic warrant for believing it. I have set this out in several other books and this one. And any one religion and its claims has to compete with all others, and offer a resounding epistemic win in order to be thoroughly warranted.

I don't think *any* religion *even comes close.*

What other revelations are there, where revelation means some kind of interaction with the source material? Well, there are artefacts, like a holy book. Perhaps books, perhaps a stele here or an inscription there.

Still, nothing on Earth that has come up with the goods, nothing overcomes the very lower prior probabilities with evidence that even remotely satisfies a Bayesian calculation. And even if, say, an ancient inscription did, or an ancient holy book did really come from a particular divine truth, we still couldn't *really know that.* Such claims are still not believable in the present world as we know it. The Christian God doesn't seem to be in the business of planting crosses on the moon or regrowing limbs or appearing to us all in a world of video recording and global news.

So we are left with personal revelation – including personal revelations to others who then impress them onto ourselves.

Essentially, personal witness and experience of revelation from any source is highly problematic:

(1) You can't use them to convince others. Even theologians and apologists like William Lane Craig recognise this. You cannot rationally convince someone else with a divine revelation or experience. Especially given the

vast array of these over time and place that are mutually exclusive. It would employ special pleading and double standards.

(2) Even for yourself, they are problematic. We can use inductive reasoning to cast serious doubt on divine revelations. After all, one recent shooter in America, who killed his family, claimed God asked him to do it.[1] Every religion in the world over time and place has had adherents experiencing gods that are mutually exclusive. In order to say that your revelation was true, and that you understood it correctly and thus it had 1-to-1 correspondence (or close to), you would have to overcome an exceptionally low prior probability (the vast amount, if not all, previous personal revelations have been incorrect) with epistemic certainty and special pleading that yours was, indeed, veridical.

(3) But, seriously, how many believers have actually had real, veridical personal revelations that allow them to have beliefs that they somehow know are 1-to-1 correspondences to the source material (God and moral rules or some Platonic realm). Seriously, how many people have ever said, "I know every moral rule in the world because I have been personally revealed them by my god"?

(4) Irrespective of all this, you *still* build up your world from a subjective, experiential scenario. First comes subjective experience, then everything else. Indeed, this is the fundamental of idealism. Idealism is the main threat to my worldview (not belief in God, or even evolution, but what I believe of the world – that there is a material reality outside of my mind.

The fact that there are 42,000 different denominations is evidence that the Christian God hasn't clearly communicated or interacted with humanity. We have 42,000 denominations of Christians, each with their own personal interpretations of God and God's desires and commands (and that's not to mention the myriad other religions and their multitudinous denominations and sects, and all of their individual interpreters), all claiming that they have it right, that their beliefs have the closest correspondence.

Of course, to do this, you need to…

(1) define your god;
(2) rationally show that gods are possible and then probable;
(3) establish that *your* god, "God", exists;
(4) by establishing that you have the right god;
(5) establish that your god is moral;

---

[1] Levenson (2021).

(6) establish that you know your god's attributes, desires and commands so that

(7) when you are being moral, you are aligning your morality accurately with your god.

I'm sure you could add more reasonable hoops that the theist has to jump through.

There are all the obvious epistemological problems with this, some detailed earlier in this book, and throughout the catalogue of my previous writing. I just don't know how you can know, with any level of certitude, that you are aligning your morality, short of God coming down and verifying this in person and in a way that you were confident actually (and verifiably) happened.

But on a day-to-day basis, you are still using ordinary morality, morality that doesn't require God or gods. You are hopefully knowing that rape is bad. Not from divine revelation, mind – after all, rape is countenanced often in the Old Testament. As is slavery and many other moral ills.

No, morality is based on reasoning, and the abstracts and reasoning exist in, because they are constructed by, our subjective minds.

And the best understanding of Christianity that I give you is this: it's not true. God doesn't exist; gods don't exist. Hopefully, I have given you just enough of the many reasons as to why I think this is the case. I have also furnished you with a smattering of epistemology so that you can understand some of the problems and some of the methods involved at coming to something like a truth. I think that "there are no gods" is a truth claim that almost certainly corresponds with reality. I can use rational arguments to support this, and I can assess evidence presented by theists to support this, employing tools like Bayes' Theorem to evaluate those claims.

Philosophy is as much about building up knowledge bases as it is rejecting claims, and this is where the scientific method and induction come in handy. As tools (together with Bayes' Theorem), they work: they are reliable. The system is self-correcting when it works well. And all of my beliefs and findings, truth claims and philosophies, are coherent. They fit snuggly, like well-crafted bricks, into a solid wall; a wall where there are no holes, no gaps, no structural problems.

In short, this wall shouldn't fall on my head.

What about meaning and morality? I could be overly succinct here in answering this question: it's up to us to solve our own problems. I actually think that is a very good starting point. We're alone here, as far as supernatural, divine entities are concerned. We are our own gods in that *we* can set our goals, *we* can give our lives meaning, *we* can produce our own moral systems, and *we* can strive for greater knowledge as effectively and as morally as possible. The problem is agreement, and to be more precise, agreement by genuine consensus, not by force.

If we can throw off the lies and mistruths, if we can jettison our collection of gods into the annals of history, then we can give ourselves a better chance of surviving and flourishing, alongside a healthy planet full of wonder. Because it is not about some promissory note of heaven that is waiting to make our lives better than they presently are. It is about the here and now, and we really have to do the spadework to make our present Earthly existences (and those of our children) better.

Yes, we might just be a fleeting spec of insignificance in the history of the whole universe – finite and unknown beyond our Earthly sphere of influence. Or maybe not. Who *really knows*? But, in the same way that a movie in a cinema might not last forever, and might not have any impact beyond its immediate time and space, if I'm watching it, I want it to be as enjoyable as possible, to make me feel good. And it is all the more warming to know others around me feel the same, that we are in some kind of collective joy that is not harming others around us, or the cinema itself, so that those due in for the next showing will derive the same pleasure we were privileged to garner.

Is it all self-serving?

If being good makes us feel good, let us at least try to think of it as the collateral, even if it really turns out to be the driver.

Finally, to return to personal revelation: it won't cut the mustard because every religion in the world in all places and times have adherents who believe they have received such. The Christian doesn't believe the Muslim's personal revelation and vice versa.

The atheist believes neither and doesn't welcome in special pleading and double standards.

So I just jettison all that bother and do it myself, and in doing so, try to make the world a better place. There is no heaven for me bribing me to act in a certain way, colouring every moral action so that they are, in effect, entirely self-centred. Likewise, there is no threat of hell, beating me with the worst stick in human conception, making me act a certain way.

Instead, I develop – as is the purpose and content of this book – moral frameworks that are coherent, pragmatic and useful, and philosophically legible.

I suggest you do the same.

235

BIBLIOGRAPHY

Alston, William (1989), "Some Suggestions for Divine Command Theorists", from *Christian Theism and the Problems of Philosophy,* Ed. Beaty, Michael D., University of Notre Dame Press.

Aquinas, T., "Summa Theologica'.

Aristotle, (1982 edn), *'Eudemian Ethics',* 1215b, M. Woods (trans), Oxford: Oxford University Press.

Aristotle (2000 edn), *Nicomachean Ethics,* Roger Crisp (ed./trans.), Cambridge: Cambridge University Press.

Armstrong, David M. (1983), *What is a Law of Nature?,* Cambridge: Cambridge University Press.

Audi, R. (Ed.)(1999 2nd edition), *'The Cambridge Dictionary Of Philosophy',* Cambridge: Cambridge University Press.

Bentham, Jeremy (1789), The Principles of Morals and Legislation.

Beyerstein, Barry L. (1991), "The Brain and Consciousness: Implications for Psi Phenomena." In *The Hundredth Monkey.* Edited Kendrick Frazier. Buffalo, NY: Prometheus Books, p. 43-53.

Bird, Alexander & Tobin, *Emma* (2017), "Natural Kinds", *The Stanford Encylopedia of Philosophy,* https://plato.stanford.edu/entries/natural-kinds (retrieved 13/02/2021).

Blackburn, S. (1994;2008), *Oxford Dictionary of Philosophy,* Oxford: Oxford University Press.

Blackburn, S. (1999), *'Think',* Oxford: Oxford University Press.

Blanchflower, D.G., Oswald A.J., (2004), "Money, Sex, and Happiness: An Empirical Study", NBER Working Paper No. 10499, The National Bureau of Economic Research, Issued May 2004.

Brown, Lydia (2011), "The Significance of Semantics: Person-First Language: Why It Matters", *Autistic Hoya,* https://www.autistichoya.com/2011/08/significance-of-semantics-person-first.html, (retrieved 06/09/2021).

Carrier, Richard (2006), "Carrier's Opening Statement: Naturalism Is True, Theism is Not", *The Secular Web,* https://infidels.org/library/modern/richard-carrier-carrier-wanchick-carrier1/ (retrieved 20/12/2020).

Carrier, Richard (2015), "Open Letter to Academic Philosophy: All Your Moral Theories Are the Same", *Richard Carrier Blogs,* https://www.richardcarrier.info/archives/8903 (retrieved 03/02/2021).

Carroll, Sean (2011), "Physics and the Immortality of the Soul", *Preposterous Universe,* https://www.preposterousuniverse.com/blog/2011/05/23/physics-and-the-immortality-of-the-soul/ (retrieved 02/09/2021).

Chignell, Andrew & Pereboom, Derk (2020), "Natural Theology and Natural Religion", *The Stanford Encyclopedia of Philosophy*, https://plato.stanford.edu/entries/natural-theology/ (retrieved 02/02/2021).

Colleti, Lucio (1969), "From Hegel to Marcuse", in *From Rousseau to Lenin: Studies in Ideology and Society* [orig. *Ideologia e Società*, 1969], translated by John Merrington and Judith White (New York: Monthly Review Press, 1972), pp. 111-140.

Copan, Paul and Craig, William Lane (2007), *Passionate Conviction: Contemporary Discourses on Christian Apologetics*, Nashville, TN: B&H Publishing Group.

Craig, William Lane and Moreland, J.P. (2003), *Philosophical Foundations for a Christian Worldview*, IVP Academic: Illinois.

Craig, William Lane and Moreland, J.P. (2009), *The Blackwell Companion to Natural Theology*, Wiley-Blackwell: New Jersey.

Craig, William Lane (n.d.), "The Problem of Evil", *Be Thinking*, https://www.bethinking.org/suffering/the-problem-of-evil (retrieved 01/01/2021)".

Craig, William Lane (1997), "The Indispensability of Theological Meta-Ethical Foundations for Morality", *Reasonable Faith with William Lane Craig*, https://www.reasonablefaith.org/writings/scholarly-writings/the-existence-of-god/the-indispensability-of-theological-meta-ethical-foundations-for-morality/ (retrieved 03/02/2021).

Craig, William Lane (2007), "Slaughter of the Canaanites", *Reasonable Faith with William Lane Craig*, https://www.reasonablefaith.org/writings/question-answer/slaughter-of-the-canaanites (retrieved 21/12/2020).

Craig, William Lane (2008; 3rd Ed), *A Reasonable Faith*, Wheaton, IL: Crossway Books.

Craig, William Lane (2008b), "Subject: Abortion and Presidential Politics", *Reasonable Faith with William Lane Craig*, https://www.reasonablefaith.org/writings/question-answer/abortion-and-presidential-politics (retrieved 30/12/2011).

Craig, William Lane (2008c), "How are Morals Objectively Grounded in God?", *Reasonable Faith with William Lane Craig,* https://www.reasonablefaith.org/media/reasonable-faith-podcast/how-are-morals-objectively-grounded-in-god (retrieved 03/02/2021).

Craig, William Lane (2011), "Moral Values and Abstract Objects", *Reasonable Faith with William Lane Craig,,* https://www.reasonablefaith.org/writings/question-answer/moral-values-and-abstract-objects (retrieved 21/09/2021).

Davies, P. (1993), The Mind of God: The Scientific Basis for a Rational World, Simon & Schuster.

Davies, Stephen T. (1993), *Risen Indeed,* Grand Rapids: William B. Eerdmans.

Descartes, R. (1984), *Meditations on First Philosophy* [1641] and *Passions of the Soul* [1649], in *The Philosophical Writings of Descartes,* vol. I-III, translated by Cottingham, J., Stoothoff, R., & Murdoch, D.. Cambridge: Cambridge University Press, v.I, 343.

Descartes, R., (1664) *Treatise on Man.*

Descartes, R., (1649) *The Passions of the Soul.*

Descartes, R., (1641) "Reply to Fourth Set of Objections" in *Meditations.*

Descartes, R. (2008), *Meditations on first philosophy* (M. Moriarty, Trans.), Oxford University Press.

Descartes, R. (1989), *Passions of the Soul,* trans. Stephen H. Voss. Indianapolis: Hackett.

Descartes, R., (1964–76), *Oeuvres de Descartes,* 11 vols., ed. Charles Adam and Paul Tannery, new edn. Paris: Vrin/CNRS.

Eagleton, T., (2007), The Meaning of Life: A Very Short Introduction, Oxford: OUP.

Edwards, P. Wesley (2018), "Does Morality Depend on God?", *Freethought Debater,* https://www.freethoughtdebater.org/2018/11/28/does-morality-depend-on-god/ (retrieved 21/09/2021).

Foot, Philippa (1978), The Problem of Abortion and the Doctrine of the Double Effect in Virtues and Vices, Oxford: Basil Blackwell.

Gert, Bernard (2002), "The Definition of Morality", *The Stanford Encyclopedia of Philosophy,* https://plato.stanford.edu/entries/morality-definition/ (retrieved 07/05/20).

Glanzberg, Michael (2006), "Truth", Michael, *The Stanford Encyclopedia of Philosophy,* https://plato.stanford.edu/entries/truth/ (retrieved 07/05/2012).

Goldhaber, Alfred Scharff; Nieto, Michael Martin (January–March 2010), "Photon and graviton mass limits", *Rev. Mod. Phys.* (American Physical Society) 82: 939, doi:10.1103/RevModPhys.82.939. pages 939-979.

Grayling, A.C. (2003), *What is Good?*, London: Weidenfeld & Nicolson

Gupta, Anil (2015), "Definitions", *Stanford Encyclopedia of Philosophy,* https://plato.stanford.edu/entries/definitions/ (retrieved 10/01/2021).

Habermas, Gary (n.d.), "Minimal Facts on the Resurrection that Even Skeptics Accept", *Southern Evangelical Seminary & Bible College,* https://ses.edu/minimal-facts-on-the-resurrection-that-even-skeptics-accept/ (retrieved 15/11/2020).

Habermas, Gary (2009), 'Why The "Minimal Facts" Model is Unpersuasive'. *Evaluating Christianity,* https://evaluatingchristianity.wordpress.com/2009/03/05/why-the-minimal-facts-model-is-unpersuasive/ (retrieved 18/09/2020).

Haidt, Jonathan (2001), "The Emotional Dog and Its Rational Tail: A Social Intuitionist Approach to Moral Judgment", *Psychological Review*, 108 (4): p. k814-834.

Hare, R.M. (1955), "Universalisability", *Proceedings of the Aristotelian Society,* 55:295 - 312 (1955).

Hare, R.M. (1963), *Freedom and Reason*, Oxford: OUP.

Harris, C. E. (1956), The Ethics of Natural Law, from *Applying Moral Theories*, Belmont, CA: Wadworth.

Harris, Sam (2012), *The Moral Landscape*, London: Bantam Press.

Hegel, G. W. F. (1969), *The Science of Logic,* trans. A. V. Miller: London.

Himma, Kenneth Einar (n.d.), "Design Arguments for the Existence of God", *The Internet Encyclopedia of Philosophy*, https://iep.utm.edu/design/ (retrieved 20/05/2020).

Hanfling, O. (1987), '*The Quest for Meaning (Life & Death)*', Oxford: Blackwell.

Hanfling, O. (1987a), Life and Meaning: A Philosophical Reader (Life & Death), Oxford: Blackwell.

Hare, John (2006), "Religion and Morality", *The Stanford Encyclopedia of Philosophy*, https://plato.stanford.edu/entries/religion-morality/ (retrieved 10/01/2021).

Henderson, Leah (2018), "The Problem of Induction", *The Stanford Encyclopedia of Philosophy*, https://plato.stanford.edu/entries/induction-problem/ (retrieved 30/01/2021).

Hofweber, Thomas "Logic and Ontology", *The Stanford Encylopedia of Philosophy*, https://plato.stanford.edu/entries/logic-ontology/ (retrieved 10/01/2021).

Hossenfelder, Sabine (2021), "The Simulation Hypothesis is Pseudoscience", *BackRe(Action),* https://backreaction.blogspot.com/2021/02/the-simulation-hypothesis-is.html, (retrieved 02/09/2021).

Howson, C. (2000), Hume's Problem: Induction and the Justification of Belief, Oxford: Oxford University Press.

Hume, D. (1779) *Dialogues Concerning Natural Religion,* Project Gutenberg, https://www.gutenberg.org/ebooks/4583 (retrieved 21/09/2021).

Hume, D. (1902, 2nd ed./2006), *An Enquiry Concerning Human Understanding*, Project Gutenberg, https://www.gutenberg.org/ebooks/9662, (retrieved 06/09/2021 from 2006 Project Gutenberg posting).

Kant, Immanuel (1993), *Grounding for the Metaphysics of Morals*, trans. Ellington, James W., 3rd ed., Indianapolis: Hackett.

Khazan, Olga (2014), "Is One of the Most Popular Psychology Experiments Worthless?", *The Atlantic*, July 24, 2014 https://www.theatlantic.com/health/archive/2014/07/what-if-one-of-the-most-popular-experiments-in-psychology-is-worthless/374931/ (retrieved 01/02/2021).

Kiekeben, Franz (2015), *The Truth About God*, Independently published.

Kocsis, S., et al (2011), "Observing the Average Trajectories of Single Photons in a Two-Slit Interferometer", Science, 3 June 2011: Vol. 332 no. 6034 pp. 1170-1173.

Kurtz, Paul (1990), Philosophical Essays in Pragmatic Naturalism, Amherst: Prometheus.

LK (2014), "Berkeley's Idealism: A Critique", *Social Democracy for the 21st Century: A Realist Alternative to the Modern Left*, https://socialdemocracy21stcentury.blogspot.com/2014/02/berkeleys-idealism-critique.html (retrieved 23/02/2021).

Lamont, Corliss (1990, 5th ed.), *The Illusion of Immortality*. New York: Unger/Continuum.

Lerner, Lawrence, "Methodological Naturalism vs Ontological or Philosophical Naturalism", *Answers in Science*, http://answersinscience.org/MethodologicalNaturalism.htm (retrieved 02/02/2021).

Levenson, Eric (2021), "An ex-Marine sharpshooter said he killed a baby and 3 others because God told him to, affidavit states", *CNN*, September 7th 2021, https://edition.cnn.com/2021/09/06/us/florida-shooting-infant-what-we-know/ (retrieved 12/09/2021).

Lipton, P. (2002), 'Review: Colin Howson - Hume's Problem: Induction and the Justification of Belief', British Journal For The Philosophy of Science (2002) 53 (4): 579-583.

Loftus, John W. (2016), *Christianity in the Light of Science*, Amherst, NY: Prometheus.

Loftus, John W. (2020), "What's Wrong With Using Bayes Theorem to Evaluate Miracles?", *Debunking Christianity*, https://www.debunking-christianity.com/2020/11/whats-wrong-with-using-bayes-theorem-to.html (retrieved 06/09/2021).

Lokhorst, Gert-Jan (2005), "Descartes and the Pineal Gland", *Stanford Encyclopedia of Philosophy* https://plato.stanford.edu/entries/pineal-gland/ (retrieved 29/08/2011).

Lombardi, Joseph L. (2005), "Against God's Moral Goodness", *American Catholic Philosophical Quarterly*, Volume 79, Issue 2, Spring 2005.

Lowder, Jeffrey Jay (2012), "The Evidential Argument from the History of Science (AHS)", *The Secular Outpost*, https://www.patheos.com/blogs/secularoutpost/2012/06/16/the-evidential-argument-from-the-history-of-science-ahs/#ixzz3PwEz8UxQ (retrieved 25/11/2020).

Lyubomirsky, S., Schkade, D., and Sheldon K.M., "Pursuing Happiness: The Architecture of Sustainable Change," *Review of General Psychology*, Vol. 9, No. 2, 111–131, 2005.

McNaughton, David (2003), "Is God (almost) a consequentialist? Swinburne's moral theory", https://www.academia.edu/287978/Is_God_Almost_a_Consequentialist_Swinburnes_Moral_Theory (retrieved 20/05/2020).

McQuillan, Colin (2012), "German Idealism", *The Internet Encyclopedia of Philosophy*, https://iep.utm.edu/germidea/ (retrieved 20/05/2020).

Maher, M., & Bolland, J., (1912), "Soul", *The Catholic Encyclopedia*. New York: Robert Appleton Company. retrieved January 6, 2021 from New Advent: https://www.newadvent.org/cathen/14153a.htm (retrieved 20/05/2020).

Martin, Michael (2007), *Cambridge Companion to Atheism,* New York: Cambridge University Press.

Merrill, K. (2003), "Review of COLIN HOWSON. Hume's Problem: Induction and the Justification of Belief", *Hume Studies*, Volume XXVIX, Number 1 (April, 2003) 155-162.

Murdoch, D. (2002), "Induction, Hume and Probability", *The Journal of Philosophy*, Vol. 99, No. 4, April 2002, 185-199.

Niiniluoto, Ilkka (2011), "Scientific Progress", *The Internet Encyclopedia of Philosophy*, https://plato.stanford.edu/entries/scientific-progress/ (retrieved 20/05/2020).

Norenzayan A, Gervais WM, Trzesniewski KH (2012). "Mentalizing Deficits Constrain Belief in a Personal God". PLoS ONE 7(5): e36880. https://doi.org/10.1371/journal.pone.0036880 (retrieved 22/09/2020).

Oderberg, David S. (2007), "Why I am not a Consequentialist", a talk delivered at the University of Lisbon.

Pearce, Jonathan M.S. (2010), Free Will? An investigation into whether we have free will, or whether I was always going to write this book', Fareham: Ginger Prince Publications.

Pearce, Jonathan M.S. (2011), *The Little Book of Unholy Questions*, Fareham: Onus Books.

Pearce, Jonathan M.S. (2014), "Islam vs Christianity: The Care Differences", *A Tippling Philosopher*, https://www.patheos.com/blogs/tippling/2014/08/24/islam-vs-christianity-the-core-differences/ (retrieved on 02/02/2021).

Pearce, Jonathan M.S. (2015), "'True Islam' and Violent Extremism - REDUX", *A Tippling Philosopher*, https://www.patheos.com/blogs/tippling/2015/11/14/true-islam-and-violent-extremism-redux-2/ (retrieved on 02/02/2021).

Pearce, Jonathan M.S. (2016), Did God Create the Universe from Nothing?: Countering William Lane Craig's Kalam Cosmological Argument, Fareham: Onus Books.

Pearce, Jonathan M.S. (2016b), "16 Problems with Divine Command Theory", *A Tippling Philosopher*, https://www.patheos.com/blogs/tippling/2016/09/04/16-problems-with-divine-command-theory/ (retrieved on 02/02/2021).

Pearce, Jonathan M.S. (2016c), "Heaven & Hell Stop You From Genuinely Morally Evaluating", *A Tippling Philosopher*, https://www.patheos.com/blogs/tippling/2016/05/09/heaven-hell-stop-you-from-genuinely-morally-evaluating/ (retrieved 02/02/2021)

Pearce, Jonathan M.S. (2017), *Not Seeing God: Atheism in the 21st Century*, Fareham: Onus Books.

Pearce, Jonathan M.S. (2018), "My Atheistic Moral Philosophy; Objective, Subjective and Theistic Morality", *A Tippling Philosopher*, https://www.patheos.com/blogs/tippling/2018/09/22/my-atheistic-moral-philosophy-objective-subjective-and-theistic-morality/ (retrieved 20/09/2021).

Pearce, Jonathan M.S. (2020), "Philosophy 101 (philpapers induced) #11 – Laws of nature: Humean or non-Humean?", *A Tippling Philosopher*, https://www.patheos.com/blogs/tippling/2020/03/18/philosophy-101-philpapers-induced-10-laws-of-nature-humean-or-non-humean/ (retrieved 02/02/2021).

Pearce, Jonathan M.S. (2020b), "Concerning Metaphysical and Methodological Naturalism", *A Tippling Philosopher*, https://www.patheos.com/blogs/tippling/2020/05/01/concerning-metaphysical-and-methodological-naturalism/ (retrieved 03/02/2021)

Pearce, Jonathan M.S. (2021), The Problem with "God": Classical Theism Under the Spotlight, Fareham: Onus Books.

Price, Robert M. & Lowder, Jeffery Jay (2005), *The Empty Tomb: Jesus Beyond the Grave*, Amherst: Prometheus.

Redding, Paul (2010), "Georg Wilhelm Friedrich Hegel", *The Stanford Encyclopedia of Philosophy*, https://plato.stanford.edu/entries/hegel/ (retrieved 12/04/2020).

Rosen, G. (2001), 'Abstract Objects', *The Stanford Encyclopedia of Philosophy*, https://plato.stanford.edu/entries/abstract-objects/ (retrieved 30/08/2011).

Russell, B. (1961, 2nd ed.), *The History of Western Philosophy*, London: Routledge.

Schopenhauer, Arthur (2015), *The World as Will and Idea (Vol. 2 of 3)*, VM ebooks.

Sinnott-Armstrong, Walter (2011), *Morality Without God*, Oxford: OUP.

Smith, David Woodrup (2008), "Phenomenology", *The Stanford Encyclopedia of Philosophy*, https://plato.stanford.edu/entries/phenomenology/ (retrieved 20/01/2021).

Spear, Andrew (n.d.), "Edmund Husserl: Intentionality and Intentional Content", *Internet Encyclopedia of Philosophy*, https://iep.utm.edu/huss-int/ (retrieved 26/02/2021).

Stecher, Carl & Blomberg (2019), *Resurrection: Faith or Fact?*, Durham, NC: Pitchstone Publishing.

Steup, Matthias (2005), "Epistemology", *The Stanford Encyclopedia of Philosophy*, https://plato.stanford.edu/entries/epistemology/ (retrieved 20/04/2021).

Stump, Eleonore (1992), "God's Obligations", *Philosophical Perspectives*, Vol. 6, Ethics (1992), pp. 475-491.

Swinburne, Richard (1997), *The Evolution of the Soul*, Oxford: Oxford University Press.

Swinburne, Richard, (1998), *Providence and the Problem of Evil*, Oxford: Clarendon Press.

Thompson, M. (1995;2006), 'Teach Yourself Philosophy', London: Hachette Livre UK.

Trakakis, Nick (n.d.), "The Evidential Problem of Evil", *The Internet Encyclopedia of Philosophy*, https://iep.utm.edu/evil-evi/ (retrieved 03/02/2021).

Tremblay, Francois (2005), "The Case for Objective Morality", *strongatheism.net*, http://www.strongatheism.net/library/philosophy/case_for_objective_morality (retrieved 04/02/2021).

Wegner, D. M. (2002), *The Illusion of Conscious Will*,' Cambridge, Mass.: MIT Press/Bradford Books.

Williams, Bernard (1981) "Internal and External Reasons", in Williams's *Moral Luck*, Cambridge: Cambridge University Press.

Woolf, L. (1960), 'Sowing: an autobiography of the years, 1880–1904', London: The Hogarth Press Ltd.

Vickers, John (2009), "The Problem of Induction", *The Stanford Encyclopedia of Philosophy*, though originally here: https://plato.stanford.edu/entries/induction-problem/, it is now superseded by Henderson (2018) and archived here: https://stanford.library.sydney.edu.au/archives/spr2009/entries/induction-problem/ (retrieved 30/01/2021).

Zimmerman, Michael J. & Bradley, Ben (2019), "Intrinsic Vs. Extrinsic Value", *The Stanford Encyclopedia of Philosophy*, https://plato.stanford.edu/entries/value-intrinsic-extrinsic/ (retrieved 24/03/2021).

General websites/sources without author attribution:

Stanford Encyclopedia of Philosophy – https://plato.stanford.edu/

"The Philpapers Survey", (2009), *Philpapers*, https://philpapers.org/surveys/ (retrieved 20/09/2021).

Reasonable Faith/William Lane Craig – https://www.reasonablefaith.org/

"The United Nations Charter (full text), *The United Nations*, https://www.un.org/en/about-us/un-charter/full-text (retrieved 22/09/2021).

9 781838 239114

Printed by BoD™in Norderstedt, Germany